769
SE

Seaver, Tom

Tom Seaver's
baseball card book

DATE			
OC 12 '85	JY 2 '90		
NO 04 '85	AG 10 '90		
AP 26 '88	MR 26 '91		
MY 28 '88	JY 26 '91		
JA 29 '88	DE 14 '91		
NO 14 '88	FE 23 '93		
AP 26 '89	JE 2 '99		
JE 7 '89			
JE 29 '89			
AP 28 '90			
MY 29 '90			

© THE BAKER & TAYLOR CO.

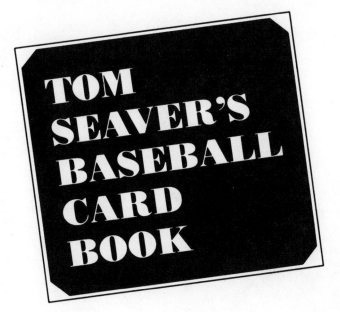

TOM
SEAVER'S
BASEBALL
CARD
BOOK

TOM SEAVER'S BASEBALL CARD BOOK

**by Tom Seaver
with Alice Siegel
and Margo McLoone-Basta**

Julian Messner **New York**

For our beloved
parents, husbands
and children

Copyright © 1985 by Alice Siegel and Margo McLoone–Basta
All rights reserved
including the right of reproduction
in whole or in part in any form
Published by JULIAN MESSNER
A Division of Simon & Schuster, Inc.
Simon & Schuster Building
1230 Avenue of the Americas
New York, New York 10020
Designed by Stanley S. Drate/Folio Graphics Co., Inc.
Manufactured in the United States of America
10 9 8 7 6 5 4 3 2 1
JULIAN MESSNER and colophon are trademarks
of Simon & Schuster, Inc.
Also available in Wanderer paperback edition.
Library of Congress Cataloging in Publication Data

Seaver, Tom, 1944-
  The Tom Seaver baseball card book.

  Includes index.
  1. Baseball cards—Catalogs. I. McLoone-Basta, Margo.
II. Siegel, Alice. III. Title.
GV875.3.S4   1984   769′.49796357   84-2191
ISBN 0-671-49525-9 (pbk.)
ISBN 0-671-53106-9 (lib. bdg.)

CONTENTS

1 Personal Recollections

My earliest memories of baseball cards date back thirty years. I was a nine-year-old Little League ball player. I loved baseball. Professional ball players were my idols. I collected baseball cards because I wanted to know everything about the game of baseball and the players.

In those days we listened to baseball games on the radio. The only way I could see all the players and their uniforms was to look at my baseball cards. It was fascinating to see the faces of the players I followed so closely. I also enjoyed looking at the different styles of baseball uniforms worn by the Major League teams. I studied those uniforms carefully—from the belt loops to the insignias on the hats.

I was a student of the game of baseball. I read sports magazines and newspapers to learn everything I could about baseball. But I can honestly say that the best way I had of learning about the game was by studying my baseball cards. I spent hours reading the back sides of cards. I memorized the statistics of most of the players. My favorite players were Hank Aaron, Eddie Mathews and Warren Spahn. My favorite teams were the Milwaukee Braves, Detroit Tigers and Pittsburgh Pirates.

Of all the cards I collected, the ones I cherished most were my Ted Williams cards. In 1959 Fleers

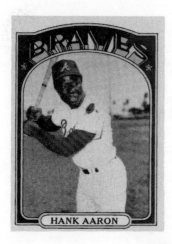

HANK AARON

Ted Turns Professional

issued a set of eighty cards devoted to the life and career of Ted Williams. I tried to collect all eighty but was never able to complete the set. Perhaps that's why those cards were so important to me. Since then I've learned that one card in the set—Number 68, "Ted Signs for 1959"—was difficult to obtain. Even now no one knows why. The lucky few who did collect it own a valuable card today.

Baseball cards were an important part of my youth. Even though I'm a professional baseball player today, baseball cards are still important to me. I can vividly remember how I felt when I first saw myself on a baseball card; it was exciting. My rookie card was a 1967 Topps card in which I was pictured with Bill Denehy (who was also a Met rookie pitcher that year). I still have that card.

Every player is eager to see his first card. In spring, when the new cards come out, there is quite a commotion at the training camp. Rookies get a first look at their cards. The rest of us look through the new cards carefully. We all search for the card of the player who took the worst picture, so we can tease him. On the more serious side, there are many players who have baseball cards in their lockers. These pictures of baseball buddies are reminders of good friends and good times.

I've been playing baseball for a long time and I know how much kids like baseball cards. Every year I get hundreds of requests to autograph cards. Kids write to me to ask about baseball cards and my collection. Collecting baseball cards is a marvelous hobby, which brings joy and fun to millions of kids and grownups.

TOM SEAVER

2 Baseball Cards: The First Hundred Years

The first professional baseball game in America was played in 1876 between the Boston Red Stockings and the Philadelphia A's. Only ten years after, in 1886, the first baseball cards appeared. The companies that made those cards had no way of knowing how popular the cards would someday be. Today, almost a hundred years later, baseball card collecting is a hobby enjoyed by millions of people around the world.

Many people think that baseball cards were always packaged with bubble gum. In fact, the first baseball cards were put in cigarette packs. They were used to stiffen the package and to promote the sale of cigarettes. Adults were the earliest collectors of baseball cards. Later, when baseball cards were put in bubble gum packages, kids took up the hobby of collecting.

The Old Judge Cigarette Company manufactured some of the first cigarettes. In 1886 they inserted baseball cards in the packs to keep the cigarettes from breaking. The cards proved to be so popular that other cigarette companies began to insert them in their cigarette packs. Mayo, Allen and Ginter, and Gold Coin are the names of some of those tobacco companies.

The first baseball cards were quite different from the cards of today. They were 1½ by 2 inches. The picture of the baseball player was taken in a studio. The player posed by swinging at, or pretending to catch, a ball hanging from a string. The player's photograph was pasted to a piece of cardboard. The back side of the card was blank.

Many tobacco companies began to issue baseball cards between the years 1908 and 1919. At least seventeen companies were in the business. The most well known of the companies of this era were Piedmont, Sweet Caporal and Polar Bear. For the first time, baseball cards had a picture on the front and information about the player on the back. These cards are known to collectors as T cards.

The first candy company to make baseball cards was the Cracker Jack Company. In 1914 it began promoting Crackerjacks with baseball cards. Soon after, caramels, peanut bars and other candies were sold with baseball cards. The candy cards of that time are known to collectors as E cards.

The now famous combination of baseball cards and bubble gum was born in the 1930s. The Goudey Gum Company was the first to sell gum with baseball cards. Within a short time other gum companies like

"WHIT" WYATT

National Chickle, DeLong and Gum Inc. manufactured baseball cards. The bubble gum cards of this time are especially popular today. They featured some of the greatest baseball players of all time, like Babe Ruth, Lou Gehrig and Dizzy Dean.

During World War II baseball cards were not produced. After the war, in 1948, two bubble gum companies, Leaf Gum and Bowman, brought back baseball cards and bubble gum. In 1951 the Topps Bubble Gum Co. entered the market.

33 — BILLY (The Bull) JOHNSON

Third Base—New York Yankees

Born: Montclair, N. J. Aug. 30, 1918

Bats: Right   Throws: Right

Height: 5:9½   Weight: 178

He led the American League's third basemen in 1943 in put-outs and assists, and tied for most double plays. He's a heavy hitter. His 141 base hits in 1947 batted in 95 runs. In the World Series that year, three of his seven hits were triples. He was named for the All Star Team in 1943. He spent two years in war service. He lives in Augusta, Georgia. 1947 average .285.

ASK FOR BLONY BUBBLE GUM

The Bubble Gum with
the three different flavors
BOWMAN GUM, INC. Copyright 1948

The 1950s are known as the "Golden Age" of baseball cards. The rivalry between Bowman and Topps for the market resulted in good quality cards with accurate statistics and biographies of the players printed on the back. These are some of the most popular cards of hobbyists today. In 1956 Topps bought out the Bowman Company and became the leading producer of baseball cards.

Today's standard size baseball card is 2½ x 3 inches. Topps issued these cards in 1957. Over the

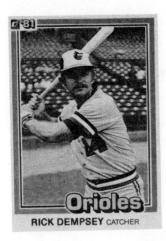

RICK DEMPSEY CATCHER

JOHN CANDELARIA PITCHER

years Topps introduced new and unusual kinds of baseball cards. In addition to the player cards, it printed baseball cards with a theme. "All-Star" cards and "Greatest Moments in Baseball" cards are two examples. Topps had a winning way with baseball cards. It produced almost all of the cards from 1957 through 1980.

In 1981 Topps was joined by the Fleer and Donruss corporations in distributing baseball cards. They are the three major baseball card manufacturers today.

For a hundred years baseball and baseball cards have been part of the American way of life. Baseball is the "American pastime," and baseball cards mirror the image of the sport as nothing else can.

3 Baseball Card Firsts

1. The *first time players' statistics appeared on the back of baseball cards* was in 1911 when the Mecca Tobacco Company issued the T-201 cards.

2. The *first Cubans to appear on baseball cards* were Rafael Almeida and Armando Marsans. They were pictured on tobacco cards in 1911.

ALMEIDA-CINN.-NAT.

Rafael Almeida

Senor Rafael Almeida is one of the first two Cubans to operate in the big leagues. Almeida is considered the strongest hitter ever developed in Cuba. Almeida is of Portuguese descent and first came to this country as a member of the New Britain team of the Connecticut League. He was sold to Cincinnati and played there in 1911. His failure to report promptly in 1912 brought about his release to Birmingham but he will return to Cincinnati as he is playing a fine third base and hitting the ball hard in the Southern League. In 1911 Almeida batted .313 and fielded .890 for Cincinnati.

CYCLE CIGARETTES

MARSANS-CINN.-NAT.

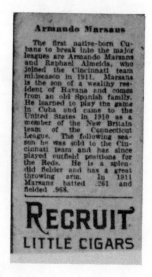

Armando Marsans

The first native-born Cubans to break into the major leagues are Armando Marsans and Raphael Almeida, who joined the Cincinnati team midseason in 1911. Marsans is the son of a wealthy resident of Havana and comes from an old Spanish family. He learned to play the game in Cuba and came to the United States in 1910 as a member of the New Britain team of the Connecticut League. The following season he was sold to the Cincinnati team and has since played outfield positions for the Reds. He is a splendid fielder and has a great throwing arm. In 1911 Marsans batted .261 and fielded .968.

RECRUIT LITTLE CIGARS

3. The *first team cards* were issued by the Fatima Tobacco Company in 1913.

4. The *first player baseball card issued after World War II* (no cards were printed during the war) was the Bob Elliot card. It was the 1948 Bowman Bubble Gum card number 1.

1 — BOB ELLIOTT

Third Base—Boston Braves

Born:
San Francisco, Cal. 1916
Bats: Right   Throws: Right
Height: 6:00   Weight: 185

Voted 1947's Most Valuable Player and batting .317. Bob made a spectacular come back after 1946, his poorest year with the Pirates since he had joined them in 1939. The trade did something for him for he also led the National League's 3rd basemen in fielding. He began in the South Atlantic League playing with Savannah. He has been chosen for three All Star Teams.

ASK FOR BLONY BUBBLE GUM

The Bubble Gum with
the three different flavors
BOWMAN GUM, INC. Copyright 1948

5. The *first Major League black ballplayer to appear on a baseball card* was Jackie Robinson. The Leaf Company issued his card in 1948.

6. The *first Little League baseball player to appear on a baseball card* was Joey Jay. His first baseball card was issued by Topps in 1954.

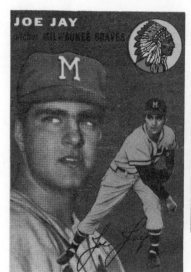
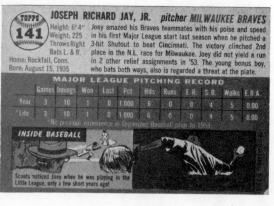

7. The *first baseball cards to feature umpires* were put out in 1955 by the Bowman Bubble Gum Company.

8. The *first twins to appear on a baseball card together* were Johnny and Eddie O'Brien in their 1954 Topps card.

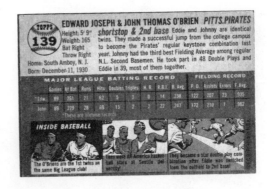

9. The *first checklist card* (a card listing all the cards in a series) was issued by Topps in 1956.

10. The *first baseball cards with the players' complete Major League career statistics* were issued in 1957 by Topps.

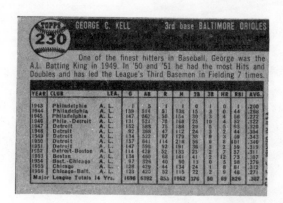

11. The *first baseball cards featuring rookies* were issued by Topps in 1963.

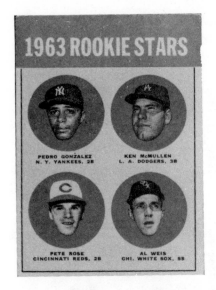

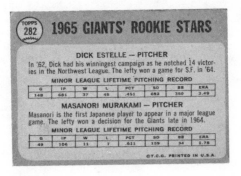

12. The *first Japanese baseball player to appear on a baseball card* was Masonuri Murakami. His rookie card was issued in 1965.

13. The *first player to be designated "pinch runner" on his baseball card* was Herb Washington in his 1975 Topps card.

14. The *first team mascot to appear on a baseball card* was the San Diego Chicken, whose card was issued by Donruss in 1982.

4 The Making of a Topps Baseball Card

The process of creating baseball cards begins long before the pictures of the players are taken. Topps Chewing Gum has been selling baseball bubble gum cards since 1951. Here is a description of Topps creative and manufacturing process.

A huge staff of people work together to put Topps baseball cards in the stores every year. Decision makers, designers, writers, photographers,

statisticians, gum makers and packers are some of these workers.

To begin, every year important decisions have to be made about the next year's set of baseball cards. How many cards will be in the series? What number card will each player have? What will be the special features of this year's cards? In 1983, as part of the entire series of 792 cards, Topps featured the twenty-six Major League managers. They also had a special feature of "Super Veterans" which showed rookie and current photos of each player.

The designers' jobs are very challenging. They must design the baseball cards so that they are traditional looking and yet, at the same time, stand out as "this year's cards." For example, in 1983 Topps designed cards with two photos on the front of the cards. There was a large action shot and a smaller close-up portrait. The back of the cards always list the complete Major League career statistics of the player along with highlights of the previous seasons.

The photographers for Topps begin to take pictures of the players at spring training. They continue to snap shots at the ball parks throughout the season. The photographers take many poses, including photos of baseball players with and without caps, with and without a visible team insignia, action and still shots.

All of the photographs, which are in color, are brought to the enormous Topps file so that they are available for selection by the Topps Sports Department. The best photos to be used on the cards are selected with the help of the art director. It is important that the photographs have excellent color qualities in order to maintain realistic reproductions. The photos must clearly show the baseball player, and the action photos must be excellent demonstrations of the player's capabilities.

When the photos are selected and the cards are designed, all the statistical information about the players must be ready. A staff of writers and statisticians prepare, check and double-check the information. Even the youngest consumers are avid fans and they want and appreciate accurate information. Baseball cards are often the most important source of ballplayer information for many children.

In the Art Department all of the photos, designs and copy are put together on boards which are used for the printing process. When all the artwork has been prepared, the material is sent to the print shop where cards are printed on giant sheets that feature 264 individual pictures.

From the printing presses, the sheets go to the cutting and packaging departments. Special collating machines cut the sheets into individual cards and mix them to provide an assortment and prevent duplication of cards in individual packages.

The cards are put into packages with the gum (which is manufactured in another part of the big plant in Pennsylvania). These packages are then placed in counter display boxes. The boxes are shipped in cartons, which are sent to candy distributors throughout the country. Stores buy the cards from the distributors and put them on the counter when the baseball card selling season begins.

5 Fascinating Facts About Baseball Cards

1. There are over 500,000 known *baseball card collectors* in the United States today.

2. The two *most valuable baseball cards in the world* are the Honus Wagner T-card, worth now about $20,000, and the Eddie Plank T-card, worth about $7,500. The stories of how these cards came to be so valuable are familiar to most collectors. Because Wagner strongly opposed cigarette smoking, he insisted that his card be discontinued. Therefore only a few were circulated. The plate which was used to print the Plank card broke before all the cards were made. A new plate was not made and no more of his cards were issued. In the case of both cards, they became valuable because there are so few of them in existence today.

3. The *most valuable Topps* baseball card is the 1952 Mickey Mantle card. This card is valuable today because Mickey Mantle was one of the greatest and most popular baseball players of all time and because this was his rookie card.

4. The Topps Pete Rose rookie card is the *most valuable card of a present-day baseball player.* It is worth about $350 in mint condition. The popularity of this card is due to Rose's record-breaking career.

5. *The world's largest collection of baseball cards*

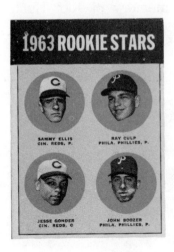

for public viewing is called the Burdick collection. Named after its original owner, Jefferson Burdick, it is on display at the Metropolitan Museum of Art on Fifth Avenue and 82nd Street in New York City. Appointments to see this collection (which includes American baseball cards and other advertising picture cards) must be made in advance. Children who are under the age of twelve must have an adult with them when viewing the collection.

6. The *most common complaint of baseball players* about their baseball card pictures is that they look better in person than in the photograph.

7. *If a player is traded after his baseball card picture is taken,* Topps prints a card with a photo showing the player hatless or hiding his team ensignia.

8. According to Topps, although *kids* are not the majority of serious card collectors, they *pick up the most errors on baseball cards.*

9. The *first baseball card ever issued in memory of a deceased player* was a 1964 Topps card. It was issued in memory of Ken Hubbs, who died two months before the season began.

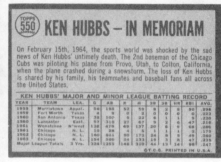

10. *Many Major League baseball players collect baseball cards.* Some of these players are Steve Garvey, Gary Carter, Duane Kuiper and Dale Murphy.

11. It is a known fact that some players have corrected faulty baseball mechanics by viewing their action baseball cards.

6 Baseball Card Photo Gallery

Tom Seaver's Personal Picks for the All-Time All Star Team

1. Hank Aaron   Outfield
2. Mickey Mantle   Outfield
3. Willie Mays   Outfield
4. Sandy Koufax   Pitcher
5. Johnny Bench   Catcher
6. Willie McCovey   First Base
7. Jackie Robinson   Second Base
8. Eddie Mathews   Third Base
9. Honus Wagner   Shortstop

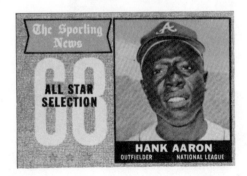

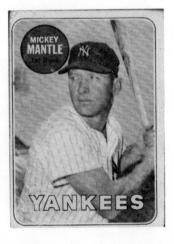

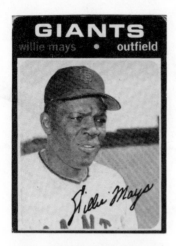

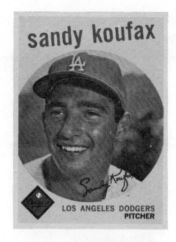

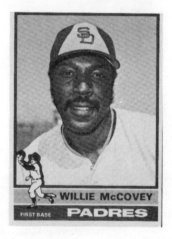

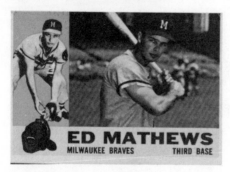

Tom Seaver's Personal Picks for Toughest Batters

1. Willie McCovey
2. Willie Stargell
3. Ted Simmons
4. Roger Maris
5. Woody Woodward

6. Tom Hutton
7. Roberto Clemente
8. Joe Morgan
9. Pete Rose

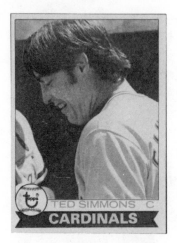

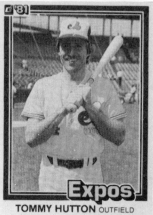

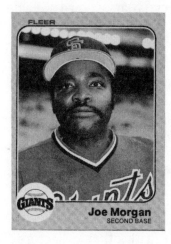

7 The Hobby of Collecting

I often tell kids who are baseball fans that collecting baseball cards is a great hobby for them. It's one of the best ways I know of to learn more about the game and its players. When you look at the front of a baseball card, you see the player and the name of his team and position close-up. The back of the card is a ready reference source of information about the player's statistics and personal history.

Kids also like to know that card collecting can be a valuable investment. They can buy and trade new cards cheaply and every year a card's value increases, if it is cared for properly.

My favorite reason for collecting baseball cards is that it builds a storehouse of memories. In future years a look at your collection will help you recall the players and teams of your youth.

The following guidelines will help you get started in the hobby of baseball card collecting.

How to Acquire Baseball Cards

Buy new cards from your local stores. They cost approximately 2¢ a card.

Buy and trade cards with other collectors. The *Official Price Guide* in this book will help you to purchase and swap cards at equal value. The names of card collectors can be located in these hobby magazines.

Baseball Cards
700 East State Street
Iola, Wisconsin 54990
   (published twice a year)

Sports Collectors Digest
700 East State Street
Iola, Wisconsin 54990
   (published twice a month)

The Trader Speaks
3 Pleasant Drive
Lake Ronkonkoma, New York 11779
   (published once a month)

If there are certain cards that you want to buy or swap, put an ad in a hobby magazine or your local newspaper. The message you write should be simple and brief. For example, "WANTED: Baseball cards. All Tom Seaver, mint only. Call or write to _____ (your name, address and phone number)."

Buy cards from dealers at baseball card conventions. Conventions are held throughout the year in cities all across the country. The dates and locations are listed in hobby magazines and local newspapers. Before you go to a convention, it's a good idea to make a list. Write down the cards you want and the prices you are willing to pay for them. You are almost certain to find any cards you want at these conventions. You can bring your own cards with you to trade or you can just look around and learn more about the hobby by asking questions of the dealers. They are usually helpful to new collectors. Each year baseball card collectors hold a national convention. Every year a different city hosts this convention which attracts thousands of card collectors from all over the country. Try to attend a national convention; it can be a great experience.

How to Care for Your Collection

There are four things every collector should remember when storing his or her cards: keep them clean, keep them dry, keep them in order, keep them safe and out of the way. Following is a chart showing some of the ways collectors store their cards.

TYPE OF STORAGE	ADVANTAGES	DISADVANTAGES
Shoe Boxes	There is no cost, and they are easily available. An old-time favorite, good for beginners.	Cards are not readily visible for locating. Cards are not well protected for handling.
Cardboard Base-ball Card Box	Inexpensive (25¢ to 30¢ per box). Sturdy, made of heavy-duty cardboard. Will hold a complete series or up to 800 cards.	Cards are not readily visible for locating. Cards are not well protected for handling.

Clear Plastic Sheets with Pockets (known as P.V.C.s)	Both sides of cards are visible while protected.	Costly (about 15¢ per nine-card sheet plus the cost of a three-ring binder). Cards must be placed very carefully to avoid creasing.

| Lucite Card Holder for display of valuable and favorite cards. | Sturdy, permanent display of cards. | Expensive, 50¢ for a one-card holder. |

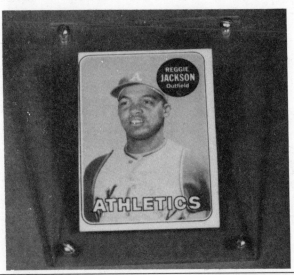

| Multi Drawer Steel File Cabinets (index card size) | Cards can be sorted numerically by years. Cards are easily available by pulling out the drawers. Cards can be locked to protect from theft. Extremely durable, these are mostly used by dealers. | Very expensive ($40 and up for new). They take up a lot of space. |

8 How to Judge the Condition of a Baseball Card

Buyers and sellers of baseball cards need standards to reach an agreement on the value of a card. There is no uniform grading system for baseball cards. The staff of SPORTS COLLECTORS DIGEST has written some guidelines for hobbyists to follow. I think they will help you in assessing the value of your cards.

Mint (Mt.) A perfect card. No signs of wear (rounded corners, edge dents, surface scratches) or aging (yellowing of white areas). Additionally, no imperfectly printed card (markedly off center, out of register, etc.) or card stained by contact with gum or other substance can be truly Mint in condition.

Excellent to Mint (Ex.–Mt.) A nearly perfect card, showing barely perceptible signs of handling. May have one or two corners which are no longer perfectly sharp. May have minor printing imperfections. No creases or scruffiness on surface. May show hint of aging.

Excellent (Ex.) A well-printed, well-preserved card that is beginning to show signs of wear. Corners and edges no longer razor sharp, though not noticeably

Mint

Ex.-Mt.

Excellent

Very Good

Fair

Poor

rounded. Centering may be off, but all borders must show. No creases. Surfaces may show slightest loss of original gloss from rubbing across other cards.

Very Good (VG) A card that has obviously been handled. Corners will be rounded and, perhaps, creased. Edges may show dents from having been rubber-banded. Surface will exhibit some loss of luster, but all printing is intact. May show moderate gum staining. No major creases, tape marks or stains, or extraneous writing. Exhibits no damage, just honest handling.

Good (G) A card that shows signs of excessive wear or abuse. Top or corners may have thumbtack holes. Heavily rounded corners, edge nicks and/or surface scratches. Will have several creases of varying intensity, though showing no major loss of ink at the creases. May show minor added pen or pencil writing. May show heavy gum stains, tape stains, or evidence that it has been mounted in scrapbook. Nearly all printing, front and back, will be intact, though there may be one or two small "chips" of design missing. May well show very heavy surface wear and resulting loss of luster.

Fair (F) A badly mishandled card. Many heavy creases, including those breaking the paper. Corners may be rounded into design of card. Tape and/or paper on which card may once have been mounted, may still be adhered. May have pen or pencil writing added so as to detract from design. Major areas of back may be missing due to tape or paper removal.

Poor (P) A card that has been tortured to death. Corners or other areas may have been torn off. Card may have been trimmed, have holes from paper punch or have been used for BB gun practice. Major portions of front or back printing may be missing from contact with heaven-only-knows-what substance. Face may exhibit added writing in form of derogatory comments on the player's ability, ethnic heritage or legitimacy.

COURTESY OF SPORTS COLLECTORS DIGEST

Collection Categories

9

When you accumulate baseball cards, you need to put them in some kind of order. The best way to do this is to sort your cards into categories. Baseball card collectors call these categories collections. Your collections should reflect your special interests in baseball. Make up your own, or choose some of the common types of collections from the following list.

Complete Set (Series)

A complete set includes every card issued by a company in a single year. A checklist baseball card lists the cards and their designated numbers for the year. When you have checked off every card on the list, you know you have a complete set. This is the most popular way of collecting baseball cards.

Teams

A team collection is made up of the cards of every player on a given team during a single season. Team collecting is an excellent way to show your loyalty toward your favorite ball club and its players. There is no set way to start a team collection. You can blend your Topps, Fleers and Donruss cards into one team, taking the best picture of each player. Because players are traded and managers change yearly, this kind of collection provides a sort of time capsule.

Themes

Collecting by theme is creative collecting. There are many different and unique themes you can think of yourself. Collecting theme cards is fun and will enliven your collection. Some good examples of theme collections are listed below.

A collection of father and son cards, i.e., Yogi and Dale Berra. There have been almost 100 players whose sons have also played Major League Baseball. Over the years this collection could include grandsons.

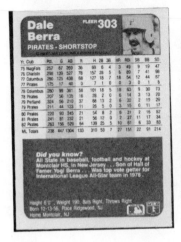
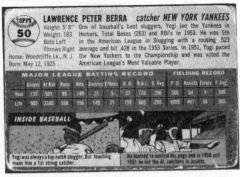

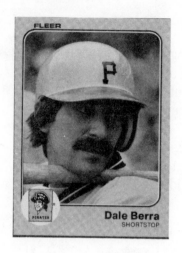

A collection of players whose last names are the same as American presidents, i.e., Gary Carter, U. L. Washington.

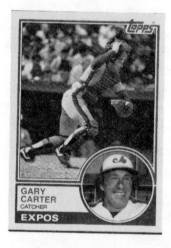

A collection of players whose names are the same as animals, i.e., Ray Lamb, Steve Trout.

 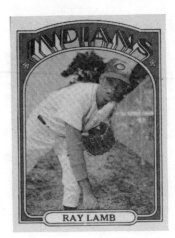

A collection of players whose names are the same as occupations, i.e., John Butcher, Dusty Baker.

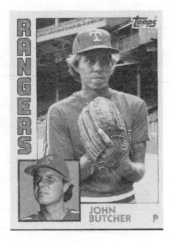 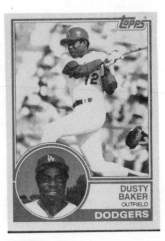

A collection of players who have nicknames, i.e., Dennis "Oilcan" Boyd, Tug McGraw.

A collection of cards of all the players who have been inducted into the Baseball Hall of Fame, i.e., Willie Mays, Duke Snider.

Autographed Cards

You must have the players autograph their own cards in order to have this kind of collection. Some cards have the players' autographs already printed on them. These are not true autographed cards.

There are several ways to have your cards autographed. One way is to have the player autograph it in person. You may go to the stadium before the game and try your luck. The players are busy at this time and some of them don't like to give autographs before the game. But others do, so see for yourself. In person autographs are easiest to get at spring training camp, before the season begins, when players have more time. On page 71 you will find a guide to spring training camp locations.

If you can't get to a training camp or ball park, you can send your cards through the mail. The best way to do this is to mail your cards (with a self-addressed, stamped return envelope) in care of the ball park. On page 67 you will find a list of the addresses of Major League ball parks. If you time it so that your letter arrives just before a team's long home stand, you have a better chance of getting a response. Some collectors mail cards to be autographed to the players' homes. Many hobby magazines print the home addresses of players. Again, pick the right time to mail your cards. The All Star break and off-season are the best times to catch the players at home. Most players will return your cards with an autograph, but some may not. Never send valuable cards through the mail. Also, you must be patient. Players are busy and many kids want autographed cards. You may have to wait a long time to have your autographed cards returned.

Errors and Variations

Error cards are those with mistakes. Common errors are as follows: incorrect statistics, misspelling of names, wrong teams and wrong positions. A collection of error cards can be very valuable. Once the company finds an error, it sometimes corrects it and reissues the card. The cards with errors may become scarce and therefore valuable. A card that corrects an error is called a variation. A helpful guide for people who collect error and variation cards is *THE MISTAKE MANUAL,* written by Ralph Nozaki.

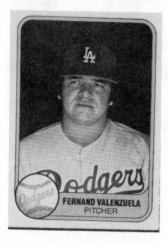

FERNAND VALENZUELA
PITCHER

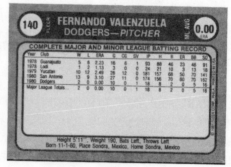

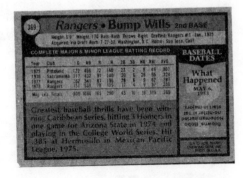

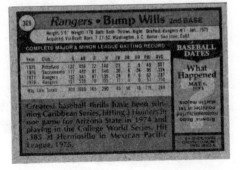

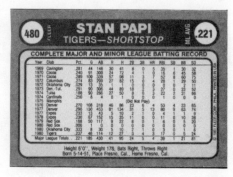

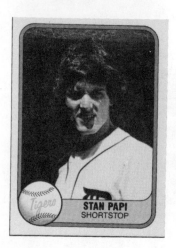

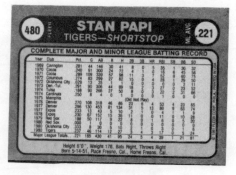

Players' First Cards

Usually a player first appears on a baseball card when he's in the Minor Leagues. A collection of players' first Minor League cards is a unique one. These cards cannot be purchased in stores. They are available by writing to TCMA Company, Box #2, Amawalk, New York 10501. Another way of getting

these cards is by writing to the Minor League teams
that issue them. A list of leagues and their addresses
can be found on page 69.

Rookies

A rookie card is the first Major League baseball card of a player. Sometimes the designation *Rookie* is on the card. Sometimes it is just a regular player card in the series. This may be a worthwhile collection because the first card of a player who has become a superstar can be very valuable.

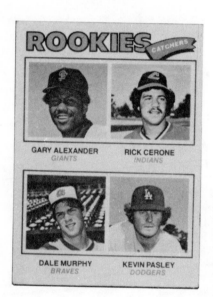

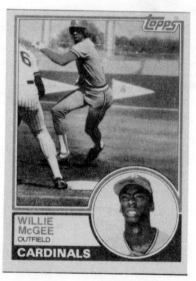

Single Player

A single player collection includes all of one player's cards since he began playing baseball. For example, if you want to collect all of my baseball cards you will need the following cards:

Tom Seaver
Baseball Card Checklist

TOPPS

1967	#581	(Rookie)
1968	#45	
1969	#480	
1970	#300	
1971	#160	
1972	#445	(In Action #446)
1973	#350	
1974	#80	
1975	#370	
1976	#600	(Record Breaker #5)
1977	#150	
1978	#450	
1979	#100	
1980	#500	
1981	#220	
1982	#30	(In Action #31) (All Star #346)
1983	#580	
1984	#740	

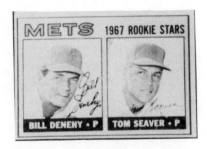

DONRUSS

1981	#422	
1982	#148	(Diamond King #16)
1983	#122	
1984	#116	

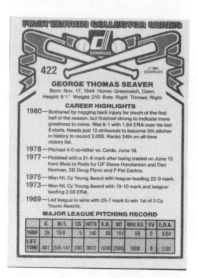

FLEERS

1981	#200	
1982	#82	(Most Wins #645)
1983	#601	
1984	#595	

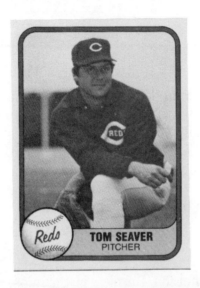

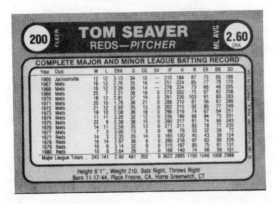

10 **Five Famous Collectors**

Among the many people who collect baseball cards, there are five outstanding ones. They are Jefferson Burdick, Leopold Goulston, Renata Galasso, Barry Halper and Edward Wharton-Tigar. These collectors are famous because of the size and quality of their collections and because of their contributions to the hobby of baseball card collecting.

Jefferson Burdick

Jefferson Burdick is the most famous baseball card collector in America. His collection, which has been called "the finest collection of American cards," is located in the *Print Room* of the Metropolitan Museum of Art, New York City. Among the 300,000 items in the room is an extensive collection of *Old Judge* tobacco baseball cards and other baseball cards from every part of the country.

He presented the first of his collection to the museum in 1948. For twelve years he continued to ship two to six cartons to the museum annually. After all the cards reached the museum, Burdick spent years working there to catalogue each of them in the collection. His designations for baseball cards are used by hobbyists today (for example, T-cards). Shortly after his collection was labeled and in place at the musuem, Jefferson Burdick died.

Leopold Goulston

The New York City Public Library is the home of another famous collection. It is called the Goulston Collection, named after Leopold Morse Goulston. He was responsible for the 1,000 portraits of baseball players and old baseball teams on tobacco cards of the 1800s. This collection, which was donated to the library in 1946, can be viewed at the main branch (42nd Street) of the library.

Renata Galasso

Among today's collectors is Renata Galasso, one of the few women collectors and dealers in the field. She started collecting when she was eighteen years old and a college freshman. She was looking for a part-time job when someone suggested she invest in baseball cards as a business. Today, she and her husband are very successful baseball card dealers. They also publish their own baseball card collecting magazine called *The Hobby Card Report*. Among her private collection of cards, Ms. Galasso has four of the valuable Eddie Plank cards and several complete sets of tobacco cards.

Ms. Galasso advises kids to collect what they like in baseball cards. If they are trying to buy cards that will become valuable, they should look for cards of young players who may be superstars in future years.

Barry Halper

Barry Halper is considered the ultimate collector of our time. His private collection is kept in his own home. It has been called a "private museum that would make the Hall of Fame envious."

As an eight-year-old, Halper, like most of his friends, collected baseball cards. Luckily his mother didn't throw any of them away. Today he has more than a million baseball cards in his collection. Among them is the rare and very valuable Honus Wagner card. His collection is so famous that he has appeared on many television programs to talk about it.

Edward Wharton-Tigar

Edward Wharton-Tigar is an international card collector. A successful British businessman, he travels throughout the world for his company. He has found card collectors in every country he has visited. His weekly mailbag is filled with letters from these collectors who seek advice on card collecting.

Despite his multi-million-dollar dealings, his greatest satisfaction comes from collecting baseball cards. He has one of the most complete collections of baseball tobacco cards in the world today, including the rare Honus Wagner, about which he said, "I paid $250 for my card twenty-five years ago and my friends told me I was foolish to pay such a price for a cigarette card—one sold in New York in 1981 for $25,000."

Mr. Wharton-Tigar started collecting cards at the early age of four. His mother wanted him to collect stamps; his father encouraged him to collect baseball cards. He can locate any of these cards in a minute. How does he do it? He uses an index system which he developed and is presently used by tobacco card collectors all over the world.

I hope the stories of these five collectors are an inspiration to you. Who knows, maybe some day you too may make a contribution to the hobby of baseball card collecting.

11

A Guide to Baseball Card Abbreviations

The back side of baseball cards are loaded with information about the players baseball statistics. Most of it is abbreviated. The following list will help you to understand the meaning of the information.

	PLAYERS
AL	American League
NL	National League
G	Games
AB	At Bats
RBI	Runs Batted In
HR	Home Runs
3B	Triples
2B	Doubles
H	Hits
R	Runs
AVG	Batting Average

The baseball cards of pitchers have special abbreviations. They are as follows:

	PITCHERS
G	Games Pitched
IP	Innings Pitched
W	Wins

L   Losses
PCT   Percentage of Games Won and Lost
R   Runs
ER   Earned Runs
SO   Strikeouts
BB   Bases on Balls (Walks)
ERA   Earned Run Average
CG   Complete Games
S   Saves

When collectors advertise in newspapers and hobby magazines, they use abbreviations to identify the cards they want to buy, sell or swap. Following is a list of standard hobby abbreviations used by baseball card collectors.

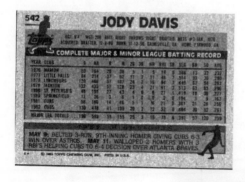

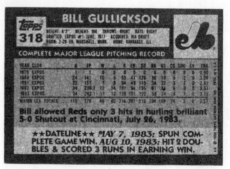

Standard Hobby Abbreviations

ABT	About
AUTO	Autographed
B	Bottom
BK	Back
C	Corner
CR	Crease
CRS	Creases
DAM	Damaged
F	Front
GB	Glue on Back
HC	Heavily Creased
IK	Ink Marks
MB	Minimum Bid
PH	Pin Hole
PM	Pencil Marks
PUH	Punch Hole
S	Stained
SASE	Self-Addressed Stamped Envelope
SB	Suggested Bid
SC	Slightly Creased
SH	Staple Holes
SL	Slight
ST	Slight Trimming
T	Top
TH	Tack Hole
TM	Tape Marks
TP	Taped
W	With

The following is a list of letter prefixes used to classify the cards issued before 1948.

1. N-cards Nineteenth-century tobacco cards
2. T-cards Twentieth-century tobacco cards
3. E-cards Pre–1930 candy and gum cards

4. R-cards   Candy and gum issued from 1930 to present

5. F-cards   Food cards also known as premiums. They are given away with hot dogs, ice cream, etc.

6. D-cards   Bakery product cards also known as premiums. They are given away with bread and cookies.

12 Professional Baseball Team Directory

NATIONAL LEAGUE

Atlanta Braves
PO Box 4064
Atlanta, GA 30302

Chicago Cubs
Wrigley Field
Chicago, IL 60613

Cincinnati Reds
100 Riverfront Stadium
Cincinnati, OH 45202

Houston Astros
Astrodome
PO Box 218
Houston, TX 77001

Los Angeles Dodgers
Dodger Stadium
1000 Elysian Park Ave.
Los Angeles, CA 90012

Montreal Expos
PO Box 500, Station M
Montreal, Quebec H1V 3P2

New York Mets
William A. Shea Stadium
Roosevelt Ave. & 126th St.
Flushing, NY 11368

Philadelphia Phillies
PO Box 7575
Philadelphia, PA 15212

Pittsburgh Pirates
600 Stadium Circle
Pittsburgh, PA 15212

St. Louis Cardinals
Busch Memorial Stadium
250 Stadium Plaza
St. Louis, MO 63102

San Diego Padres
PO Box 2000
San Diego, CA 92120

San Francisco Giants
Candlestick Park
San Francisco, CA 94124

AMERICAN LEAGUE

Baltimore Orioles
Memorial Stadium
Baltimore, MD 21218

Boston Red Sox
24 Yawkey Way
Boston, MA 02215

California Angels
Anaheim Stadium
2000 State College Blvd.
Anaheim, CA 92806

Chicago White Sox
Comiskey Park
Dan Ryan Expressway &
  35th St.
Chicago, IL 60616

Cleveland Indians
Cleveland Stadium
Cleveland, OH 44114

Detroit Tigers
Tiger Stadium
Detroit, MI 48216

Kansas City Royals
Harry S. Truman Sports
  Complex
PO Box 1969
Kansas City, MO 64141

Milwaukee Brewers
Milwaukee County Stadium
Milwaukee, WI 53214

Minnesota Twins
Hubert H. Humphrey
  Metrodome
8001 Cedar Ave.
Bloomington, MN 55420

New York Yankees
Yankee Stadium
Bronx, NY 10451

Oakland A's
Oakland-Alameda County
  Coliseum
Oakland, CA 94621

Seattle Mariners
PO Box 4100
Seattle, WA 98104

Texas Rangers
Arlington Stadium
PO Box 1111
Arlington, TX 76010

Toronto Blue Jays
Box 7777
Adelaide St. PO
Toronto, Ontario M5C 2K7

13

A Guide to Minor League Teams

You can locate the teams in your area by contacting the following league offices.

AAA
American Association   Box 382; Wichita,
                             KS 67201

AAA
International League   Box 608; Grove City,
                             OH 43123

AAA
Pacific Coast League   2101 E. Broadway Rd.;
                             Tempe, AZ 85282

AA
Eastern League   PO Box 318; Bristol,
                             CT 06010

AA
Southern League   235 Main St.; Suite 200,
                             Trussville, AL 35173

AA
Texas League   1501 N. University; Suite
                             412, Little Rock,
                             AR 72207

A
California League

1060 Willow; San Jose,
CA 95125

A
Carolina League

219 W. Chatham St.;
Apex, NC 27502

A
Florida State League

Box 414; Lakeland,
FL 33802

A
Midwest League

Box 444, Burlington,
IA 52601

A
New York/Penn League

220 Brookside Dr.,
Buffalo, NY 14220

A
Northwest League

1840 Tabor St., Eugene,
OR 97401

A
South Atlantic League

Box 49; Kings Mountain,
NC 28086

Rookie
Appalachian League

157 Carson Lane; Bristol,
VA 24201

Rookie
Pioneer League

Box 1144; Billings, MT
59103

Rookie
Gulf Coast League

Sunset Towers, Suite
905, 11 Sunset Drive,
Sarasota, FL 33577

14 Spring Training Camps

Atlanta Braves
West Palm Beach Municipal
 Stadium
Palm Beach, Florida

Baltimore Orioles
Miami Stadium
Northwest 10th Avenue
Miami, Florida

Boston Red Sox
Chain O'Lakes Park
Cypress Gardens Boulevard
Winter Haven, Florida

California Angels
Angel Stadium
Sunrise Way
Palm Springs, California

Chicago Cubs
Hoho Kam Park
Mesa, Arizona

Cincinnati Reds
Al Lopez Field
Dale Maboy Highway and
 Tampa Boulevard
Tampa, Florida

Cleveland Indians
Hy Corbet Field
Randolph Park
Ruscon, Arizona

Detroit Tigers
Joker Marchant
Stadium Hills Boulevard
Lakeland, Florida

Houston Astros
Astrotown Complex
Interstate 95
Cocoa, Florida

Kansas City Royals
Pijott Stadium
Fort Meyers, Florida

Los Angeles Dodgers
Dodgertown
Vero Beach, Florida

Milwaukee Brewers
Sun City Stadium
Sun City, Arizona

Minnesota Twins
Tinker Field
Tampa and Church Streets
Tampa, Florida

Montreal Expos
West Palm Beach Municipal
    Stadium
Palm Beach Lakes Boulevard
West Palm Beach, Florida

New York Mets
Payson Complex
7902 30th Avenue North
St. Petersburg, Florida

New York Yankees
Yankee Stadium
5301 Northwest 12th Avenue
Fort Lauderdale, Florida

Oakland A's
Phoenix Stadium
5999 East Van Buren
Phoenix, Arizona

Philadelphia Phillies
Carpenter Complex
Coachman Road
Clearwater, Florida

St. Louis Cardinals
Busch Complex
62n Avenue
St. Petersburg, Florida

San Francisco Giants
Scottsdale Stadium
7408 East Osborn Road
Scottsdale, Arizona

Seattle Mariners
Diablo Stadium
2525 South 48th St.
Tempe, Arizona

Texas Rangers
Pompano Beach Municipal
    Stadium
Field on Northeast Eighth
    Street
Pompano Beach, Florida

Toronto Blue Jays
Grant Field
Douglas Avenue
Dunedin, Florida

15 Price Guide and Checklist

TOPPS—1980

(2½″ × 3½″, Numbered 1–726, Color) Mint Condition

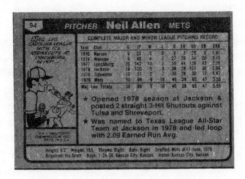

Complete Set	$23.00
1 Highlights, 1979	.15
2 Highlights, 1979	.10
3 Highlights, 1979	.10
4 Highlights, 1979	.10
5 Highlights, 1979	.10
6 Highlights, 1979	.10
7 Mike Lum	.05
8 Craig Swan	.05
9 Steven Braun	.05
10 Denny Martinez	.05
11 Jimmy Sexton	.05
12 John Curtis	.05
13 Ron Pruitt	.05
14 Dave Cash	.05
15 Bill Campbell	.05
16 Jerry Narron	.05
17 Bruce Sutter	.15
18 Ron Jackson	.05
19 Balor Moore	.05

20	Dan Ford	.05	64	Joe Nolan	.05
21	Manny Sarmiento	.05	65	Al Bumbry	.05
22	Pat Putnam	.05	66	Kansas City Royals	.05
23	Derrel Thomas	.05	67	Doyle Alexander	.05
24	Jim Slaton	.05	68	Larry Harlow	.05
25	Lee Mazzilli	.05	69	Rick Williams	.05
26	Marty Pattin	.05	70	Gary Carter	.40
27	Del Unser	.05	71	John Milner	.05
28	Bruce Kison	.05	72	Fred Howard	.05
29	Mark Wagner	.05	73	Dave Collins	.05
30	Vida Blue	.10	74	Sid Monge	.05
31	Jay Johnstone	.05	75	Bill Russell	.05
32	Julio Cruz	.05	76	John Stearns	.05
33	Tony Scott	.05	77	Dave Stieb	1.50
34	Jeff Newman	.05	78	Ruppert Jones	.05
35	Luis Tiant	.10	79	Bob Owchinko	.05
36	Rusty Torres	.05	80	Ron LeFlore	.05
37	Kiko Garcia	.05	81	Ted Sizemore	.05
38	Dan Spillner	.05	82	Houston Astros	.05
39	Rowland Office	.07	83	Steve Trout	.05
40	Carlton Fisk	.10	84	Gary Lavelle	.05
41	Texas Rangers	.05	85	Ted Simmons	.10
42	Dave Palmer	.05	86	Dave Hamilton	.05
43	Bombo Rivera	.05	87	Pepe Frias	.05
44	Bill Fahey	.05	88	Ken Landreaux	.05
45	Frank White	.10	89	Don Hood	.05
46	Rico Carty	.05	90	Manny Trillo	.05
47	Bill Bonham	.05	91	Rick Dempsey	.05
48	Rick Miller	.05	92	Rick Rhoden	.05
49	Mario Guerrero	.05	93	Dave Roberts	.05
50	J. Rodney Richard	.10	94	Neil Allen	.05
51	Joe Ferguson	.05	95	Cecil Cooper	.15
52	Warren Brusstar	.05	96	Oakland A's	.05
53	Ben Oglivie	.10	97	Bill Lee	.05
54	Dennis Lamp	.05	98	Jerry Terrell	.05
55	Bill Madlock	.15	99	Victor Cruz	.05
56	Bobby Valentine	.05	100	Johnny Bench	.50
57	Pete Vuckovich	.15	101	Aurelio Lopez	.05
58	Doug Flynn	.05	102	Rich Dauer	.05
59	Eddy Putman	.05	103	Bill Caudill	.05
60	Bucky Dent	.05	104	Manny Mota	.05
61	Gary Serum	.05	105	Frank Tanana	.05
62	Mike Ivie	.05	106	Jeff Leonard	.05
63	Bob Stanley	.05	107	Francisco Barrios	.05

108	Bob Horner	.35	152	John Fulgham	.05
109	Bill Travers	.05	153	Tim Blackwell	.05
110	Fred Lynn	.35	154	Lary Sorensen	.05
111	Bob Knepper	.05	155	Jerry Remy	.05
112	Chicago White Sox	.05	156	Tony Brizzolara	.05
113	Geoff Zahn	.05	157	Willie Wilson	.15
114	Juan Beniquez	.05	158	Rob Picciolo	.05
115	Sparky Lyle	.05	159	Ken Clay	.05
116	Larry Cox	.05	160	Eddie Murray	.35
117	Dock Ellis	.05	161	Larry Christenson	.05
118	Phil Garner	.05	162	Bob Randall	.05
119	Sammy Stewart	.05	163	Steve Swisher	.05
120	Greg Luzinski	.20	164	Greg Pryor	.05
121	Checklist #1	.05	165	Omar Moreno	.05
122	Dave Rosello	.05	166	Glenn Abbott	.05
123	Lynn Jones	.05	167	Jack Clark	.10
124	Dave Lemanczyk	.05	168	Rick Waits	.05
125	Tony Perez	.10	169	Luis Gomez	.05
126	Dave Tomlin	.05	170	Burt Hooton	.05
127	Gary Thomasson	.05	171	Fernando Gonzalez	.05
128	Tom Burgmeier	.05	172	Ron Hodges	.05
129	Craig Reynolds	.05	173	John Henry Johnson	.05
130	Amos Otis	.10	174	Ray Knight	.05
131	Paul Mitchell	.05	175	Rick Reuschel	.05
132	Biff Pocoroba	.05	176	Champ Summers	.05
133	Jerry Turner	.05	177	Dave Heaverlo	.05
134	Matt Keough	.05	178	Tim McCarver	.05
135	Bill Buckner	.15	179	Ron Davis	.05
136	Dick Ruthven	.05	180	Warren Cromartie	.10
137	John Castino	.05	181	Moose Haas	.05
138	Ross Baumgarten	.05	182	Ken Reitz	.05
139	Dane Iorg	.05	183	Jim Anderson	.05
140	Rich Gossage	.15	184	Steve Renko	.05
141	Gary Alexander	.05	185	Hal McRae	.05
142	Phil Huffman	.05	186	Junior Moore	.05
143	Bruce Bochte	.05	187	Alan Ashby	.05
144	Steve Comer	.05	188	Terry Crowley	.05
145	Darrell Evans	.10	189	Kevin Kobel	.05
146	Bob Welch	.05	190	Buddy Bell	.05
147	Terry Puhl	.05	191	Ted Martinez	.05
148	Manny Sanguillen	.05	192	Altanta Braves	.05
149	Tom Hume	.05	193	Dave Goltz	.05
150	Jason Thompson	.05	194	Mike Easler	.10
151	Tom Hausman	.05	195	John Montefusco	.05

196 Lance Parrish	.05
197 Byron McLaughlin	.05
198 Dell Alston	.05
199 Mike LaCoss	.05
200 Jim Rice	.50
201 Batting Leaders	.10
202 Home Run Leaders	.10
203 R.B.I. Leaders	.10
204 Stolen Base Leaders	.10
205 Victory Leaders	.10
206 Strikeout Leaders	.10
207 E.R.A. Leaders	.10
208 Wayne Cage	.05
209 Von Joshua	.05
210 Steve Carlton	.80
211 Dave Skaggs	.05
212 Dave Roberts	.05
213 Mike Jorgensen	.05
214 California Angels	.05
215 Sixto Lezcano	.05
216 Phil Mankowski	.05
217 Ed Halicki	.05
218 Jose Morales	.05
219 Steve Mingori	.05
220 Dave Concepcion	.10
221 Joe Cannon	.05
222 Ron Hassey	.05
223 Bob Sykes	.05
224 Willie Montanez	.05
225 Lou Piniella	.05
226 Bill Stein	.05
227 Len Barker	.05
228 Johnny Oates	.05
229 Jim Bibby	.05
230 Dave Winfield	.35
231 Steve McCatty	.05
232 Alan Trammell	.05
233 LaRue Washington	.05
234 Vern Ruhle	.05
235 Andre Dawson	.20
236 Marc Hill	.05
237 Scott McGregor	.10
238 Rob Wilfong	.05
239 Don Aase	.05

240 Dave Kingman	.10
241 Checklist #2	.05
242 Lamar Johnson	.05
243 Jerry Augustine	.05
244 St. Louis Cardinals	.05
245 Phil Niekro	.10
246 Tim Foli	.05
247 Frank Riccelli	.05
248 Jamie Quirk	.05
249 Jim Clancy	.05
250 Jim Kaat	.10
251 Kip Young	.05
252 Ted Cox	.05
253 John Montague	.05
254 Paul Dade	.05
255 Dusty Baker	.10
256 Roger Erickson	.05
257 Larry Herndon	.05
258 Paul Moskau	.05
259 New York Mets	.05
260 Al Oliver	.25
261 Dave Chalk	.05
262 Benny Ayala	.05
263 Dave LaRoche	.05
264 Bill Robinson	.05
265 Robin Yount	.50
266 Bernie Carbo	.05
267 Dan Schatzeder	.05
268 Rafael Landestoy	.05
269 Dave Tobik	.05
270 Mike Schmidt	1.00
271 Dick Drago	.05
272 Ralph Garr	.05
273 Eduardo Rodriguez	.05
274 Dale Murphy	1.00
275 Jerry Koosman	.05
276 Tom Veryzer	.05
277 Rick Bosetti	.05
278 Jim Spencer	.05
279 Rob Andrews	.05
280 Gaylord Perry	.15
281 Paul Blair	.05
282 Seattle Mariners	.05
283 John Ellis	.05

284	Larry Murray	.05	328	Minnesota Twins		.05
285	Don Baylor	.10	329	Bert Roberge		.05
286	Darold Knowles	.05	330	Al Cowens		.05
287	John Lowenstein	.05	331	Rich Hebner		.05
288	Dave Rozema	.05	332	Enrique Romo		.05
289	Bruce Bochy	.05	333	Jim Norris		.10
290	Steve Garvey	.50	334	Jim Beattie		.05
291	Randy Scarbery	.05	335	Willie McCovey		.50
292	Dale Berra	.05	336	George Medich		.05
293	Elias Sosa	.05	337	Carney Lansford		.10
294	Charlie Spikes	.05	338	Johnny Wockenfuss		.05
295	Larry Gura	.05	339	John D'Acquisto		.05
296	Dave Rader	.05	340	Ken Singleton		.10
297	Tim Johnson	.05	341	Jim Essian		.05
298	Ken Holtzman	.05	342	Odell Jones		.05
299	Steve Henderson	.05	343	Mike Vail		.05
300	Ron Guidry	.35	344	Randy Lerch		.05
301	Mike Edwards	.05	345	Larry Parrish		.05
302	Los Angeles Dodgers	.05	346	Buddy Solomon		.05
303	Bill Castro	.05	347	Harry Chappas		.05
304	Butch Wynegar	.05	348	Checklist #3		.05
305	Randy Jones	.05	349	Jack Brohamer		.05
306	Denny Walling	.05	350	George Hendrick		.15
307	Rick Honeycutt	.05	351	Bob Davis		.05
308	Mike Hargrove	.05	352	Dan Briggs		.05
309	Larry McWilliams	.05	353	Andy Hassler		.05
310	Dave Parker	.25	354	Rick Auerbach		.05
311	Roger Metzger	.05	355	Gary Matthews		.05
312	Mike Barlow	.05	356	San Diego Padres		.05
313	Johnny Grubb	.05	357	Bob McClure		.05
314	Tim Stoddard	.05	358	Lou Whitaker		.10
315	Steve Kemp	.10	359	Randy Moffitt		.05
316	Bob Lacey	.05	360	Darrell Porter		.05
317	Mike Anderson	.05	361	Wayne Garland		.05
318	Jerry Reuss	.05	362	Danny Goodwin		.05
319	Chris Speier	.05	363	Wayne Gross		.05
320	Dennis Eckersley	.05	364	Ray Burris		.05
321	Keith Hernandez	.25	365	Bobby Murcer		.05
322	Claudell Washington	.05	366	Rob Dressler		.05
323	Mick Kelleher	.05	367	Billy Smith		.05
324	Tom Underwood	.05	368	Willie Aikens		.05
325	Dan Driessen	.10	369	Jim Kern		.05
326	Bo McLaughlin	.05	370	Cesar Cedeno		.10
327	Ray Fosse	.05	371	Jack Morris		.10

372	Joel Youngblood	.05	416	Tom Brookens	.05
373	Dan Petry	.05	417	Craig Chamberlain	.05
374	Jim Gantner	.10	418	Roger Freed	.05
375	Ross Grimsley	.05	419	Vic Correll	.05
376	Gary Allenson	.05	420	Butch Hobson	.05
377	Junior Kennedy	.05	421	Doug Bird	.05
378	Jerry Mumphrey	.05	422	Larry Milbourne	.05
379	Kevin Bell	.05	423	Dave Frost	.05
380	Garry Maddox	.05	424	New York Yankees	.05
381	Chicago Cubs	.05	425	Mark Belanger	.05
382	Dave Freisleben	.05	426	Grant Jackson	.05
383	Ed Ott	.05	427	Tom Hutton	.05
384	Joey McLaughlin	.05	428	Pat Zachry	.05
385	Enos Cabell	.05	429	Duane Kuiper	.05
386	Darrell Jackson	.05	430	Larry Hisle	.05
387	Fred Stanley	.05	431	Mike Krukow	.05
388	Mike Paxton	.05	432	Willie Norwood	.05
389	Pete LaCock	.05	433	Rich Gale	.05
390	Fergie Jenkins	.10	434	Johnnie LeMaster	.05
391	Tony Armas	.10	435	Don Gullett	.05
392	Milt Wilcox	.10	436	Billy Almon	.05
393	Ozzie Smith	.05	437	Joe Niekro	.05
394	Reggie Cleveland	.05	438	Dave Revering	.05
395	Ellis Valentine	.05	439	Mike Phillips	.05
396	Dan Meyer	.05	440	Don Sutton	.15
397	Roy Thomas	.05	441	Eric Soderholm	.05
398	Barry Foote	.05	442	Jorge Orta	.05
399	Mike Proly	.05	443	Mike Parrott	.05
400	George Foster	.20	444	Alvis Woods	.05
401	Pete Falcone	.05	445	Mark Fidrych	.05
402	Merv Rettenmund	.05	446	Duffy Dyer	.05
403	Pete Redfern	.05	447	Nino Espinosa	.05
404	Baltimore Orioles	.05	448	Jim Wohlford	.05
405	Dwight Evans	.05	449	Doug Bair	.05
406	Paul Molitor	.15	450	George Brett	.75
407	Tony Solaita	.05	451	Cleveland Indians	.05
408	Bill North	.05	452	Steve Dillard	.05
409	Paul Splittorff	.05	453	Mike Bacsik	.05
410	Bobby Bonds	.05	454	Tom Donohue	.05
411	Frank LaCorte	.05	455	Mike Torrez	.05
412	Thad Bosley	.05	456	Frank Taveras	.05
413	Allen Ripley	.05	457	Bert Blyleven	.05
414	George Scott	.05	458	Billy Sample	.05
415	Bill Atkinson	.05	459	Mickey Lolich	.05

460	Willie Randolph	.05
461	Dwayne Murphy	.05
462	Mike Sadek	.05
463	Jerry Royster	.05
464	John Denny	.05
465	Rick Monday	.05
466	Mike Squires	.05
467	Jesse Jefferson	.05
468	Aurelio Rodriguez	.05
469	Randy Niemann	.05
470	Bob Boone	.05
471	Hosken Powell	.05
472	Willie Hernandez	.05
473	Bump Wills	.05
474	Steve Busby	.05
475	Cesar Geronimo	.05
476	Bob Shirley	.05
477	Buck Martinez	.05
478	Gil Flores	.05
479	Montreal Expos	.05
480	Bob Watson	.10
481	Tom Paciorek	.05
482	Rickey Henderson	4.00
483	Bo Diaz	.05
484	Checklist #4	.05
485	Mickey Rivers	.05
486	Mike Tyson	.05
487	Wayne Nordhagen	.05
488	Roy Howell	.05
489	Preston Hanna	.05
490	Lee May	.05
491	Steve Mura	.05
492	Todd Cruz	.05
493	Jerry Martin	.05
494	Craig Minetto	.05
495	Bake McBride	.05
496	Silvio Martinez	.05
497	Jim Mason	.05
498	Danny Darwin	.05
499	San Francisco Giants	.05
500	Tom Seaver	.50
501	Rennie Stennett	.05
502	Rich Wortham	.05
503	Mike Cubbage	.05
504	Gene Garber	.05
505	Bert Campaneris	.05
506	Tom Buskey	.05
507	Leon Roberts	.05
508	U. L. Washington	.05
509	Ed Glynn	.05
510	Ron Cey	.10
511	Eric Wilkins	.05
512	Jose Cardenal	.05
513	Tom Dixon	.05
514	Steve Ontiveros	.05
515	Mike Caldwell	.05
516	Hector Cruz	.05
517	Don Stanhouse	.05
518	Nelson Norman	.05
519	Steve Nicosia	.05
520	Steve Rogers	.10
521	Ken Brett	.05
522	Jim Morrison	.05
523	Ken Henderson	.05
524	Jim Wright	.05
525	Clint Hurdle	.05
526	Philadelphia Phillies	.05
527	Doug Rau	.05
528	Adrian Devine	.05
529	Jim Barr	.05
530	Jim Sundberg	.05
531	Eric Rasmussen	.05
532	Willie Horton	.05
533	Checklist #5	.05
534	Andre Thornton	.05
535	Bob Forsch	.05
536	Lee Lacy	.05
537	Alex Trevino	.05
538	Joe Strain	.05
539	Rudy May	.05
540	Pete Rose	1.50
541	Miguel Dilone	.05
542	Joe Coleman	.05
543	Pat Kelly	.05
544	Rick Sutcliffe	.05
545	Jeff Burroughs	.05
546	Rick Langford	.05
547	John Wathan	.05

548 Dave Rajsich	.05	593 Jesus Alou	.05
549 Larry Wolfe	.05	594 Dick Tidrow	.05
550 Ken Griffey	.10	595 Don Money	.05
551 Pittsburgh Pirates	.05	596 Rick Matula	.05
552 Bill Nahorodny	.05	597 Tom Poquette	.05
553 Dick Davis	.05	598 Fred Kendall	.05
554 Art Howe	.05	599 Mike Norris	.10
555 Ed Figueroa	.05	600 Reggie Jackson	.75
556 Joe Rudi	.05	601 Buddy Schultz	.05
557 Mark Lee	.05	602 Brian Downing	.05
558 Alfredo Griffin	.05	603 Jack Billingham	.05
559 Dale Murray	.05	604 Glenn Adams	.05
560 Dave Lopes	.05	605 Terry Forster	.05
561 Eddie Whitson	.05	606 Cincinnati Reds	.05
562 Joe Wallis	.05	607 Woodie Fryman	.05
563 Will McEnaney	.05	608 Alan Bannister	.05
564 Rick Manning	.05	609 Ron Reed	.05
565 Dennis Leonard	.05	610 Willie Stargell	.50
566 Bud Harrelson	.05	611 Jerry Garvin	.05
567 Skip Lockwood	.05	612 Cliff Johnson	.05
568 Gary Roenicke	.05	613 Randy Stein	.05
569 Terry Kennedy	.10	614 John Hiller	.05
570 Roy Smalley	.05	615 Doug DeCinces	.05
571 Joe Sambito	.05	616 Gene Richards	.05
572 Jerry Morales	.05	617 Joaquin Andujar	.05
573 Kent Tekulve	.05	618 Bob Montgomery	.05
574 Scot Thompson	.05	619 Sergio Ferrer	.05
575 Ken Kravec	.05	620 Richie Zisk	.05
576 Jim Dwyer	.05	621 Bob Grich	.05
577 Toronto Blue Jays	.05	622 Mario Soto	.10
578 Scott Sanderson	.05	623 Gorman Thomas	.05
579 Charlie Moore	.05	624 Lerrin LaGrow	.05
580 Nolan Ryan	.50	625 Chris Chambliss	.10
581 Bob Bailor	.05	626 Detroit Tigers	.05
582 Brian Doyle	.05	627 Pedro Borbon	.05
583 Bob Stinson	.05	628 Doug Capilla	.05
584 Kurt Bevacqua	.05	629 Jim Todd	.05
585 Al Hrabosky	.05	630 Larry Bowa	.10
586 Mitchell Page	.05	631 Mark Littell	.05
587 Garry Templeton	.10	632 Barry Bonnell	.05
588 Greg Minton	.05	633 Bob Apodaca	.05
589 Chet Lemon	.05	634 Glenn Borgmann	.05
590 Jim Palmer	.25	635 John Candelaria	.05
591 Rick Cerone	.05	636 Toby Harrah	.05
592 Jon Matlack	.05	637 Joe Simpson	.05

638 Mark Clear	.05	683 Prospects for the Pirates	.05
639 Larry Biittner	.05	684 Prospects for the Cardinals	.05
640 Mike Flanagan	.05	685 Prospects for the Padres	.05
641 Ed Kranepool	.05	686 Prospects for the Giants	.05
642 Ken Forsch	.05	687 Mike Heath	.05
643 John Mayberry	.05	688 Steve Stone	.05
644 Charlie Hough	.05	689 Boston Red Sox	.05
645 Rick Burleson	.05	690 Tommy John	.20
646 Checklist #6	.05	691 Ivan De Jesus	.05
647 Milt May	.05	692 Rawly Eastwick	.05
648 Roy White	.05	693 Craig Kusick	.05
649 Tom Griffin	.05	694 Jim Rooker	.05
650 Joe Morgan	.15	695 Reggie Smith	.05
651 Rollie Fingers	.25	696 Julio Gonzalez	.05
652 Mario Mendoza	.05	697 David Clyde	.05
653 Stan Bahnsen	.05	698 Oscar Gamble	.05
654 Bruce Boisclair	.05	699 Floyd Bannister	.05
655 Tug McGraw	.05	700 Rod Carew	.75
656 Larvell Blanks	.05	701 Ken Oberkfell	.05
657 Dave Edwards	.05	702 Ed Farmer	.05
658 Chris Knapp	.05	703 Otto Velez	.05
659 Milwaukee Brewers	.05	704 Gene Tenace	.05
660 Rusty Staub	.05	705 Freddie Patek	.05
661 Prospects for the Orioles	.05	706 Tippy Martinez	.05
662 Prospects for the Red Sox	.05	707 Elliott Maddox	.05
663 Prospects for the Angels	.05	708 Bob Tolan	.05
664 Prospects for the White Sox	.05	709 Pat Underwood	.05
665 Prospects for the Indians	.05	710 Graig Nettles	.10
666 Prospects for the Tigers	.05	711 Bob Galasso	.05
667 Prospects for the Royals	1.00	712 Rodney Scott	.05
668 Prospects for the Brewers	.05	713 Terry Whitfield	.05
669 Prospects for the Twins	.05	714 Fred Norman	.05
670 Prospects for the Yankees	.05	715 Sal Bando	.05
671 Prospects for the Oakland A's	.05	716 Lynn McGlothen	.05
672 Prospects for the Mariners	.05	717 Mickey Klutts	.05
673 Prospects for the Rangers	.05	718 Greg Gross	.05
674 Prospects for the Blue Jays	.05	719 Don Robinson	.05
675 Prospects for the Braves	.05	720 Carl Yastrzemski	.75
676 Prospects for the Cubs	.05	721 Paul Hartzell	.05
677 Prospects for the Reds	.05	722 Jose Cruz	.05
678 Prospects for the Astros	.05	723 Shane Rawley	.05
679 Prospects for the Dodgers	.05	724 Jerry White	.05
680 Prospects for the Expos	.05	725 Rick Wise	.05
681 Prospects for the Mets	.05	726 Steve Yeager	.05
682 Prospects for the Phillies	.05		

TOPPS—1981

(2¹/₂″ × 3¹/₂″, Numbered 1–726, Color) Mint Condition

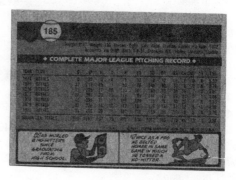

Complete Set		$21.00
1	Brett/Buckner	.15
2	Jackson/Oglivie, Schmidt	.15
3	Cooper/Schmidt	.10
4	Henderson/LeFlore	.10
5	Stone/Carlton	.10
6	Barker/Carlton	.10
7	May/Sutton	.10
8	Quisenberry/Fingers/Hume	.05
9	Pete LaCock	.05
10	Mike Flanagan	.05
11	Jim Wohlford	.05
12	Mark Clear	.05
13	Joe Charboneau	.10
14	John Tudor	.05
15	Larry Parrish	.05
16	Ron Davis	.05
17	Cliff Johnson	.05
18	Glenn Adams	.05
19	Jim Clancy	.05
20	Jeff Burroughs	.05
21	Ron Oester	.05
22	Danny Darwin	.05
23	Alex Trevino	.05
24	Don Stanhouse	.05
25	Sixto Lezcano	.05
26	U. L. Washington	.05
27	Champ Summers	.05
28	Enrique Romo	.05
29	Gene Tenace	.05
30	Jack Clark	.10
31	Checklist #1	.05
32	Ken Oberkfell	.05
33	Rick Honeycutt	.05
34	Aurelio Rodriguez	.05
35	Mitchell Page	.05
36	Ed Farmer	.05
37	Gary Roenicke	.05

38	Win Remmerswall	.05
39	Tom Veryzer	.05
40	Tug McGraw	.05
41	Rangers Future Stars	.05
42	Jerry White	.05
43	Jose Morales	.05
44	Larry McWilliams	.05
45	Enos Cabell	.05
46	Rick Bosetti	.05
47	Ken Brett	.05
48	Dave Skaggs	.05
49	Bob Shirley	.05
50	Dave Lopes	.05
51	Bill Robinson	.05
52	Hector Cruz	.05
53	Kevin Saucier	.05
54	Ivan De Jesus	.05
55	Mike Norris	.05
56	Buck Martinez	.05
57	Dave Roberts	.05
58	Joel Youngblood	.05
59	Dan Petry	.05
60	Willie Randolph	.05
61	Butch Wynegar	.05
62	Joe Pettini	.05
63	Steve Renko	.05
64	Brian Asselstine	.05
65	Scott McGregor	.05
66	Royals Future Stars	.05
67	Ken Kravec	.05
68	Matt Alexander	.05
69	Ed Halicki	.05
70	Al Oliver	.20
71	Hal Dues	.05
72	Barry Evans	.05
73	Doug Bair	.05
74	Mike Hargrove	.05
75	Reggie Smith	.10
76	Mario Mendoza	.05
77	Mike Barlow	.05
78	Steve Dillard	.05
79	Bruce Robbins	.05
80	Rusty Staub	.05
81	Dave Stapleton	.05
82	Astros Future Stars	.05
83	Mike Proly	.05
84	Johnnie LeMaster	.05
85	Mike Caldwell	.05
86	Wayne Gross	.05
87	Rick Camp	.05
88	Joe Lefebvre	.05
89	Darrell Jackson	.05
90	Bake McBride	.05
91	Tim Stoddard	.05
92	Mike Easler	.10
93	Ed Glynn	.05
94	Harry Spilman	.05
95	Jim Sundberg	.05
96	A's Future Stars	.05
97	Chris Speier	.05
98	Clint Hurdle	.05
99	Eric Wilkins	.05
100	Rod Carew	.50
101	Benny Ayala	.05
102	Dave Tobik	.05
103	Jerry Martin	.05
104	Terry Forster	.05
105	Jose Cruz	.05
106	Don Money	.05
107	Rich Wortham	.05
108	Bruce Benedict	.05
109	Mike Scott	.05
110	Carl Yastrzemski	.75
111	Greg Minton	.05
112	Future Stars of the White Sox	.05
113	Mike Phillips	.05
114	Tom Underwood	.05
115	Roy Smalley	.05
116	Joe Simpson	.05
117	Pete Falcone	.05
118	Kurt Bevacqua	.05
119	Tippy Martinez	.05
120	Larry Bowa	.10
121	Larry Harlow	.05
122	John Denny	.05
123	Al Cowens	.05
124	Jerry Garvin	.05
125	Andre Dawson	.20

126 Charlie Leibrandt	.05	
127 Rudy Law	.05	
128 Gary Allenson	.05	
129 Art Howe	.05	
130 Larry Gura	.05	
131 Keith Moreland	.05	
132 Tommy Boggs	.05	
133 Jeff Cox	.05	
134 Steve Mura	.05	
135 Gorman Thomas	.10	
136 Doug Capilla	.05	
137 Hosken Powell	.05	
138 Rich Dotson	.05	
139 Oscar Gamble	.05	
140 Bob Forsch	.05	
141 Miguel Dilone	.05	
142 Jackson Todd	.05	
143 Dan Meyer	.05	
144 Allen Ripley	.05	
145 Mickey Rivers	.05	
146 Bobby Castillo	.05	
147 Dale Berra	.05	
148 Randy Niemann	.05	
149 Joe Nolan	.05	
150 Mark Fidrych	.05	
151 Claudell Washington	.05	
152 John Urrea	.05	
153 Tom Poquette	.05	
154 Rick Langford	.05	
155 Chris Chambliss	.10	
156 Bob McClure	.05	
157 John Wathan	.05	
158 Fergie Jenkins	.05	
159 Brian Doyle	.05	
160 Garry Maddox	.05	
161 Dan Graham	.05	
162 Doug Corbett	.05	
163 Billy Almon	.05	
164 LaMarr Hoyt	1.00	
165 Tony Scott	.05	
166 Floyd Bannister	.05	
167 Terry Whitfield	.05	
168 Don Robinson	.05	
169 John Mayberry	.05	

170 Ross Grimsley	.05
171 Gene Richards	.05
172 Gary Woods	.05
173 Bump Wills	.05
174 Doug Rau	.05
175 Dave Collins	.05
176 Mike Krukow	.05
177 Rick Peters	.05
178 Jim Essian	.05
179 Rudy May	.05
180 Pete Rose	1.00
181 Elias Sosa	.05
182 Bob Grich	.05
183 Dick Davis	.05
184 Jim Dwyer	.05
185 Dennis Leonard	.05
186 Wayne Nordhagen	.05
187 Mike Parrot	.05
188 Doug DeCinces	.05
189 Craig Swan	.05
190 Cesar Cedeno	.05
191 Rick Sutcliffe	.05
192 Braves Future Stars	.05
193 Pete Vuckovich	.10
194 Rod Scurry	.05
195 Rich Murray	.05
196 Duffy Dyer	.05
197 Jim Kern	.05
198 Jerry Dybzinski	.05
199 Chuck Rainey	.05
200 George Foster	.20
201 Record Breaker: Bench	.15
202 Record Breaker: Carlton	.15
203 Record Breaker: Gullickson	.15
204 Record Breaker: LeFlore	.15
205 Record Breaker: Rose	.15
206 Record Breaker: Schmidt	.15
207 Record Breaker: Smith	.15
208 Record Breaker: Wilson	.15
209 Dickie Thon	.10
210 Jim Palmer	.25
211 Derrel Thomas	.05
212 Steve Nicosia	.05
213 Al Holland	.05

214 Future Stars of the Angels	.05
215 Larry Hisle	.10
216 John Henry Johnson	.05
217 Rich Hebner	.05
218 Paul Splittorff	.05
219 Ken Landreaux	.05
220 Tom Seaver	.35
221 Bob Davis	.05
222 Jorge Orta	.05
223 Roy Lee Jackson	.05
224 Pat Zachry	.05
225 Ruppert Jones	.05
226 Manny Sanguillen	.05
227 Fred Martinez	.05
228 Tom Paciorek	.05
229 Rollie Fingers	.25
230 George Hendrick	.20
231 Joe Beckwith	.05
232 Mickey Klutts	.05
233 Skip Lockwood	.05
234 Lou Whitaker	.10
235 Scott Sanderson	.05
236 Mike Ivie	.05
237 Charlie Moore	.05
238 Willie Hernandez	.05
239 Rick Miller	.05
240 Nolan Ryan	.35
241 Checklist #2	.05
242 Chet Lemon	.05
243 Sal Butera	.05
244 Future Stars of the Cardinals	.05
245 Ed Figueroa	.05
246 Ed Ott	.05
247 Glen Hubbard	.05
248 Joey McLaughlin	.05
249 Larry Cox	.05
250 Ron Guidry	.20
251 Tom Brookens	.05
252 Victor Cruz	.05
253 Dave Bergman	.05
254 Ozzie Smith	.10
255 Mark Littell	.05
256 Bombo Rivera	.05
257 Rennie Stennett	.05

258 Joe Prios	.05
259 Future Stars of the Mets	1.00
260 Ron Cey	.10
261 Rickey Henderson	.30
262 Sammy Stewart	.05
263 Brian Downing	.05
264 Jim Norris	.05
265 John Candelaria	.05
266 Tom Herr	.05
267 Stan Bahnsen	.05
268 Jerry Royster	.05
269 Ken Forsch	.05
270 Greg Luzinski	.10
271 Bill Castro	.05
272 Bruce Kimm	.05
273 Stan Papi	.05
274 Craig Chamberlain	.05
275 Dwight Evans	.05
276 Dan Spillner	.05
277 Alfredo Griffin	.05
278 Rick Sofield	.05
279 Bob Knepper	.05
280 Ken Griffey	.10
281 Fred Stanley	.05
282 Future Stars of the Mariners	.05
283 Billy Sample	.05
284 Brian Kingman	.05
285 Jerry Turner	.05
286 Dave Frost	.05
287 Lenn Sakata	.05
288 Bob Clark	.05
289 Mickey Hatcher	.05
290 Bob Boone	.05
291 Aurelio Lopes	.05
292 Mike Squires	.05
293 Charlie Lea	.05
294 Mike Tyson	.05
295 Hal McRae	.05
296 Bill Nahorodny	.05
297 Bob Bailor	.05
298 Buddy Solomon	.05
299 Elliott Maddox	.05
300 Paul Molitor	.20
301 Matt Keough	.05

302	Dodgers Future Stars	1.50	346	Larry Christenson	.05
303	Johnny Oates	.05	347	Harold Baines	.30
304	John Castino	.05	348	Bob Sykes	.05
305	Ken Clay	.05	349	Glenn Hoffman	.05
306	Juan Beniquez	.05	350	J. Rodney Richard	.10
307	Gene Garber	.05	351	Otto Velez	.05
308	Rick Manning	.05	352	Dick Tidrow	.05
309	Luis Salazar	.05	353	Terry Kennedy	.10
310	Vida Blue	.10	354	Mario Soto	.10
311	Freddie Patek	.05	355	Bob Horner	.50
312	Rick Rhoden	.05	356	Future Stars of the Padres	.05
313	Luis Pujols	.05	357	Jim Slaton	.05
314	Rich Dauer	.05	358	Mark Wagner	.05
315	Kirk Gibson	.50	359	Tom Hausman	.05
316	Craig Minetto	.05	360	Willie Wilson	.25
317	Lonnie Smith	.35	361	Joe Strain	.05
318	Steve Yeager	.05	362	Bo Diaz	.05
319	Rowland Office	.05	363	Geoff Zahn	.05
320	Tom Burgmeier	.05	364	Mike Davis	.05
321	Leon Durham	.35	365	Graig Nettles	.10
322	Neil Allen	.05	366	Mike Ramsey	.05
323	Jim Morrison	.05	367	Denny Martinez	.05
324	Mike Willis	.05	368	Leon Roberts	.05
325	Ray Knight	.05	369	Frank Tanana	.05
326	Biff Pocoroba	.05	370	Dave Winfield	.35
327	Moose Haas	.05	371	Charlie Hough	.05
328	Twins Future Stars	.05	372	Jay Johnstone	.05
329	Joaquin Andujar	.05	373	Pat Underwood	.05
330	Frank White	.05	374	Tom Hutton	.05
331	Dennis Lamp	.05	375	Dave Concepcion	.10
332	Lee Lacy	.05	376	Ron Reed	.05
333	Sid Monge	.05	377	Jerry Morales	.05
334	Dane Iorg	.05	378	Dave Rader	.05
335	Rick Cerone	.05	379	Lary Sorensen	.05
336	Eddie Whitson	.05	380	Willie Stargell	.50
337	Lynn Jones	.05	381	Future Stars of the Cubs	.05
338	Checklist #3	.05	382	Paul Mirabella	.05
339	John Ellis	.05	383	Eric Soderholm	.05
340	Bruce Kison	.05	384	Mike Sadek	.05
341	Dwayne Murphy	.05	385	Joe Sambito	.05
342	Eric Rasmussen	.05	386	Dave Edwards	.05
343	Frank Travers	.05	387	Phil Niekro	.10
344	Bryon McLaughlin	.05	388	Andre Thornton	.05
345	Warren Cromartie	.05	389	Marty Pattin	.05

390	Cesar Geronimo	.05
391	Dave Lemanczyk	.05
392	Lance Parrish	.05
393	Broderick Perkins	.05
394	Woodie Fryman	.05
395	Scot Thompson	.05
396	Bill Campbell	.05
397	Julio Cruz	.05
398	Ross Baumgarten	.05
399	Future Stars of the Orioles	.75
400	Reggie Jackson	.50
401	A.L. Playoffs	.05
402	N.L. Playoffs	.05
403	World Series—1980	.05
404	World Series—1980	.05
405	Nino Espinosa	.05
406	Dickie Noles	.05
407	Ernie Whitt	.05
408	Fernando Arroyo	.05
409	Larry Herndon	.05
410	Bert Campaneris	.05
411	Terry Puhl	.05
412	Britt Burns	.20
413	Tony Bernazard	.05
414	John Pacella	.05
415	Ben Oglivie	.05
416	Gary Alexander	.05
417	Dan Schatzeder	.05
418	Bobby Brown	.05
419	Tom Hume	.05
420	Keith Hernandez	.20
421	Bob Stanley	.05
422	Dan Ford	.05
423	Shane Rawley	.05
424	Future Stars of the Yankees	.10
425	Al Bumbry	.05
426	Warren Brusstar	.05
427	John D'Acquisto	.05
428	John Stearns	.05
429	Mick Kelleher	.05
430	Jim Bibby	.05
431	Dave Roberts	.05
432	Len Barker	.05
433	Rance Mulliniks	.05
434	Roger Erickson	.05
435	Jim Spencer	.05
436	Gary Lucas	.05
437	Mike Heath	.05
438	John Montefusco	.05
439	Denny Walling	.05
440	Jerry Reuss	.05
441	Ken Reitz	.05
442	Ron Pruitt	.05
443	Jim Beattie	.05
444	Garth Iorg	.05
445	Ellis Valentine	.05
446	Checklist #4	.05
447	Junior Kennedy	.05
448	Tim Corcoran	.05
449	Paul Mitchell	.05
450	Dave Kingman	.10
451	Future Stars of the Indians	.05
452	Renie Martin	.05
453	Rob Wilfong	.05
454	Andy Hassler	.05
455	Rick Burleson	.05
456	Jeff Reardon	.05
457	Mike Lum	.05
458	Randy Jones	.05
459	Greg Gross	.05
460	Rich Gossage	.10
461	Dave McKay	.05
462	Jack Brohamer	.05
463	Milt May	.05
464	Adrian Devine	.05
465	Bill Russell	.05
466	Bob Molinaro	.05
467	Dave Stieb	.15
468	Johnny Wockenfuss	.05
469	Jeff Leonard	.05
470	Manny Trillo	.05
471	Mike Vail	.05
472	Dyar Miller	.05
473	Jose Cardenal	.05
474	Mike LaCoss	.05
475	Buddy Bell	.05
476	Jerry Koosman	.05
477	Luis Gomez	.05

478 Juan Eichelberger	.05	
479 Future Stars of the Expos	1.50	
480 Carlton Fisk	.10	
481 Bob Lacey	.05	
482 Jim Gantner	.05	
483 Mike Griffin	.05	
484 Max Venable	.05	
485 Garry Templeton	.10	
486 Marc Hill	.05	
487 Dewey Robinson	.05	
488 Damaso Garcia	.05	
489 John Littlefield	.05	
490 Eddie Murray	.25	
491 Gordy Pladson	.05	
492 Barry Foote	.05	
493 Dan Quisenberry	.20	
494 Bob Walk	.05	
495 Dusty Baker	.10	
496 Paul Dade	.05	
497 Fred Norman	.05	
498 Pat Putnam	.05	
499 Frank Pastore	.05	
500 Jim Rice	.25	
501 Tim Foli	.05	
502 Future Stars of the Giants	.05	
503 Steve McCatty	.05	
504 Dale Murphy	.75	
505 Jason Thompson	.05	
506 Phil Huffman	.05	
507 Jamie Quirk	.05	
508 Bob Dressler	.05	
509 Pete Mackanin	.05	
510 Lee Mazzilli	.05	
511 Wayne Garland	.05	
512 Gary Thomasson	.05	
513 Frank LaCorte	.05	
514 George Riley	.05	
515 Robin Yount	.50	
516 Doug Bird	.05	
517 Richie Zisk	.05	
518 Grant Jackson	.05	
519 John Tamargo	.05	
520 Steve Stone	.05	
521 Sam Mejias	.05	

522 Mike Colbern	.05
523 John Fulgham	.05
524 Willie Aikens	.05
525 Mike Torrez	.05
526 Future Stars of the Phillies	.05
527 Danny Goodwin	.05
528 Gary Matthews	.05
529 Dave LaRoche	.05
530 Steve Garvey	.50
531 John Curtis	.05
532 Bill Stein	.05
533 Jesus Figueroa	.05
534 Dave Smith	.05
535 Omar Moreno	.05
536 Bob Owchinko	.05
537 Ron Hodges	.05
538 Tom Griffin	.05
539 Rodney Scott	.05
540 Mike Schmidt	.75
541 Steve Swisher	.05
542 Larry Bradford	.05
543 Terry Crowley	.05
544 Rich Gale	.05
545 Johnny Grubb	.05
546 Paul Moskau	.05
547 Mario Guerrero	.05
548 Dave Goltz	.05
549 Jerry Remy	.05
550 Tommy John	.10
551 Future Stars to the Pirates	.05
552 Steve Trout	.05
553 Tim Blackwell	.05
554 Bert Blyleven	.05
555 Cecil Cooper	.15
556 Jerry Mumphrey	.05
557 Chris Knapp	.05
558 Barry Bonnell	.05
559 Willie Montanez	.05
560 Joe Morgan	.15
561 Dennis Littlejohn	.05
562 Checklist #5	.05
563 Jim Kaat	.10
564 Ron Hassey	.05
565 Burt Hooton	.05

566 Del Unser	.05
567 Mark Bomback	.05
568 Dave Revering	.05
569 Al Williams	.05
570 Ken Singleton	.10
571 Todd Cruz	.05
572 Jack Morris	.10
573 Phil Garner	.05
574 Bill Caudill	.05
575 Tony Perez	.10
576 Reggie Cleveland	.05
577 Future Stars of the Blue Jays	.05
578 Bill Gullickson	.05
579 Tim Flannery	.05
580 Don Baylor	.10
581 Roy Howell	.05
582 Gaylord Perry	.20
583 Larry Milbourne	.05
584 Randy Lerch	.05
585 Amos Otis	.10
586 Silvio Martinez	.05
587 Jeff Newman	.05
588 Gary Lavelle	.05
589 Lamar Johnson	.05
590 Bruce Sutter	.15
591 John Lowenstein	.05
592 Steve Comer	.05
593 Steve Kemp	.05
594 Preston Hanna	.05
595 Butch Hobson	.05
596 Jerry Augustine	.05
597 Rafael Landestoy	.05
598 George Vukovich	.05
599 Dennis Kinney	.05
600 Johnny Bench	.50
601 Don Aase	.05
602 Bobby Murcer	.05
603 John Verhoeven	.05
604 Rob Picciolo	.05
605 Don Sutton	.15
606 Future Stars of the Reds	.05
607 Dave Palmer	.05
608 Greg Pryor	.05
609 Lynn McGlothen	.05

610 Darrell Porter	.05
611 Rick Matula	.05
612 Duane Kuiper	.05
613 Jim Anderson	.05
614 Dave Rozema	.05
615 Rick Dempsey	.05
616 Rick Wise	.05
617 Craig Reynolds	.05
618 John Milner	.05
619 Steve Henderson	.05
620 Dennis Eckersley	.05
621 Tom Donohue	.05
622 Randy Moffitt	.05
623 Sal Bando	.05
624 Bob Welch	.05
625 Bill Buckner	.10
626 Future Stars of the Tigers	.05
627 Luis Tiant	.05
628 Vic Correll	.05
629 Tony Armas	.10
630 Steve Carlton	.35
631 Ron Jackson	.05
632 Al Bannister	.05
633 Bill Lee	.05
634 Doug Flynn	.05
635 Bobby Bonds	.05
636 Al Hrabosky	.05
637 Jerry Narron	.05
638 Checklist #6	.05
639 Carney Lansford	.10
640 Dave Parker	.30
641 Mark Belanger	.05
642 Vern Ruhle	.05
643 Lloyd Moseby	.05
644 Ramon Aviles	.05
645 Rick Reuschel	.05
646 Marvis Foley	.05
647 Dick Drago	.05
649 Darrell Evans	.05
649 Manny Sarmiento	.05
650 Bucky Dent	.05
651 Pedro Guerrero	.15
652 John Montague	.05
653 Bill Fahey	.05

654 Ray Burris	.05
655 Dan Driessen	.05
656 Jon Matlack	.05
657 Mike Cubbage	.05
658 Milt Wilcox	.05
659 Future Stars of the Brewers	.05
660 Gary Carter	.35
661 Baltimore Orioles	.05
662 Boston Red Sox	.05
663 California Angels	.05
664 Chicago White Sox	.05
665 Cleveland Indians	.05
666 Detroit Tigers	.05
667 Kansas City Royals	.05
668 Milwaukee Brewers	.05
669 Minnesota Twins	.05
670 New York Yankees	.05
671 Oakland A's	.05
672 Seattle Mariners	.05
673 Texas Rangers	.05
674 Toronto Blue Jays	.05
675 Atlanta Braves	.05
676 Chicago Cubs	.05
677 Cincinnati Reds	.05
678 Houston Astros	.05
679 Los Angeles Dodgers	.05
680 Montreal Expos	.05
681 New York Mets	.05
682 Philadelphia Phillies	.05
683 Pittsburgh Pirates	.05
684 St. Louis Cardinals	.05
685 San Diego Padres	.05
686 San Francisco Giants	.05
687 Jeff Jones	.05
688 Kiko Garcia	.05
689 Future Stars of the Red Sox	.05
690 Bob Watson	.10

691 Dick Ruthven	.05
692 Lenny Randle	.05
693 Steve Howe	.05
694 Bud Harrelson	.05
695 Kent Tekulve	.05
696 Alan Ashby	.05
697 Rick Waits	.05
698 Mike Jorgensen	.05
699 Glenn Abbott	.05
700 George Brett	.75
701 Joe Rudi	.05
702 George Medich	.05
703 Alvis Woods	.05
704 Bill Travers	.05
705 Ted Simmons	.05
706 Dave Ford	.05
707 Dave Cash	.05
708 Doyle Alexander	.05
709 Alan Trammell	.05
710 Ron LeFlore	.05
711 Joe Ferguson	.05
712 Bill Bonham	.05
713 Bill North	.05
714 Pete Redfern	.05
715 Bill Madlock	.15
716 Glenn Borgmann	.05
717 Jim Barr	.05
718 Larry Biittner	.05
719 Sparky Lyle	.05
720 Fred Lynn	.35
721 Toby Harrah	.05
722 Joe Niekro	.05
723 Bruce Bochte	.05
724 Lou Piniella	.05
725 Steve Rogers	.10
726 Rick Monday	.05

TOPPS—1982

(2¹/₂″ × 3¹/₂″, Numbered 1–726, Color) Mint Condition

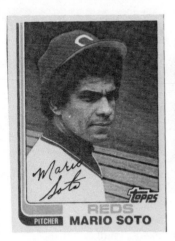

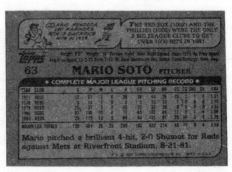

Complete Set		$18.50
1	'81 Highlight: Carlton	.20
2	'81 Highlight: Davis	.10
3	'81 Highlight: Raines	.20
4	'81 Highlight: Rose	.25
5	'81 Highlight: Ryan	.20
6	'81 Highlight: Valenzuela	.20
7	Scott Sanderson	.05
8	Rich Dauer	.05
9	Ron Guidry	.15
10	Super Action: Guidry	.10
11	Gary Alexander	.05
12	Moose Haas	.05
13	Lamar Johnson	.05
14	Steve Howe	.05
15	Ellis Valentine	.05
16	Steve Comer	.05
17	Darrell Evans	.05
18	Fernando Arroyo	.05
19	Ernie Whitt	.05
20	Garry Maddox	.05
21	Baltimore Orioles Future Stars	2.50
22	Jim Beattie	.05
23	Willie Hernandez	.05
24	Dave Frost	.05
25	Jerry Remy	.05
26	Jorge Orta	.05
27	Tom Herr	.05
28	John Urrea	.05
29	Dwayne Murphy	.05
30	Tom Seaver	.25
31	Super Action: Seaver	.20
32	Gene Garber	.05
33	Jerry Morales	.05
34	Joe Sambito	.05

35	Willie Aikens	.05
36	Texas Rangers Team Card	.05
37	Dan Graham	.05
38	Charlie Lea	.05
39	Lou Whitaker	.05
40	Dave Parker	.20
41	Super Action: Parker	.15
42	Rick Sofield	.05
43	Mike Cubbage	.05
44	Britt Burns	.10
45	Rick Cerone	.05
46	Jerry Augustine	.05
47	Jeff Leonard	.05
48	Bobby Castillo	.05
49	Alvis Woods	.05
50	Buddy Bell	.05
51	Chicago Cubs Future Stars	.05
52	Larry Anderson	.05
53	Greg Gross	.05
54	Ron Hassey	.05
55	Rick Burleson	.05
56	Mark Littell	.05
57	Craig Reynolds	.05
58	John D'Acquisto	.05
59	Rich Gedman	.05
60	Tony Armas	.10
61	Tommy Boggs	.05
62	Mike Tyson	.05
63	Mario Soto	.05
64	Lynn Jones	.05
65	Terry Kennedy	.10
66	Houston Astros Team Card	.05
67	Rich Gale	.05
68	Roy Howell	.05
69	Al Williams	.05
70	Tim Raines	.40
71	Roy Lee Jackson	.05
72	Rick Auerbach	.05
73	Buddy Solomon	.05
74	Bob Clark	.05
75	Tommy John	.15
76	Greg Pryor	.05
77	Miguel Dilone	.05
78	George Medich	.05

79	Bob Bailor	.05
80	Jim Palmer	.20
81	Super Action: Palmer	.15
82	Bob Welch	.05
83	New York Yankees Future Stars	.05
84	Rennie Stennett	.05
85	Lynn McGlothen	.05
86	Dane Iorg	.05
87	Matt Keough	.05
88	Biff Pocoroba	.05
89	Steve Henderson	.05
90	Nolan Ryan	.35
91	Carney Lansford	.10
92	Brad Havens	.05
93	Larry Hisle	.05
94	Andy Hassler	.05
95	Ozzie Smith	.10
96	Kansas City Royals Team Card	.05
97	Paul Moskau	.05
98	Terry Bulling	.05
99	Barry Bonnell	.05
100	Mike Schmidt	.35
101	Super Action: Schmidt	.25
102	Dan Briggs	.05
103	Bob Lacey	.05
104	Rance Mulliniks	.05
105	Kirk Gibson	.20
106	Enrique Romo	.05
107	Wayne Krenchicki	.05
108	Bob Sykes	.05
109	Dave Revering	.05
110	Carlton Fisk	.10
111	Super Action: Fisk	.10
112	Billy Sample	.05
113	Steve McCatty	.05
114	Ken Landreaux	.05
115	Gaylord Perry	.15
116	Jim Wohlford	.05
117	Rawly Eastwick	.05
118	Montreal Expos Future Stars	.05
119	Joe Pittman	.05
120	Gary Lucas	.05
121	Ed Lynch	.05
122	Jamie Easterly	.05

123	Danny Goodwin	.05
124	Reid Nichols	.05
125	Danny Ainge	.05
126	Atlanta Braves Team Card	.05
127	Lonnie Smith	.10
128	Frank Pastore	.05
129	Checklist #1-132	.05
130	Julio Cruz	.05
131	Stan Bahnsen	.05
132	Lee May	.05
133	Pat Underwood	.05
134	Dan Ford	.05
135	Andy Rincon	.05
136	Lenn Sakata	.05
137	George Cappuzzello	.05
138	Tony Pena	.05
139	Jeff Jones	.05
140	Ron LeFlore	.05
141	Cleveland Indians Future Stars	.05
142	Dave LaRoche	.05
143	Mookie Wilson	.10
144	Fred Breining	.05
145	Bob Horner	.25
146	Mike Griffin	.05
147	Denny Walling	.05
148	Mickey Klutts	.05
149	Pat Putnam	.05
150	Ted Simmons	.10
151	Dave Edwards	.05
152	Ramon Aviles	.05
153	Roger Erickson	.05
154	Dennis Werth	.05
155	Otto Velez	.05
156	Oakland A's Team Card	.05
157	Steve Crawford	.05
158	Brian Downing	.05
159	Larry Biittner	.05
160	Luis Tiant	.05
161	'81 Batting Leaders	.10
162	'81 Home Run Leaders	.10
163	'81 Runs Batted In Leaders	.10
164	'81 Stolen Base Leaders	.10
165	'81 Victory Leaders	.10
166	'81 Strikeout Leaders	.10
167	'81 Earned Run Average	.10
168	'81 Leading Firemen	.10
169	Charlie Leibrandt	.05
170	Jim Bibby	.05
171	San Francisco Giants Future Stars	.05
172	Bill Gullickson	.05
173	Jamie Quirk	.05
174	Dave Ford	.05
175	Jerry Mumphrey	.05
176	Dewey Robinson	.05
177	John Ellis	.05
178	Dyar Miller	.05
179	Steve Garvey	.35
180	Super Action: Garvey	.25
181	Silvio Martinez	.05
182	Larry Herndon	.05
183	Mike Proly	.05
184	Mick Kelleher	.05
185	Phil Niekro	.10
186	St. Louis Cardinals Team Card	.05
187	Jeff Newman	.05
188	Randy Martz	.05
189	Glenn Hoffman	.05
190	J. R. Richard	.10
191	Tim Wallach	.10
192	Broderick Perkins	.05
193	Darrell Jackson	.05
194	Mike Vail	.05
195	Paul Molitor	.15
196	Willie Upshaw	.05
197	Shane Rawley	.05
198	Chris Speier	.05
199	Dan Aase	.05
200	George Brett	.40
201	Super Action: Brett	.25
202	Rick Manning	.05
203	Toronto Blue Jays Future Stars	.05
204	Gary Roenicke	.05
205	Neil Allen	.05
206	Tony Bernazard	.05
207	Rod Scurry	.05
208	Bobby Murcer	.05
209	Gary Lavelle	.05

210	Keith Hernandez	.15	253	Chuck Baker	.05
211	Dan Petry	.05	254	Jorge Bell	.05
212	Mario Mendoza	.05	255	Tony Perez	.10
213	Dave Stewart	.05	256	Super Action: Perez	.10
214	Brian Asselstine	.05	257	Larry Harlow	.05
215	Mike Krukow	.05	258	Bo Diaz	.05
216	Chicago White Sox Team Card	.05	259	Rodney Scott	.05
217	Bo McLaughlin	.05	260	Bruce Sutter	.15
218	Dave Roberts	.05	261	Detroit Tigers Future Stars	.05
219	John Curtis	.05	262	Doug Bair	.05
220	Manny Trillo	.05	263	Victor Cruz	.05
221	Jim Slaton	.05	264	Dan Quisenberry	.10
222	Butch Wynegar	.05	265	Al Bumbry	.05
223	Lloyd Moseby	.05	266	Rick Leach	.05
224	Bruce Bochte	.05	267	Kurt Bevacqua	.05
225	Mike Torrez	.05	268	Rickey Keeton	.05
226	Checklist #133-264	.05	269	Jim Essian	.05
227	Ray Burris	.05	270	Rusty Staub	.05
228	Sam Mejias	.05	271	Larry Bradford	.05
229	Geoff Zahn	.05	272	Bump Wills	.05
230	Willie Wilson	.15	273	Doug Bird	.05
231	Philadelphia Phillies Future Stars	.05	274	Bob Ojeda	.10
			275	Bob Watson	.10
232	Terry Crowley	.05	276	California Angels Team Card	.05
233	Duane Kuiper	.05	277	Terry Puhl	.05
234	Ron Hodges	.05	278	John Littlefield	.05
235	Mike Easler	.05	279	Bill Russell	.05
236	John Martin	.05	280	Ben Oglivie	.05
237	Rusty Kuntz	.05	281	John Verhoeven	.05
238	Kevin Saucier	.05	282	Ken Macha	.05
239	Jon Matlack	.05	283	Brian Allard	.05
240	Bucky Dent	.05	284	Bob Grich	.05
241	Super Action: Dent	.05	285	Sparky Lyle	.05
242	Milt May	.05	286	Bill Fahey	.05
243	Bob Owchinko	.05	287	Alan Bannister	.05
244	Rufino Linares	.05	288	Garry Templeton	.10
245	Ken Reitz	.05	289	Bob Stanley	.05
246	New York Mets Team Card	.05	290	Ken Singleton	.10
247	Pedro Guerrero	.15	291	Pittsburgh Pirates Future Stars	.50
248	Frank LaCorte	.05	292	Dave Palmer	.05
249	Tim Flannery	.05	293	Ron Picciolo	.05
250	Tug McGraw	.05	294	Mike LaCoss	.05
251	Fred Lynn	.25	295	Jason Thompson	.05
252	Super Action: Lynn	.15	296	Bob Walk	.05

297	Clint Hurdle	.05	339	N.L. All-Star: Schmidt	.25
298	Danny Darwin	.05	340	N.L. All-Star: Concepcion	.10
299	Steve Trout	.05	341	N.L. All-Star: Dawson	.20
300	Reggie Jackson	.50	342	N.L. All-Star: Foster	.20
301	Super Action: Jackson	.25	343	N.L. All-Star: Parker	.15
302	Doug Flynn	.05	344	N.L. All-Star: Carter	.15
303	Bill Caudill	.05	345	N.L. All-Star: Valenzuela	.25
304	Johnnie LeMaster	.05	346	N.L. All-Star: Seaver	.25
305	Don Sutton	.10	347	N.L. All-Star: Sutter	.15
306	Super Action: Sutton	.10	348	Derrel Thomas	.05
307	Randy Bass	.05	349	George Frazier	.05
308	Charlie Moore	.05	350	Thad Bosley	.05
309	Pete Redfern	.05	351	Cincinnati Reds Future Stars	.05
310	Mike Hargrove	.05	352	Dick Davis	.05
311	Los Angeles Dodgers Team Card	.05	353	Jack O'Connor	.05
			354	Roberto Ramos	.05
312	Lenny Randle	.05	355	Dwight Evans	.05
313	John Harris	.05	356	Denny Lewallyn	.05
314	Buck Martinez	.05	357	Butch Hobson	.05
315	Burt Hooton	.05	358	Mike Parrott	.05
316	Steve Braun	.05	359	Jim Dwyer	.05
317	Dick Ruthven	.05	360	Len Barker	.05
318	Mike Heath	.05	361	Rafael Landestoy	.05
319	Dave Rozema	.05	362	Jim Wright	.05
320	Chris Chambliss	.10	363	Bob Molinaro	.05
321	Super Action: Chambliss	.10	364	Doyle Alexander	.05
322	Garry Hancock	.05	365	Bill Madlock	.10
323	Bill Lee	.05	366	San Diego Padres Team Card	.05
324	Steve Dillard	.05	367	Jim Kaat	.10
325	Jose Cruz	.05	368	Alex Trevino	.05
326	Pete Falcone	.05	369	Champ Summers	.05
327	Joe Nolan	.05	370	Mike Norris	.05
328	Ed Farmer	.05	371	Jerry Don Gleaton	.05
329	U. L. Washington	.05	372	Luis Gomez	.05
330	Rick Wise	.05	373	Gene Nelson	.05
331	Benny Ayala	.05	374	Tim Blackwell	.05
332	Don Robinson	.05	375	Dusty Baker	.05
333	Milwaukee Brewers Future Stars	.05	376	Chris Welsh	.05
			377	Kiko Garcia	.05
334	Aurelio Rodriguez	.05	378	Mike Caldwell	.05
335	Jim Sundberg	.05	379	Rob Wilfong	.05
336	Seattle Mariners Team Card	.05	380	Dave Stieb	.10
337	N.L. All-Star: Rose	.50	381	Boston Red Sox Future Stars	.05
338	N.L. All-Star: Lopes	.10	382	Joe Simpson	.05

383 Pascual Perez	.05
384 Keith Moreland	.05
385 Ken Forsch	.05
386 Jerry White	.05
387 Tom Veryzer	.05
388 Joe Rudi	.05
389 George Vukovich	.05
390 Eddie Murray	.15
391 Dave Tobik	.05
392 Rick Bosetti	.05
393 Al Hrabosky	.05
394 Checklist #265-396	.05
395 Omar Moreno	.05
396 Minnesota Twins Team Card	.05
397 Ken Brett	.05
398 Mike Squires	.05
399 Pat Zachry	.05
400 Johnny Bench	.35
401 Super Action: Bench	.20
402 Bill Stein	.05
403 Jim Tracy	.05
404 Dickie Thon	.05
405 Rick Reuschel	.05
406 Al Holland	.05
407 Danny Boone	.05
408 Ed Romero	.05
409 Don Cooper	.05
410 Ron Cey	.10
411 Super Action: Cey	.10
412 Luis Leal	.05
413 Dan Meyer	.05
414 Elias Sosa	.05
415 Don Baylor	.05
416 Marty Bystrom	.05
417 Pat Kelly	.05
418 Texas Rangers Future Stars	.05
419 Steve Stone	.05
420 George Hendrick	.10
421 Mark Clear	.05
422 Cliff Johnson	.05
423 Stan Papi	.05
424 Bruce Benedict	.05
425 John Candelaria	.05
426 Baltimore Orioles Team Card	.05

427 Ron Oester	.05
428 LaMarr Hoyt	.10
429 John Wathan	.05
430 Vida Blue	.10
431 Super Action: Blue	.10
432 Mike Scott	.05
433 Alan Ashby	.05
434 Joe Lefebvre	.05
435 Robin Yount	.25
436 Joe Strain	.05
437 Juan Berenguer	.05
438 Pete Mackanin	.05
439 Dave Righetti	1.00
440 Jeff Burroughs	.05
441 Houston Astros Future Stars	.05
442 Bruce Kison	.05
443 Mark Wagner	.05
444 Terry Forster	.05
445 Larry Parrish	.05
446 Wayne Garland	.05
447 Darrell Porter	.10
448 Super Action: Porter	.10
449 Luis Aguayo	.05
450 Jack Morris	.05
451 Ed Miller	.05
452 Lee Smith	.05
453 Art Howe	.05
454 Rick Langford	.05
455 Tom Burgmeier	.05
456 Chicago Cubs Team Card	.05
457 Tim Stoddard	.05
458 Willie Montanez	.05
459 Bruce Berenyi	.05
460 Jack Clark	.10
461 Rich Dotson	.05
462 Dave Chalk	.05
463 Jim Kern	.05
464 Juan Bonilla	.05
465 Lee Mazzilli	.05
466 Randy Lerch	.05
467 Mickey Hatcher	.05
468 Floyd Bannister	.05
469 Ed Ott	.05
470 John Mayberry	.05

471	Kansas City Royals Future Stars	.05	514	Joe Ferguson	.05
472	Oscar Gamble	.05	515	Larry Bowa	.10
473	Mike Stanton	.05	516	Super Action: Bowa	.10
474	Ken Oberkfell	.05	517	Mark Brouhard	.05
475	Alan Trammell	.05	518	Garth Iorg	.05
476	Brian Kingman	.05	519	Glenn Adams	.05
477	Steve Yeager	.05	520	Mike Flanagan	.05
478	Ray Searage	.05	521	Billy Almon	.05
479	Rowland Office	.05	522	Chuck Rainey	.05
480	Steve Carlton	.35	523	Gary Gray	.05
481	Super Action: Carlton	.25	524	Tom Hausman	.05
482	Glenn Hubbard	.05	525	Ray Knight	.05
483	Gary Woods	.05	526	Montreal Expos Team Card	.05
484	Ivan De Jesus	.05	527	John Henry Johnson	.05
485	Kent Tekulve	.05	528	Matt Alexander	.05
486	New York Yankees Team Card	.05	529	Allen Ripley	.05
487	Bob McClure	.05	530	Dickie Noles	.05
488	Ron Jackson	.05	531	Oakland A's Future Stars	.05
489	Rick Dempsey	.05	532	Toby Harrah	.05
490	Dennis Eckersley	.05	533	Joaquin Andujar	.05
491	Checklist #397-528	.05	534	Dave McKay	.05
492	Joe Price	.05	535	Lance Parrish	.05
493	Chet Lemon	.05	536	Rafael Ramirez	.05
494	Hubie Brooks	.05	537	Doug Capilla	.05
495	Dennis Leonard	.05	538	Lou Piniella	.05
496	Johnny Grubb	.05	539	Vern Ruhle	.05
497	Jim Anderson	.05	540	Andre Dawson	.15
498	Dave Bergman	.05	541	Barry Evans	.05
499	Paul Mirabella	.05	542	Ned Yost	.05
500	Rod Carew	.50	543	Bill Robinson	.05
501	Super Action: Carew	.35	544	Larry Christenson	.05
502	Atlanta Braves Future Stars	.05	545	Reggie Smith	.10
503	Julio Gonzalez	.05	546	Super Action: Smith	.10
504	Rick Peters	.05	547	A. L. All-Star Carew	.25
505	Graig Nettles	.10	548	A. L. All-Star: Randolph	.10
506	Super Action: Nettles	.10	549	A. L. All-Star: Brett	.25
507	Terry Harper	.05	550	A. L. All-Star: Dent	.10
508	Jody Davis	.05	551	A. L. All-Star: Jackson	.25
509	Harry Spilman	.05	552	A. L. All-Star: Singleton	.10
510	Fernando Valenzuela	.35	553	A. L. All-Star: Winfield	.15
511	Ruppert Jones	.05	554	A. L. All-Star: Fisk	.10
512	Jerry Dybzinski	.05	555	A. L. All-Star: McGregor	.10
513	Rick Rhoden	.05	556	A. L. All-Star: Morris	.10
			557	A. L. All-Star: Gossage	.10

558 John Tudor	.05
559 Cleveland Indians Team Card	.05
560 Doug Corbett	.05
561 St. Louis Cardinals Future Stars	.05
562 Mike O'Berry	.05
563 Ross Baumgarten	.05
564 Doug DeCinces	.05
565 Jackson Todd	.05
566 Mike Jorgensen	.05
567 Bob Babcock	.05
568 Joe Pettini	.05
569 Willie Randolph	.10
570 Super Action: Randolph	.10
571 Glenn Abbott	.05
572 Juan Beniquez	.05
573 Rick Waits	.05
574 Mike Ramsey	.05
575 Al Cowens	.05
576 San Francisco Giants Team Card	.05
577 Rick Monday	.05
578 Shooty Babitt	.05
579 Rick Mahler	.05
580 Bobby Bonds	.05
581 Ron Reed	.05
582 Luis Pujols	.05
583 Tippy Martinez	.05
584 Hosken Powell	.05
585 Rollie Fingers	.15
586 Super Action: Fingers	.10
587 Tim Lollar	.05
588 Dale Berra	.05
589 Dave Stapleton	.05
590 Al Oliver	.15
591 Super Action: Oliver	.10
592 Craig Swan	.05
593 Billy Smith	.05
594 Renie Martin	.05
595 Dave Collins	.05
596 Damaso Garcia	.05
597 Wayne Nordhagen	.05
598 Bob Galasso	.05
599 Chicago White Sox Future Stars	.05
600 Dave Winfield	.20
601 Sid Monge	.05
602 Freddie Patek	.05
603 Rich Hebner	.05
604 Orlando Sanchez	.05
605 Steve Rogers	.10
606 Toronto Blue Jays Team Card	.05
607 Leon Durham	.10
608 Jerry Royster	.05
609 Rick Sutcliffe	.05
610 Rickey Henderson	.20
611 Joe Niekro	.05
612 Gary Ward	.05
613 Jim Gantner	.05
614 Juan Eichelberger	.05
615 Bob Boone	.10
616 Super Action: Boone	.10
617 Scott McGregor	.05
618 Tim Foli	.05
619 Bill Campbell	.05
620 Ken Griffey	.10
621 Super Action: Griffey	.10
622 Dennis Lamp	.05
623 New York Mets Future Stars	.05
624 Fergie Jenkins	.10
625 Hal McRae	.05
626 Randy Jones	.05
627 Enos Cabell	.05
628 Bill Travers	.05
629 Johnny Wockenfuss	.05
630 Joe Charboneau	.05
631 Gene Tenace	.05
632 Bryan Clark	.05
633 Mitchell Page	.05
634 Checklist #529-660	.05
635 Ron Davis	.05
636 Philadelphia Phillies Team Card	.05
637 Rick Camp	.05
638 John Milner	.05
639 Ken Kravec	.05
640 Cesar Cedeno	.05
641 Steve Mura	.05
642 Mike Scioscia	.05
643 Pete Vuckovich	.10

644	John Castino	.05	
645	Frank White	.10	
646	Super Action: White	.10	
647	Warren Brusstar	.05	
648	Jose Morales	.05	
649	Ken Clay	.05	
650	Carl Yastrzemski	.50	
651	Super Action: Yastrzemski	.35	
652	Steve Nicosia	.05	
653	California Angels Future Stars	.50	
654	Jim Morrison	.05	
655	Joel Youngblood	.05	
656	Eddie Whitson	.05	
657	Tom Poquette	.05	
658	Tito Landrum	.05	
659	Fred Martinez	.05	
660	Dave Concepcion	.10	
661	Super Action: Concepcion	.10	
662	Luis Salazar	.05	
663	Hector Cruz	.05	
664	Dan Spillner	.05	
665	Jim Clancy	.05	
666	Detroit Tigers Team Card	.05	
667	Jeff Reardon	.05	
668	Dale Murphy	.50	
669	Larry Milbourne	.05	
670	Steve Kemp	.05	
671	Mike Davis	.05	
672	Bob Knepper	.05	
673	Keith Drumright	.05	
674	Dave Goltz	.05	
675	Cecil Cooper	.15	
676	Sal Butera	.05	
677	Alfredo Griffin	.05	
678	Tom Paciorek	.05	
679	Sammy Stewart	.05	
680	Gary Matthews	.05	
681	Los Angeles Dodgers Future Stars	1.00	
682	Jesse Jefferson	.05	
683	Phil Garner	.05	
684	Harold Baines	.10	
685	Bert Blyleven	.05	
686	Gary Allenson	.05	
687	Greg Minton	.05	

688	Leon Roberts	.05
689	Lary Sorensen	.05
690	Dave Kingman	.10
691	Dan Schatzeder	.05
692	Wayne Gross	.05
693	Cesar Geronimo	.05
694	Dave Wehrmeister	.05
695	Warren Cromartie	.05
696	Pittsburgh Pirates Team Card	.05
697	John Montefusco	.05
698	Tony Scott	.05
699	Dick Tidrow	.05
700	George Foster	.20
701	Super Action: Foster	.15
702	Steve Renko	.05
703	Milwaukee Brewers Team Card	.05
704	Mickey Rivers	.10
705	Super Action: Rivers	.10
706	Barry Foote	.05
707	Mark Bomback	.05
708	Gene Richards	.05
709	Don Money	.05
710	Jerry Reuss	.05
711	Seattle Mariners Future Stars	.05
712	Denny Martinez	.05
713	Del Unser	.05
714	Jerry Koosman	.05
715	Willie Stargell	.25
716	Super Action: Stargell	.15
717	Rick Miller	.05
718	Charlie Hough	.05
719	Jerry Narron	.05
720	Greg Luzinski	.10
721	Super Action: Luzinski	.10
722	Jerry Martin	.05
723	Junior Kennedy	.05
724	Dave Rosello	.05
725	Amos Otis	.10
726	Super Action: Otis	.10
727	Sixto Lezcano	.05
728	Aurelio Lopez	.05
729	Jim Spencer	.05
730	Gary Carter	.25
731	San Diego Padres Future Stars	.05
732	Mike Lum	.05

733 Larry McWilliams	.05
734 Mike Ivie	.05
735 Rudy May	.05
736 Jerry Turner	.05
737 Reggie Cleveland	.05
738 Dave Engle	.05
739 Joey McLaughlin	.05
740 Dave Lopes	.10
741 Super Action: Lopes	.10
742 Dick Drago	.05
743 John Stearns	.05
744 Mike Witt	.05
745 Bake McBride	.05
746 Andre Thornton	.05
747 John Lowenstein	.05
748 Marc Hill	.05
749 Bob Shirley	.05
750 Jim Rice	.35
751 Rick Honeycutt	.05
752 Lee Lacy	.05
753 Tom Brookens	.05
754 Joe Morgan	.15
755 Super Action: Morgan	.10
756 Cincinnati Reds Team Card	.05
758 Claudell Washington	.05
759 Paul Splittorff	.05
760 Bill Buckner	.10
761 Dave Smith	.05
762 Mike Phillips	.05
763 Tom Hume	.05

764 Steve Swisher	.05
765 Gorman Thomas	.10
766 Minnesota Twins Future Stars	1.00
767 Roy Smalley	.05
768 Jerry Garvin	.05
769 Richie Zisk	.05
770 Rich Gossage	.10
771 Super Action: Gossage	.10
772 Bert Campaneris	.05
773 John Denny	.05
774 Jay Johnstone	.05
775 Bob Forsch	.05
776 Mark Belanger	.05
777 Tom Griffin	.05
778 Kevin Hickey	.05
779 Grant Jackson	.05
780 Pete Rose	.75
781 Super Action: Rose	.35
782 Frank Taveras	.05
783 Greg Harris	.05
784 Milt Wilcox	.05
785 Dan Driessen	.05
786 Boston Red Sox Team Card	.05
787 Fred Stanley	.05
788 Woodie Fryman	.05
789 Checklist #661-792	.05
790 Larry Gura	.05
791 Bobby Brown	.05
792 Frank Tanana	.05

TOPPS—1983

(2¹/₂″ × 3¹/₂″, Numbered 1–792, Color) Mint Condition

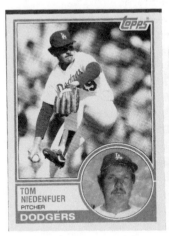
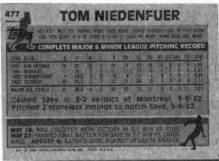

Complete Set		$17.50
1	1982 Record Breaker, Tony Armas	.10
2	1982 Record Breaker, Rickey Henderson	.15
3	1982 Record Breaker, Greg Minton	.10
4	1982 Record Breaker, Lance Parrish	.10
5	1982 Record Breaker, Manny Trillo	.10
6	1982 Record Breaker, John Wathan	.10
7	Gene Richards	.04
8	Steve Balboni	.04
9	Joey McLaughlin	.04
10	Gorman Thomas	.10
11	Billy Gardner	.04
12	Paul Mirabella	.04
13	Larry Herndon	.04
14	Frank LaCorte	.04
15	Ron Cey	.10
16	George Vukovich	.04
17	Kent Tekulve	.04
18	Super Veteran, Kent Tekulve	.04
19	Oscar Gamble	.04
20	Carlton Fisk	.10
21	Baltimore Orioles Team Leaders	.04
22	Randy Martz	.04
23	Mike Heath	.04
24	Steve Mura	.04
25	Hal McRae	.04
26	Jerry Royster	.04
27	Doug Corbett	.04
28	Bruce Bochte	.04
29	Randy Jones	.04
30	Jim Rice	.25
31	Bill Gullickson	.04
32	Dave Bergman	.04

33	Jack O'Connor	.04
34	Paul Householder	.05
35	Rollie Fingers	.15
36	Super Veteran, Rollie Fingers	.10
37	Darrell Johnson	.04
38	Tim Flannery	.04
39	Terry Puhl	.04
40	Fernando Valenzuela	.30
41	Jerry Turner	.04
42	Dale Murray	.04
43	Bob Dernier	.04
44	Don Robinson	.04
45	John Mayberry	.04
46	Richard Dotson	.04
47	Dave McKay	.04
48	Lary Sorensen	.04
49	Willie McGee	.75
50	Bob Horner	.25
51	Chicago Cubs Team Leaders	.04
52	Onix Concepcion	.04
53	Mike Witt	.04
54	Jim Maler	.04
55	Mookie Wilson	.04
56	Chuck Rainey	.04
57	Tim Blackwell	.04
58	Al Holland	.04
59	Benny Ayala	.04
60	Johnny Bench	.25
61	Super Veteran, Johnny Bench	.20
62	Bob McClure	.04
63	Rick Monday	.04
64	Bill Stein	.04
65	Jack Morris	.04
66	Bob Lillis	.04
67	Sal Butera	.04
68	Eric Show	.04
69	Lee Lacy	.04
70	Steve Carlton	.35
71	Super Veteran, Steve Carlton	.25
72	Tom Paciorek	.04
73	Allen Ripley	.04
74	Julio Gonzalez	.04
75	Amos Otis	.04
76	Rick Mahler	.04
77	Hosken Powell	.04
78	Bill Caudill	.04
79	Mick Kelleher	.04
80	George Foster	.25
81	New York Yankees Team Leaders	.04
82	Bruce Hurst	.04
83	Ryne Sandberg	.25
84	Milt May	.04
85	Ken Singleton	.10
86	Tom Hume	.04
87	Joe Rudi	.04
88	Jim Gantner	.04
89	Leon Roberts	.04
90	Jerry Reuss	.04
91	Larry Milbourne	.04
92	Mike LaCoss	.04
93	John Castino	.04
94	Dave Edwards	.04
95	Alan Trammell	.04
96	Dick Howser	.04
97	Ross Baumgarten	.04
98	Vance Law	.04
99	Dickie Noles	.04
100	Pete Rose	.75
101	Super Veteran, Pete Rose	.50
102	Dave Beard	.04
103	Darrell Porter	.04
104	Bob Walk	.04
105	Don Baylor	.04
106	Gene Nelson	.04
107	Mike Jorgensen	.04
108	Glenn Hoffman	.04
109	Luis Leal	.04
110	Ken Griffey	.10
111	Montreal Expos Team Leaders	.04
112	Bob Shirley	.04
113	Ron Roenicke	.04
114	Jim Slaton	.04
115	Chili Davis	.04
116	Dave Schmidt	.04
117	Alan Knicely	.04
118	Chris Welsh	.04
119	Tom Brookens	.04

120 Len Barker	.04	
121 Mickey Hatcher	.04	
122 Jimmy Smith	.04	
123 George Frazier	.04	
124 Marc Hill	.04	
125 Leon Durham	.10	
126 Joe Torre	.04	
127 Preston Hanna	.04	
128 Mike Ramsey	.04	
129 Checklist, cards 1–132	.04	
130 Dave Stieb	.04	
131 Ed Ott	.04	
132 Todd Cruz	.04	
133 Jim Barr	.04	
134 Hubie Brooks	.04	
135 Dwight Evans	.04	
136 Willie Aikens	.04	
137 Woodie Fryman	.04	
138 Rick Dempsey	.04	
139 Bruce Berenyi	.04	
140 Willie Randolph	.04	
141 Cleveland Indians Team Leaders	.04	
142 Mike Caldwell	.04	
143 Joe Pettini	.04	
144 Mark Wagner	.04	
145 Don Sutton	.10	
146 Super Veteran, Don Sutton	.10	
147 Rick Leach	.04	
148 Dave Roberts	.04	
149 Johnny Ray	.04	
150 Bruce Sutter	.10	
151 Super Veteran, Bruce Sutter	.10	
152 Jay Johnstone	.04	
153 Jerry Koosman	.04	
154 Johnnie LeMaster	.04	
155 Dan Quisenberry	.04	
156 Billy Martin	.10	
157 Steve Bedrosian	.04	
158 Rob Wilfong	.04	
159 Mike Stanton	.04	
160 Dave Kingman	.10	
161 Super Veteran, Dave Kingman	.10	
162 Mark Clear	.04	

163 Cal Ripken	.25
164 Dave Palmer	.04
165 Dan Driessen	.10
166 John Pacella	.04
167 Mark Brouhard	.04
168 Juan Eichelberger	.04
169 Doug Flynn	.04
170 Steve Howe	.04
171 San Francisco Giants Team Leaders	.04
172 Vern Ruhle	.04
173 Jim Morrison	.04
174 Jerry Ujdur	.04
175 Bo Diaz	.04
176 Dave Righetti	.10
177 Harold Baines	.04
178 Luis Tiant	.04
179 Super Veteran, Luis Tiant	.10
180 Rickey Henderson	.20
181 Terry Felton	.04
182 Mike Fischlin	.04
183 Ed Vande Berg	.04
184 Bob Clark	.04
185 Tim Lollar	.04
186 Whitey Herzog	.04
187 Terry Leach	.04
188 Rick Miller	.04
189 Dan Schatzeder	.04
190 Cecil Cooper	.10
191 Joe Price	.04
192 Floyd Rayford	.04
193 Harry Spilman	.04
194 Cesar Geronimo	.04
195 Bob Stoddard	.04
196 Bill Fahey	.04
197 Jim Eisenreich	.04
198 Kiko Garcia	.04
199 Marty Bystrom	.04
200 Rod Carew	.50
201 Super Veteran, Rod Carew	.35
202 Toronto Blue Jays Team Leaders	.05
203 Mike Morgan	.05
204 Junior Kennedy	.04

205 Dave Parker	.20
206 Ken Oberkfell	.04
207 Rick Camp	.04
208 Dan Meyer	.04
209 Mike Moore	.04
210 Jack Clark	.10
211 John Denny	.04
212 John Stearns	.04
213 Tom Burgmeier	.04
214 Jerry White	.04
215 Mario Soto	.04
216 Tony LaRussa	.04
217 Tim Stoddard	.04
218 Roy Howell	.04
219 Mike Armstrong	.04
220 Dusty Baker	.04
221 Joe Niekro	.04
222 Damaso Garcia	.04
223 John Montefusco	.04
224 Mickey Rivers	.04
225 Enos Cabell	.04
226 Enrique Romo	.04
227 Chris Bando	.04
228 Joaquin Andujar	.04
229 Philadelphia Phillies Team Leaders	.04
230 Fergie Jenkins	.10
231 Super Veteran, Fergie Jenkins	.10
232 Tom Brunansky	.04
233 Wayne Gross	.04
234 Larry Andersen	.04
235 Claudell Washington	.04
236 Steve Renko	.04
237 Dan Norman	.04
238 Bud Black	.04
239 Dave Stapleton	.04
240 Rich Gossage	.10
241 Super Veteran, Rich Gossage	.10
242 Joe Nolan	.04
243 Duane Walker	.04
244 Dwight Bernard	.04
245 Steve Sax	.10
246 George Bamberger	.04
247 Dave Smith	.04
248 Bake McBride	.04

249 Checklist, cards 133–264	.04
250 Bill Buckner	.10
251 Alan Wiggins	.04
252 Luis Aguayo	.04
253 Larry Williams	.04
254 Rick Cerone	.04
255 Gene Garber	.10
256 Super Veteran, Gene Garber	.10
257 Jesse Barfield	.04
258 Manny Castillo	.04
259 Jeff Jones	.04
260 Steve Kemp	.04
261 Detroit Tigers Team Leaders	.04
262 Ron Jackson	.04
263 Renie Martin	.04
264 Jamie Quirk	.04
265 Joel Youngblood	.04
266 Paul Boris	.04
267 Terry Francona	.04
268 Storm Davis	.04
269 Ron Oester	.04
270 Dennis Eckersley	.04
271 Ed Romero	.04
272 Frank Tanana	.04
273 Mark Belanger	.04
274 Terry Kennedy	.04
275 Ray Knight	.04
276 Gene Mauch	.04
277 Rance Mulliniks	.04
278 Kevin Hickey	.04
279 Greg Gross	.04
280 Bert Blyleven	.04
281 Andre Robertson	.04
282 Reggie Smith	.10
283 Super Veteran, Reggie Smith	.10
284 Jeff Lahti	.04
285 Lance Parrish	.04
286 Rick Langford	.04
287 Bobby Brown	.04
288 Joe Crowley	.04
289 Jerry Dybzinski	.04
290 Jeff Reardon	.04
291 Pittsburgh Pirates Team Leaders	.04
292 Craig Swan	.04

293	Glenn Gulliver	.04	
294	Dave Engle	.04	
295	Jerry Remy	.04	
296	Greg Harris	.04	
297	Ned Yost	.04	
298	Floyd Chiffer	.04	
299	George Wright	.04	
300	Mike Schmidt	.35	
301	Super Veteran, Mike Schmidt	.25	
302	Ernie Whitt	.04	
303	Miguel Dilone	.04	
304	Dave Rucker	.04	
305	Larry Bowa	.05	
306	Tom Lasorda	.10	
307	Lou Piniella	.04	
308	Jesus Vega	.04	
309	Jeff Leonard	.04	
310	Greg Luzinski	.10	
311	Glenn Brummer	.04	
312	Brian Kingman	.04	
313	Gary Gray	.04	
314	Ken Dayley	.04	
315	Rick Burleson	.04	
316	Paul Splittorff	.04	
317	Gary Rajsich	.04	
318	John Tudor	.04	
319	Lenn Sakata	.04	
320	Steve Rogers	.10	
321	Milwaukee Brewers Team Leaders	.04	
322	Dave Van Gorder	.04	
323	Luis DeLeon	.04	
324	Mike Marshall	.10	
325	Von Hayes	.04	
326	Garth Iorg	.04	
327	Bobby Castillo	.04	
328	Craig Reynolds	.04	
329	Randy Niemann	.04	
330	Buddy Bell	.04	
331	Mike Krukow	.04	
332	Glenn Wilson	.10	
333	Dave LaRoche	.04	
334	Super Veteran, Dave LaRoche	.04	
335	Steve Henderson	.04	
336	Rene Lachemann	.04	
337	Tito Landrum	.04	
338	Bob Owchinko	.04	
339	Terry Harper	.04	
340	Larry Gura	.04	
341	Doug DeCinces	.04	
342	Atlee Hammaker	.04	
343	Bob Bailor	.04	
344	Roger LaFrancois	.04	
345	Jim Clancy	.04	
346	Joe Pittman	.04	
347	Sammy Stewart	.04	
348	Alan Bannister	.04	
349	Checklist, cards 265–396	.04	
350	Robin Yount	.20	
351	Cincinnati Reds Team Leaders	.04	
352	Mike Scioscia	.04	
353	Steve Comer	.04	
354	Randy Johnson	.04	
355	Jim Bibby	.04	
356	Gary Woods	.04	
357	Len Matuszek	.04	
358	Jerry Garvin	.04	
359	Dave Collins	.04	
360	Nolan Ryan	.25	
361	Super Veteran, Nolan Ryan	.20	
362	Billy Almon	.04	
363	John Stuper	.04	
364	Brett Butler	.04	
365	Dave Lopes	.04	
366	Dick Williams	.04	
367	Bud Anderson	.04	
368	Richie Zisk	.04	
369	Jesse Orosco	.04	
370	Gary Carter	.20	
371	Mike Richardt	.04	
372	Terry Crowley	.04	
373	Kevin Saucier	.04	
374	Wayne Krenchicki	.04	
375	Pete Vuckovich	.10	
376	Ken Landreaux	.04	
377	Lee May	.10	
378	Super Veteran, Lee May	.10	
379	Guy Sularz	.04	
380	Ron Davis	.04	
381	Boston Red Sox Team Leaders	.04	

382	Bob Knepper	.04
383	Ozzie Virgil	.04
384	Dave Dravecky	.04
385	Mike Easler	.10
386	A.L. All-Star: Rod Carew	.25
387	A.L. All-Star: Bob Grich	.10
388	A.L. All-Star: George Brett	.25
389	A.L. All-Star: Robin Yount	.15
390	A.L. All-Star: Reggie Jackson	.25
391	A.L. All-Star: Rickey Henderson	.15
392	A.L. All-Star: Fred Lynn	.20
393	A.L. All-Star: Carlton Fisk	.15
394	A.L. All-Star: Pete Vuckovich	.15
395	A.L. All-Star: Larry Gura	.10
396	A.L. All-Star: Dan Quisenberry	.10
397	N.L. All-Star: Pete Rose	.50
398	N.L. All-Star: Manny Trillo	.10
399	N.L. All-Star: Mike Schmidt	.25
400	N.L. All-Star: Dave Concepcion	.10
401	N.L. All-Star: Dale Murphy	.20
402	N.L. All-Star: Andre Dawson	.20
403	N.L. All-Star: Tim Raines	.15
404	N.L. All-Star: Gary Carter	.15
405	N.L. All-Star: Steve Rogers	.15
406	N.L. All-Star: Steve Carlton	.25
407	N.L. All-Star: Bruce Sutter	.15
408	Rudy May	.04
409	Marvis Foley	.04
410	Phil Niekro	.10
411	Super Veteran, Phil Niekro	.10
412	Texas Rangers Team Leaders	.04
413	Matt Keough	.04
414	Julio Cruz	.04
415	Bob Forsch	.04
416	Joe Ferguson	.04
417	Tom Hausman	.04
418	Greg Pryor	.04
419	Steve Crawford	.04
420	Al Oliver	.15
421	Super Veteran, Al Oliver	.10
422	George Cappuzzello	.04
423	Tom Lawless	.04
424	Jerry Augustine	.04
425	Pedro Guerrero	.10
426	Earl Weaver	.10
427	Roy Lee Jackson	.04
428	Champ Summers	.04
429	Eddie Whitson	.04
430	Kirk Gibson	.10
431	Gary Gaetti	.04
432	Porfirio Altamirano	.04
433	Dale Berra	.04
434	Dennis Lamp	.04
435	Tony Armas	.05
436	Bill Campbell	.04
437	Rick Sweet	.04
438	Dave LaPoint	.04
439	Rafael Ramirez	.04
440	Ron Guidry	.15
441	Houston Astros Team Leaders	.04
442	Brian Downing	.04
443	Don Hood	.04
444	Wally Backman	.04
445	Mike Flanagan	.04
447	Reid Nichols	.04
448	Darrell Evans	.04
449	Eddie Milner	.04
450	Ted Simmons	.10
451	Super Veteran: Ted Simmons	.10
452	Lloyd Moseby	.04
453	Lamar Johnson	.04
454	Bob Welch	.04
455	Sixto Lezcano	.04
456	Lee Elia	.04
457	Milt Wilcox	.04
458	Ron Washington	.04
459	Ed Farmer	.04
460	Roy Smalley	.04
461	Steve Trout	.04
462	Steve Nicosia	.04
463	Gaylord Perry	.15
464	Super Veteran, Gaylord Perry	.10
465	Lonnie Smith	.10
466	Tom Underwood	.04
467	Rufino Linares	.04
468	Dave Goltz	.04

469 Ron Gardenhire	.04	
470 Greg Minton	.04	
471 Kansas City Royals Team Leaders	.04	
472 Gary Allenson	.04	
473 John Lowenstein	.04	
474 Ray Burris	.04	
475 Cesar Cedeno	.04	
476 Rob Picciolo	.04	
477 Tom Niedenfuer	.04	
478 Phil Garner	.04	
479 Charlie Hough	.04	
480 Toby Harrah	.04	
481 Scot Thompson	.04	
482 Tony Gwynn	.04	
483 Lynn Jones	.04	
484 Dick Ruthven	.04	
485 Omar Moreno	.04	
486 Clyde King	.04	
487 Jerry Hairston	.04	
488 Alfredo Griffin	.04	
489 Tom Herr	.04	
490 Jim Palmer	.25	
491 Super Veteran: Jim Palmer	.10	
492 Paul Serna	.04	
493 Steve McCatty	.04	
494 Bob Brenly	.04	
495 Warren Cromartie	.04	
496 Tom Veryzer	.04	
497 Rick Sutcliffe	.04	
498 Wade Boggs	2.00	
499 Jeff Little	.04	
500 Reggie Jackson	.35	
501 Super Veteran: Reggie Jackson	.25	
502 Atlanta Braves Team Leaders	.04	
503 Moose Haas	.04	
504 Don Werner	.04	
505 Garry Templeton	.10	
506 Jim Gott	.04	
507 Tony Scott	.04	
508 Tom Filer	.04	
509 Lou Whitaker	.04	
510 Tug McGraw	.05	
511 Super Veteran, Tug McGraw	.05	

512 Doyle Alexander	.04
513 Fred Stanley	.04
514 Rudy Law	.04
515 Gene Tenace	.04
516 Bill Virdon	.04
517 Gary Ward	.04
518 Bill Laskey	.04
519 Terry Bulling	.04
520 Fred Lynn	.20
521 Bruce Benedict	.04
522 Pat Zachry	.04
523 Carney Lansford	.04
524 Tom Brennan	.04
525 Frank White	.04
526 Checklist, cards 397–528	.04
527 Larry Biittner	.04
528 Jamie Easterly	.04
529 Tim Laudner	.04
530 Eddie Murray	.20
531 Oakland A's Team Leaders	.04
532 Dave Stewart	.04
533 Luis Salazar	.04
534 John Butcher	.04
535 Manny Trillo	.04
536 Johnny Wockenfuss	.04
537 Rod Scurry	.04
538 Danny Heep	.04
539 Roger Erickson	.04
540 Ozzie Smith	.04
541 Britt Burns	.04
542 Jody Davis	.04
543 Alan Fowlkes	.04
544 Larry Whisenton	.04
545 Floyd Bannister	.04
546 Dave Garcia	.04
547 Geoff Zahn	.04
548 Brian Giles	.04
549 Charlie Puleo	.04
550 Carl Yastrzemski	.35
551 Super Veteran, Carl Yastrzemski	.25
552 Tim Wallach	.04
553 Denny Martinez	.04
554 Mike Vail	.04

555	Steve Yeager	.04
556	Willie Upshaw	.04
557	Rick Honeycutt	.04
558	Dickie Thon	.04
559	Pete Redfern	.04
560	Ron LeFlore	.04
561	St. Louis Cardinals Team Leaders	.04
562	Dave Rozema	.04
563	Juan Bonilla	.04
564	Sid Monge	.04
565	Bucky Dent	.04
566	Manny Sarmiento	.04
567	Joe Simpson	.04
568	Willie Hernandez	.04
569	Jack Perconte	.04
570	Vida Blue	.10
571	Mickey Klutts	.04
572	Bob Watson	.04
573	Andy Hassler	.04
574	Glenn Adams	.04
575	Neil Allen	.04
576	Frank Robinson	.10
577	Luis Aponte	.04
578	David Green	.50
579	Rich Dauer	.04
580	Tom Seaver	.25
581	Super Veteran, Tom Seaver	.20
582	Marshall Edwards	.04
583	Terry Forster	.04
584	Dave Hostetler	.04
585	Jose Cruz	.04
586	Frank Viola	.04
587	Ivan De Jesus	.04
588	Pat Underwood	.04
589	Alvis Woods	.04
590	Tony Pena	.04
591	Chicago White Sox Team Leaders	.04
592	Shane Rawley	.04
593	Broderick Perkins	.04
594	Eric Rasmussen	.04
595	Tim Raines	.15
596	Randy Johnson	.04
597	Mike Proly	.04
598	Dwayne Murphy	.04
599	Don Aase	.04
600	George Brett	.35
601	Ed Lynch	.04
602	Rich Gedman	.04
603	Joe Morgan	.15
604	Super Veteran, Joe Morgan	.10
605	Gary Roenicke	.04
606	Bobby Cox	.04
607	Charlie Leibrandt	.04
608	Don Money	.04
609	Danny Darwin	.04
610	Steve Garvey	.25
611	Bert Roberge	.04
612	Steve Swisher	.04
613	Mike Ivie	.04
614	Ed Glynn	.04
615	Garry Maddox	.04
616	Bill Nahorodny	.04
617	Butch Wynegar	.04
618	LaMarr Hoyt	.10
619	Keith Moreland	.04
620	Mike Norris	.04
621	New York Mets Team Leaders	.04
622	Dave Edler	.04
623	Luis Sanchez	.04
624	Glenn Hubbard	.04
625	Ken Forsch	.04
626	Jerry Martin	.04
627	Doug Bair	.04
628	Julio Valdez	.04
629	Charlie Lea	.04
630	Paul Molitor	.10
631	Tippy Martinez	.04
632	Alex Trevino	.04
633	Vicente Romo	.04
634	Max Venable	.04
635	Graig Nettles	.10
636	Super Veteran, Graig Nettles	.10
637	Pat Corrales	.04
638	Dan Petry	.04
639	Art Howe	.04
640	Andre Thornton	.04

641	Billy Sample	.04
642	Checklist, cards 529–660	.04
643	Bump Wills	.04
644	Joe Lefebvre	.04
645	Bill Madlock	.10
646	Jim Essian	.04
647	Bobby Mitchell	.04
648	Jeff Burroughs	.04
649	Tommy Boggs	.04
650	George Hendrick	.10
651	California Angels Team Leaders	.04
652	Butch Hobson	.04
653	Ellis Valentine	.04
654	Bob Ojeda	.04
655	Al Bumbry	.04
656	Dave Frost	.04
657	Mike Gates	.04
658	Frank Pastore	.04
659	Charlie Moore	.04
660	Mike Hargrove	.04
661	Bill Russell	.04
662	Joe Sambito	.04
663	Tom O'Malley	.04
664	Bob Molinaro	.04
665	Jim Sundberg	.04
666	Sparky Anderson	.04
667	Dick Davis	.04
668	Larry Christenson	.04
669	Mike Squires	.04
670	Jerry Mumphrey	.04
671	Lenny Faedo	.04
672	Jim Kaat	.10
673	Super Veteran, Jim Kaat	.10
674	Kurt Bevacqua	.04
675	Jim Beattie	.04
676	Biff Pocoroba	.04
677	Dave Revering	.04
678	Juan Beniquez	.04
679	Mike Scott	.04
680	Andre Dawson	.10
681	Los Angeles Dodgers Team Leaders	.04
682	Bob Stanley	.04
683	Dan Ford	.04
684	Rafael Landestoy	.04
685	Lee Mazzilli	.04
686	Randy Lerch	.04
687	U. L. Washington	.04
688	Jim Wohlford	.04
689	Ron Hassey	.04
690	Kent Hrbek	.10
691	Dave Tobik	.04
692	Denny Walling	.04
693	Sparky Lyle	.04
694	Super Veteran, Sparky Lyle	.04
695	Ruppert Jones	.04
696	Chuck Tanner	.04
697	Barry Foote	.04
698	Tony Bernazard	.04
699	Lee Smith	.04
700	Keith Hernandez	.15
701	1982 Batting Leaders	.10
702	1982 Home Run Leaders	.10
703	1982 Runs Batted In Leaders	.10
704	1982 Stolen Base Leaders	.10
705	1982 Victory Leaders	.10
706	1982 Strikeout Leaders	.10
707	1982 Earned Run Average Leaders	.10
708	1982 Leading Firemen	.10
709	Jimmy Sexton	.04
710	Willie Wilson	.10
711	Seattle Mariners Team Leaders	.04
712	Bruce Kison	.04
713	Ron Hodges	.04
714	Wayne Nordhagen	.04
715	Tony Perez	.10
716	Super Veteran, Tony Perez	.10
717	Scott Sanderson	.04
718	Jim Dwyer	.04
719	Rich Gale	.04
720	Dave Concepcion	.04
721	John Martin	.04
722	Jorge Orta	.04
723	Randy Moffitt	.04
724	Johnny Grubb	.04
725	Dan Spillner	.04

726 Harvey Kuenn	.04	
727 Chet Lemon	.04	
728 Ron Reed	.04	
729 Jerry Morales	.04	
730 Jason Thompson	.04	
731 Al Williams	.04	
732 Dave Henderson	.04	
733 Buck Martinez	.04	
734 Steve Braun	.04	
735 Tommy John	.10	
736 Super Veteran, Tommy John	.10	
737 Mitchell Page	.04	
738 Tim Foli	.04	
739 Rick Ownbey	.04	
740 Rusty Staub	.04	
741 Super Veteran, Rusty Staub	.04	
742 San Diego Padres Team Leaders	.04	
743 Mike Torrez	.04	
744 Brad Mills	.04	
745 Scott McGregor	.04	
746 John Wathan	.04	
747 Fred Breining	.04	
748 Derrel Thomas	.04	
749 Jon Matlack	.04	
750 Ben Oglivie	.04	
751 Brad Havens	.04	
752 Luis Pujols	.04	
753 Elias Sosa	.04	
754 Bill Robinson	.04	
755 John Candelaria	.04	
756 Russ Nixon	.04	
757 Rick Manning	.04	
758 Aurelio Rodriguez	.04	

759 Doug Bird	.04
760 Dale Murphy	.20
761 Gary Lucas	.04
762 Cliff Johnson	.04
763 Al Cowens	.04
764 Pete Falcone	.04
765 Bob Boone	.04
766 Barry Bonnell	.04
767 Duane Kuiper	.04
768 Chris Speier	.04
769 Checklist, cards 661–792	.04
770 Dave Winfield	.15
771 Minnesota Twins Team Leaders	.04
772 Jim Kern	.04
773 Larry Hisle	.04
774 Alan Ashby	.04
775 Burt Hooton	.04
776 Larry Parrish	.04
777 John Curtis	.04
778 Rich Hebner	.04
779 Rick Waits	.04
780 Gary Matthews	.04
781 Rick Rhoden	.04
782 Bobby Murcer	.04
783 Super Veteran, Bobby Murcer	.04
784 Jeff Newman	.04
785 Dennis Leonard	.04
786 Ralph Houk	.04
787 Dick Tidrow	.04
788 Dane Iorg	.04
789 Bryan Clark	.04
790 Bob Grich	.04
791 Gary Lavelle	.04
792 Chris Chambliss	.10

TOPPS—1984

(3½″ × 2½″, Numbered 1–792, Color) Mint Condition

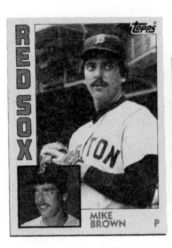

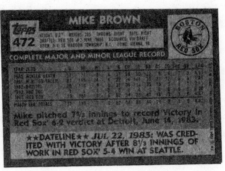

	Complete Set	$15.00
1	1983 Highlight: Steve Carlton	.10
2	1983 Highlight: Rickey Henderson	.10
3	1983 Highlight: Dan Quisenberry	.10
4	1983 Highlight: Nolan Ryan, Steve Carlton, Gaylord Perry	.10
5	1983 Highlight: Dave Righetti, Bob Forsch, Mike Warren	.10
6	1983 Highlight: Johnny Bench, Gaylord Perry, Carl Yastrzemski	.10
7	Gary Lucas	.03
8	Don Mattingly	1.00
9	Jim Gott	.03
10	Robin Yount	.25
11	Minnesota Twins Team Leaders	.03
12	Billy Sample	.03
13	Scott Holman	.03
14	Tom Brookens	.03
15	Burt Hooton	.03
16	Omar Moreno	.03
17	John Denny	.03
18	Dale Berra	.03
19	Ray Fontenot	.10
20	Greg Luzinski	.05
21	Joe Altobelli	.03
22	Bryan Clark	.03
23	Keith Moreland	.03
24	John Martin	.03
25	Glenn Hubbard	.03
26	Bud Black	.03
27	Daryl Sconiers	.03
28	Frank Viola	.03

29	Danny Heep	.03
30	Wade Boggs	.50
31	Andy McGaffigan	.03
32	Bobby Ramos	.03
33	Tom Burgmeier	.03
34	Eddie Milner	.03
35	Don Sutton	.05
36	Denny Walling	.03
37	Texas Rangers Team Leaders	.03
38	Luis DeLeon	.03
39	Garth Iorg	.03
40	Dusty Baker	.05
41	Tony Bernazard	.03
42	Johnny Grubb	.03
43	Ron Reed	.03
44	Jim Morrison	.03
45	Jerry Mumphrey	.03
46	Ray Smith	.03
47	Rudy Law	.03
48	Julio Franco	.25
49	John Stuper	.03
50	Chris Chambliss	.05
51	Jim Frey	.03
52	Paul Splittorff	.03
53	Juan Beniquez	.03
54	Jesse Orosco	.03
55	Dave Concepcion	.05
56	Gary Allenson	.03
57	Dan Schatzeder	.03
58	Max Venable	.03
59	Sammy Stewart	.03
60	Paul Molitor	.10
61	Chris Codiroli	.03
62	Dave Hostetler	.03
63	Ed Vandeberg	.03
64	Mike Scioscia	.03
65	Kirk Gibson	.05
66	Houston Astros Team Leaders	.03
67	Gary Ward	.03
68	Luis Salazar	.03
69	Rod Scurry	.03
70	Gary Matthews	.03
71	Leo Hernandez	.03
72	Mike Squires	.03
73	Jody Davis	.03
74	Jerry Martin	.03
75	Bob Forsch	.03
76	Alfredo Griffin	.03
77	Brett Butler	.05
78	Mike Torrez	.03
79	Rob Wilfong	.03
80	Steve Rogers	.10
81	Billy Martin	.05
82	Doug Bird	.03
83	Richie Zisk	.03
84	Lenny Faedo	.03
85	Atlee Hammaker	.03
86	John Shelby	.03
87	Frank Pastore	.03
88	Rob Picciolo	.03
89	Mike Smithson	.03
90	Pedro Guerrero	.15
91	Dan Spillner	.03
92	Lloyd Moseby	.03
93	Bob Knepper	.03
94	Mario Ramirez	.03
95	Aurelio Lopez	.03
96	Kansas City Royals Team Leaders	.03
97	LaMarr Hoyt	.10
98	Steve Nicosia	.03
99	Craig Lefferts	.03
100	Reggie Jackson	.20
101	Porfirio Altamirano	.03
102	Ken Oberkfell	.03
103	Dwayne Murphy	.03
104	Ken Dayley	.03
105	Tony Armas	.05
106	Tim Stoddard	.03
107	Ned Yost	.03
108	Randy Moffitt	.03
109	Brad Wellman	.03
110	Ron Guidry	.10
111	Bill Virdon	.03
112	Tom Niedenfuer	.03
113	Kelly Paris	.03
114	Checklist—Cards 1 thru 132	.03
115	Andre Thornton	.03

116	George Bjorkman	.03
117	Tom Veryzer	.03
118	Charlie Hough	.03
119	Johnny Wockenfuss	.03
120	Keith Hernandez	.10
121	Pat Sheridan	.03
122	Cecilio Guante	.03
123	Butch Wynegar	.03
124	Damaso Garcia	.03
125	Britt Burns	.10
126	Atlanta Braves Team Leaders	.03
127	Mike Madden	.03
128	Rick Manning	.03
129	Bill Laskey	.03
130	Ozzie Smith	.05
131	1983 Batting Leaders	.10
132	1983 Home Run Leaders	.10
133	1983 Runs Batted In Leaders	.10
134	1983 Stolen Base Leaders	.10
135	1983 Victory Leaders	.10
136	1983 Strikeout Leaders	.10
137	1983 Earned Run Average Leaders	.10
138	1983 Leading Firemen	.10
139	Bert Campaneris	.03
140	Storm Davis	.03
141	Pat Corrales	.03
142	Rich Gale	.03
143	Jose Morales	.03
144	Brian Harper	.03
145	Gary Lavelle	.03
146	Ed Romero	.03
147	Dan Petry	.03
148	Joe Lefebvre	.03
149	Jon Matlack	.03
150	Dale Murphy	.25
151	Steve Trout	.03
152	Glenn Brummer	.03
153	Dick Tidrow	.03
154	Dave Henderson	.03
155	Frank White	.03
156	Oakland Athletics Team Leaders	.03
157	Gary Gaetti	.03
158	John Curtis	.03
159	Darryl Cias	.03
160	Mario Soto	.05
161	Junior Ortiz	.03
162	Bob Ojeda	.03
163	Lorenzo Gray	.03
164	Scott Sanderson	.03
165	Ken Singleton	.05
166	Jamie Nelson	.03
167	Marshall Edwards	.03
168	Juan Bonilla	.03
169	Larry Parrish	.03
170	Jerry Reuss	.03
171	Frank Robinson	.05
172	Frank DiPino	.03
173	Marvell Wynne	.10
174	Juan Berenguer	.03
175	Graig Nettles	.05
176	Lee Smith	.05
177	Jerry Hairston	.03
178	Bill Krueger	.03
179	Buck Martinez	.03
180	Manny Trillo	.03
181	Roy Thomas	.03
182	Darryl Strawberry	2.00
183	Al Williams	.03
184	Mike O'Berry	.03
185	Sixto Lezcano	.03
186	St. Louis Cardinals Team Leaders	.03
187	Luis Aponte	.03
188	Bryan Little	.03
189	Tim Conroy	.03
190	Ben Oglivie	.03
191	Mike Boddicker	.10
192	Nick Esasky	.03
193	Darrell Brown	.03
194	Domingo Ramos	.03
195	Jack Morris	.05
196	Don Slaught	.03
197	Garry Hancock	.03
198	Bill Doran	.03
199	Willie Hernandez	.03
200	Andre Dawson	.15

201	Bruce Kison	.03
202	Bobby Cox	.03
203	Matt Keough	.03
204	Bobby Meacham	.03
205	Greg Minton	.03
206	Andy Van Slyke	.25
207	Donny Moore	.03
208	Jose Oquendo	.03
209	Manny Sarmiento	.03
210	Joe Morgan	.10
211	Rick Sweet	.03
212	Broderick Perkins	.03
213	Bruce Hurst	.03
214	Paul Householder	.03
215	Tippy Martinez	.03
216	Chicago White Sox Team Leaders	.03
217	Alan Ashby	.03
218	Rick Waits	.03
219	Joe Simpson	.03
220	Fernando Valenzuela	.20
221	Cliff Johnson	.03
222	Rick Honeycutt	.03
223	Wayne Krenchicki	.03
224	Sid Monge	.03
225	Lee Mazzilli	.03
226	Juan Eichelberger	.03
227	Steve Braun	.03
228	John Rabb	.03
229	Paul Owens	.03
230	Rickey Henderson	.20
231	Gary Woods	.03
232	Tim Wallach	.03
233	Checklist—Cards 133 thru 264	.03
234	Rafael Ramirez	.03
235	Matt Young	.03
236	Ellis Valentine	.03
237	John Castino	.03
238	Reid Nichols	.03
239	Jay Howell	.03
240	Eddie Murray	.20
241	Billy Almon	.03
242	Alex Trevino	.03
243	Pete Ladd	.03
244	Candy Maldonado	.03
245	Rick Sutcliffe	.03
246	New York Mets Team Leaders	.03
247	Onix Concepcion	.03
248	Bill Dawley	.03
249	Jay Johnstone	.03
250	Bill Madlock	.10
251	Tony Gwynn	.03
252	Larry Christenson	.03
253	Jim Wohlford	.03
254	Shane Rawley	.03
255	Bruce Benedict	.03
256	Dave Geisel	.03
257	Julio Cruz	.03
258	Luis Sanchez	.03
259	Sparky Anderson	.03
260	Scott McGregor	.05
261	Bobby Brown	.03
262	Tom Candiotti	.03
263	Jack Fimple	.03
264	Doug Frobel	.03
265	Donnie Hill	.03
266	Steve Lubratich	.03
267	Carmelo Martinez	.03
268	Jack O'Connor	.03
269	Aurelio Rodriguez	.03
270	Jeff Russell	.03
271	Moose Haas	.03
272	Rick Dempsey	.03
273	Charlie Puleo	.03
274	Rick Monday	.03
275	Len Matuszek	.03
276	California Angels Team Leaders	.03
277	Eddie Whitson	.03
278	Jorge Bell	.03
279	Ivan De Jesus	.03
280	Floyd Bannister	.03
281	Larry Milbourne	.03
282	Jim Barr	.03
283	Larry Biittner	.03
284	Howard Bailey	.03
285	Darrell Porter	.03

286	Lary Sorensen	.03
287	Warren Cromartie	.03
288	Jim Beattie	.03
289	Randy Johnson	.03
290	Dave Dravecky	.03
291	Chuck Tanner	.03
292	Tony Scott	.03
293	Ed Lynch	.03
294	U. L. Washington	.03
295	Mike Flanagan	.05
296	Jeff Newman	.03
297	Bruce Berenyi	.03
298	Jim Gantner	.03
299	John Butcher	.03
300	Pete Rose	.50
301	Frank LaCorte	.03
302	Barry Bonnell	.03
303	Marty Castillo	.03
304	Warren Brusstar	.03
305	Roy Smalley	.03
306	Los Angeles Dodgers Team Leaders	.03
307	Bobby Mitchell	.03
308	Ron Hassey	.03
309	Tony Phillips	.03
310	Willie McGee	.20
311	Jerry Koosman	.03
312	Jorge Orta	.03
313	Mike Jorgensen	.03
314	Orlando Mercado	.03
315	Bob Grich	.03
316	Mark Bradley	.03
317	Greg Pryor	.03
318	Bill Gullickson	.03
319	Al Bumbry	.03
320	Bob Stanley	.03
321	Harvey Kuenn	.03
322	Ken Schrom	.03
323	Alan Knicely	.03
324	Alejandro Pena	.03
325	Darrell Evans	.03
326	Bob Kearney	.03
327	Ruppert Jones	.03
328	Vern Ruhle	.03
329	Pat Tabler	.03
330	John Candelaria	.03
331	Bucky Dent	.03
332	Kevin Gross	.03
333	Larry Herndon	.03
334	Chuck Rainey	.03
335	Don Baylor	.05
336	Seattle Mariners Team Leaders	.03
337	Kevin Hagen	.03
338	Mike Warren	.03
339	Roy Lee Jackson	.03
340	Hal McRae	.05
341	Dave Tobik	.03
342	Tim Foli	.03
343	Mark Davis	.03
344	Rick Miller	.03
345	Kent Hrbek	.20
346	Kurt Bevacqua	.03
347	Allan Ramirez	.03
348	Toby Harrah	.03
349	Bob Gibson	.03
350	George Foster	.10
351	Russ Nixon	.03
352	Dave Stewart	.03
353	Jim Anderson	.03
354	Jeff Burroughs	.03
355	Jason Thompson	.03
356	Glenn Abbott	.03
357	Ron Cey	.05
358	Bob Dernier	.03
359	Jim Acker	.03
360	Willie Randolph	.05
361	Dave Smith	.03
362	David Green	.10
363	Tim Laudner	.03
364	Scott Fletcher	.03
365	Steve Bedrosian	.03
366	San Diego Padres Team Leaders	.03
367	Jamie Easterly	.03
368	Hubie Brooks	.03
369	Steve McCatty	.03
370	Tim Raines	.20
371	Dave Gumpert	.03

372	Gary Roenicke	.03
373	Bill Scherrer	.03
374	Don Money	.03
375	Dennis Leonard	.03
376	Dave Anderson	.03
377	Danny Darwin	.03
378	Bob Brenly	.03
379	Checklist—Cards 265 thru 396	.03
380	Steve Garvey	.25
381	Ralph Houk	.05
382	Chris Nyman	.03
383	Terry Puhl	.03
384	Lee Tunnell	.03
385	Tony Perez	.05
386	N. L. All-Star: George Hendrick	.05
387	N. L. All-Star: Johnny Ray	.05
388	N. L. All-Star: Mike Schmidt	.15
389	N. L. All-Star: Ozzie Smith	.05
390	N. L. All-Star: Tim Raines	.10
391	N. L. All-Star: Dale Murphy	.10
392	N. L. All-Star: Andre Dawson	.10
393	N. L. All-Star: Gary Carter	.10
394	N. L. All-Star: Steve Rogers	.05
395	N. L. All-Star: Steve Carlton	.15
396	N. L. All-Star: Jesse Orosco	.05
397	A. L. All-Star: Eddie Murray	.15
398	A. L. All-Star: Lou Whitaker	.05
399	A. L. All-Star: George Brett	.15
400	A. L. All-Star: Cal Ripken	.15
401	A. L. All-Star: Jim Rice	.15
402	A. L. All-Star: Dave Winfield	.10
403	A. L. All-Star: Lloyd Moseby	.05
404	A. L. All-Star: Ted Simmons	.05
405	A. L. All-Star: LaMarr Hoyt	.05
406	A. L. All-Star: Ron Guidry	.05
407	A. L. All-Star: Dan Quisenberry	.05
408	Lou Piniella	.03
409	Juan Agosto	.03
410	Claudell Washington	.03
411	Houston Jimenez	.03
412	Doug Rader	.03
413	Spike Owen	.03
414	Mitchell Page	.03
415	Tommy John	.05
416	Dane Iorg	.03
417	Mike Armstrong	.03
418	Ron Hodges	.03
419	John Henry Johnson	.03
420	Cecil Cooper	.10
421	Charlie Lea	.03
422	Jose Cruz	.03
423	Mike Morgan	.03
424	Dann Bilardello	.03
425	Steve Howe	.03
426	Baltimore Orioles Team Leaders	.03
427	Rick Leach	.03
428	Fred Breining	.03
429	Randy Bush	.03
430	Rusty Staub	.03
431	Chris Bando	.03
432	Charlie Hudson	.05
433	Rich Hebner	.03
434	Harold Baines	.10
435	Neil Allen	.03
436	Rick Peters	.03
437	Mike Proly	.03
438	Biff Pocoroba	.03
439	Bob Stoddard	.03
440	Steve Kemp	.03
441	Bob Lillis	.03
442	Byron McLaughlin	.03
443	Benny Ayala	.03
444	Steve Renko	.03
445	Jerry Remy	.03
446	Luis Pujols	.03
447	Tom Brunansky	.03
448	Ben Hayes	.03
449	Joe Pettini	.03
450	Gary Carter	.15
451	Bob Jones	.03
452	Chuck Porter	.03
453	Willie Upshaw	.03
454	Joe Beckwith	.03
455	Terry Kennedy	.05
456	Chicago Cubs Team Leaders	.03

457 Dave Rozema	.03	
458 Kiko Garcia	.03	
459 Kevin Hickey	.03	
460 Dave Winfield	.15	
461 Jim Maler	.03	
462 Lee Lacy	.03	
463 Dave Engle	.03	
464 Jeff Jones	.03	
465 Mookie Wilson	.03	
466 Gene Garber	.03	
467 Mike Ramsey	.03	
468 Geoff Zahn	.03	
469 Tom O'Malley	.03	
470 Nolan Ryan	.15	
471 Dick Howser	.03	
472 Mike Brown	.03	
473 Jim Dwyer	.03	
474 Greg Bargar	.03	
475 Gary Redus	.03	
476 Tom Tellmann	.03	
477 Rafael Landestoy	.03	
478 Alan Bannister	.03	
479 Frank Tanana	.03	
480 Ron Kittle	.50	
481 Mark Thurmond	.03	
482 Enos Cabell	.03	
483 Fergie Jenkins	.10	
484 Ozzie Virgil	.03	
485 Rick Rhoden	.03	
486 New York Yankees Team Leaders	.03	
487 Ricky Adams	.03	
488 Jesse Barfield	.03	
489 Dave Von Ohlen	.03	
490 Cal Ripken	.25	
491 Bobby Castillo	.03	
492 Tucker Ashford	.03	
493 Mike Norris	.03	
494 Chili Davis	.03	
495 Rollie Fingers	.05	
496 Terry Francona	.03	
497 Bud Anderson	.03	
498 Rich Gedman	.03	
499 Mike Witt	.03	

500 George Brett	.25	
501 Steve Henderson	.03	
502 Joe Torre	.03	
503 Elias Sosa	.03	
504 Mickey Rivers	.03	
505 Pete Vuckovich	.03	
506 Ernie Whitt	.03	
507 Mike LaCoss	.03	
508 Mel Hall	.20	
509 Brad Havens	.03	
510 Alan Trammell	.10	
511 Marty Bystrom	.03	
512 Oscar Gamble	.03	
513 Dave Beard	.03	
514 Floyd Rayford	.03	
515 Gorman Thomas	.05	
516 Montreal Expos Team Leaders	.03	
517 John Moses	.03	
518 Greg Walker	.03	
519 Ron Davis	.03	
520 Bob Boone	.03	
521 Pete Falcone	.03	
522 Dave Bergman	.03	
523 Glenn Hoffman	.03	
524 Carlos Diaz	.03	
525 Willie Wilson	.10	
526 Ron Oester	.03	
527 Checklist—Cards 397 thru 528	.03	
528 Mark Brouhard	.03	
529 Keith Atherton	.03	
530 Dan Ford	.03	
531 Steve Boros	.03	
532 Eric Show	.03	
533 Ken Landreaux	.03	
534 Pete O'Brien	.03	
535 Bo Diaz	.03	
536 Doug Bair	.03	
537 Johnny Ray	.05	
538 Kevin Bass	.03	
539 George Frazier	.03	
540 George Hendrick	.05	
541 Dennis Lamp	.03	
542 Duane Kuiper	.03	

543 Craig McMurtry	.10
544 Cesar Geronimo	.03
545 Bill Buckner	.05
546 Cleveland Indians Team Leaders	.03
547 Mike Moore	.03
548 Ron Jackson	.03
549 Walt Terrell	.03
550 Jim Rice	.25
551 Scott Ullger	.03
552 Ray Burris	.03
553 Joe Nolan	.03
554 Ted Power	.03
555 Greg Brock	.10
556 Joey McLaughlin	.03
557 Wayne Tolleson	.03
558 Mike Davis	.03
559 Mike Scott	.03
560 Carlton Fisk	.10
561 Whitey Herzog	.03
562 Manny Castillo	.03
563 Glenn Wilson	.05
564 Al Holland	.03
565 Leon Durham	.10
566 Jim Bibby	.03
567 Mike Heath	.03
568 Pete Filson	.03
569 Bake McBride	.03
570 Dan Quisenberry	.15
571 Bruce Bochy	.03
572 Jerry Royster	.03
573 Dave Kingman	.05
574 Brian Downing	.03
575 Jim Clancy	.03
576 San Francisco Giants Team Leaders	.03
577 Mark Clear	.03
578 Lenn Sakata	.03
579 Bob James	.03
580 Lonnie Smith	.05
581 Jose DeLeon	.25
582 Bob McClure	.03
583 Derrel Thomas	.03
584 Dave Schmidt	.03
585 Dan Driessen	.03

586 Joe Niekro	.03
587 Von Hayes	.03
588 Milt Wilcox	.03
589 Mike Easler	.05
590 Dave Stieb	.10
591 Tony LaRussa	.03
592 Andre Robertson	.03
593 Jeff Lahti	.03
594 Gene Richards	.03
595 Jeff Reardon	.03
596 Ryne Sandberg	.03
597 Rick Camp	.03
598 Rusty Kuntz	.03
599 Doug Sisk	.03
600 Rod Carew	.25
601 John Tudor	.03
602 John Wathan	.03
603 Renie Martin	.03
604 John Lowenstein	.03
605 Mike Caldwell	.03
606 Toronto Blue Jays Team Leaders	.03
607 Tom Hume	.03
608 Bobby Johnson	.03
609 Dan Meyer	.03
610 Steve Sax	.10
611 Chet Lemon	.03
612 Harry Spilman	.03
613 Greg Gross	.03
614 Len Barker	.03
615 Garry Templeton	.05
616 Don Robinson	.03
617 Rick Cerone	.03
618 Dickie Noles	.03
619 Jerry Dybzinski	.03
620 Al Oliver	.10
621 Frank Howard	.03
622 Al Cowens	.03
623 Ron Washington	.03
624 Terry Harper	.03
625 Larry Gura	.03
626 Bob Clark	.03
627 Dave LaPoint	.03
628 Ed Jurak	.03
629 Rick Langford	.03

630 Ted Simmons	.05
631 Denny Martinez	.03
632 Tom Foley	.03
633 Mike Krukow	.03
634 Mike Marshall	.10
635 Dave Righetti	.10
636 Pat Putnam	.03
637 Philadelphia Phillies Team	
Leaders	.03
638 George Vukovich	.03
639 Rick Lysander	.03
640 Lance Parrish	.03
641 Mike Richardt	.03
642 Tom Underwood	.03
643 Mike Brown	.03
644 Tim Lollar	.03
645 Tony Pena	.05
646 Checklist—Cards 529 thru	
660	.03
647 Ron Roenicke	.03
648 Len Whitehouse	.03
649 Tom Herr	.03
650 Phil Niekro	.10
651 John McNamara	.03
652 Rudy May	.03
653 Dave Stapleton	.03
654 Bob Bailor	.03
655 Amos Otis	.05
656 Bryn Smith	.03
657 Thad Bosley	.03
658 Jerry Augustine	.03
659 Duane Walker	.03
660 Ray Knight	.03
661 Steve Yeager	.03
662 Tom Brennan	.03
663 Johnnie LeMaster	.03
664 Dave Stegman	.03
665 Buddy Bell	.05
666 Detroit Tigers Team Leaders	.03
667 Vance Law	.03
668 Larry McWilliams	.03
669 Dave Lopes	.03
670 Rich Gossage	.10
671 Jamie Quirk	.03
672 Ricky Nelson	.03

673 Mike Walters	.03
674 Tim Flannery	.03
675 Pascual Perez	.05
676 Brian Giles	.03
677 Doyle Alexander	.03
678 Chris Speier	.03
679 Art Howe	.03
680 Fred Lynn	.15
681 Tom Lasorda	.05
682 Dan Morogiello	.03
683 Marty Barrett	.03
684 Bob Shirley	.03
685 Willie Aikens	.03
686 Joe Price	.03
687 Roy Howell	.03
688 George Wright	.03
689 Mike Fischlin	.03
690 Jack Clark	.10
691 Steve Lake	.03
692 Dickie Thon	.05
693 Alan Wiggins	.03
694 Mike Stanton	.03
695 Lou Whitaker	.05
696 Pittsburgh Pirates Team	
Leaders	.03
697 Dale Murray	.03
698 Marc Hill	.03
699 Dave Rucker	.03
700 Mike Schmidt	.30
701 N. L. Active Batting Leaders	.05
702 N. L. Active Hit Leaders	.05
703 N. L. Active Home Run	
Leaders	.05
704 N. L. Active Runs Batted In	
Leaders	.05
705 N. L. Active Stolen Base	
Leaders	.05
706 N. L. Active Victory Leaders	.05
707 N. L. Active Strikeout	
Leaders	.05
708 N. L. Active Earned Run Average	
Leaders	.05
709 N. L. Active Save Leaders	.05
710 A. L. Active Batting Leaders	.05
711 A. L. Active Hit Leaders	.05

712	A. L. Active Home Run Leaders	.05
713	A. L. Active Runs Batted In Leaders	.05
714	A. L. Active Stolen Base Leaders	.05
715	A. L. Active Victory Leaders	.05
716	A. L. Active Strikeout Leaders	.05
717	A. L. Active Earned Run Average Leaders	.05
718	A. L. Active Save Leaders	.05
719	Andy Hassler	.03
720	Dwight Evans	.03
721	Del Crandall	.03
722	Bob Welch	.03
723	Rich Dauer	.03
724	Eric Rasmussen	.03
725	Cesar Cedeno	.03
726	Milwaukee Brewers Team Leaders	.03
727	Joel Youngblood	.03
728	Tug McGraw	.03
729	Gene Tenace	.03
730	Bruce Sutter	.05
731	Lynn Jones	.03
732	Terry Crowley	.03
733	Dave Collins	.03
734	Odell Jones	.03
735	Rick Burleson	.03
736	Dick Ruthven	.03
737	Jim Essian	.03
738	Bill Schroeder	.03
739	Bob Watson	.03
740	Tom Seaver	.20
741	Wayne Gross	.03
742	Dick Williams	.03
743	Don Hood	.03
744	Jamie Allen	.03
745	Dennis Eckersley	.03
746	Mickey Hatcher	.03
747	Pat Zachry	.03
748	Jeff Leonard	.03
749	Doug Flynn	.03
750	Jim Palmer	.15
751	Charlie Moore	.03
752	Phil Garner	.03
753	Doug Gwosdz	.03
754	Kent Tekulve	.03
755	Garry Maddox	.03
756	Cincinnati Reds Team Leaders	.03
757	Larry Bowa	.03
758	Bill Stein	.03
759	Richard Dotson	.03
760	Bob Horner	.15
761	John Montefusco	.03
762	Rance Mulliniks	.03
763	Craig Swan	.03
764	Mike Hargrove	.03
765	Ken Forsch	03
766	Mike Vail	.03
767	Carney Lansford	.05
768	Champ Summers	.03
769	Bill Caudill	.03
770	Ken Griffey	.05
771	Billy Gardner	.03
772	Jim Slaton	.03
773	Todd Cruz	.03
774	Tom Gorman	.03
775	Dave Parker	.15
776	Craig Reynolds	.03
777	Tom Paciorek	.03
778	Andy Hawkins	.03
779	Jim Sundberg	.03
780	Steve Carlton	.25
781	Checklist—661 thru 792	.03
782	Steve Balboni	.03
783	Luis Leal	.03
784	Leon Roberts	.03
785	Joaquin Andujar	.03
786	Boston Red Sox Team Leaders	.03
787	Bill Campbell	.03
788	Milt May	.03
789	Bert Blyleven	.03
790	Doug DeCinces	03
791	Terry Forster	.03
792	Bill Russell	.03

FLEER—1981

(2½″ × 3½″, Numbered 1–660, Color) Mint Condition

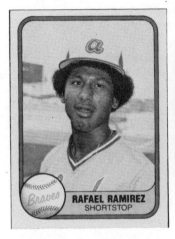

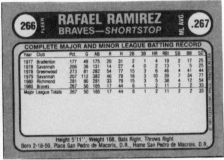

Complete Set (1st print)		$29.00
Complete Set (2nd print)		$17.00
1	Pete Rose	1.00
2	Larry Bowa	.05
3	Manny Trillo	.05
4	Bob Boone	.05
5	Mike Schmidt	.50
6	Steve Carlton	.30
7	Tug McGraw	.05
8	Larry Christenson	.05
9	Bake McBride	.05
10	Greg Luzinski	.10
11	Ron Reed	.05
12	Dickie Noles	.05
13	Keith Moreland	.05
14	Bob Walk	.05
15	Lonnie Smith	.10
16	Dick Ruthven	.05
17	Sparky Lyle	.05
18	Greg Gross	.05
19	Garry Maddox	.05
20	Nino Espinosa	.05
21	George Vukovich	.05
22	John Vukovich	.05
23	Ramon Aviles	.05
24	Kevin Saucier	.05
25	Randy Lerch	.05
26	Del Unser	.05
27	Tim McCarver	.05
28	George Brett	.50
29	Willie Wilson	.15
30	Paul Splittorff	.05
31	Dan Quisenberry	.10
32	Amos Otis	.05

33	Steve Busby	.05
34	U. L. Washington	.05
35	Dave Chalk	.05
36	Darrell Porter	.05
37	Marty Pattin	.05
38	Larry Gura	.05
39	Renie Martin	.05
40	Rich Gale	.05
41	Hal McRae	.05
42	Dennis Leonard	.05
43	Willie Aikens	.05
44	Frank White	.05
45	Clint Hurdle	.05
46	John Wathan	.05
47	Pete LaCock	.05
48	Rance Mulliniks	.05
49	Jeff Twitty	.05
50	Jamie Quirk	.05
51	Art Howe	.05
52	Ken Forsch	.05
53	Vern Ruhle	.05
54	Joe Niekro	.05
55	Frank LaCorte	.05
56	J. Rodney Richard	.10
57	Nolan Ryan	.20
58	Enos Cabell	.05
59	Cesar Cedeno	.05
60	Jose Cruz	.05
61	Bill Virdon	.05
62	Terry Puhl	.05
63	Joaquin Andujar	.05
64	Alan Ashby	.05
65	Joe Sambito	.05
66	Denny Walling	.05
67	Jeff Leonard	.05
68	Luis Pujols	.05
69	Bruce Bochte	.05
70	Rafael Landestoy	.05
71	Dave Smith	.05
72	Danny Heep	.05
73	Julio Gonzalez	.05
74	Craig Reynolds	.05
75	Gary Woods	.05
76	Dave Bergman	.05

77	Randy Niemann	.05
78	Joe Morgan	.15
79	Reggie Jackson	.35
80	Bucky Dent	.05
81	Tommy John	.10
82	Luis Tiant	.05
83	Rick Cerone	.05
84	Dick Howser	.05
85	Lou Piniella	.05
86	Ron Davis	.05
87	Graig Nettles	
	1st: "Craig"	7.00
	2nd: "Graig"	.20
88	Ron Guidry	.15
89	Rich Gossage	.10
90	Rudy May	.05
91	Gaylord Perry	.15
92	Eric Soderholm	.05
93	Bob Watson	.10
94	Bobby Murcer	.05
95	Bobby Brown	.05
96	Jim Spencer	.05
97	Tom Underwood	.05
98	Oscar Gamble	.05
99	Johnny Oates	.05
100	Fred Stanley	.05
101	Ruppert Jones	.05
102	Dennis Werth	.05
103	Joe Lefebvre	.05
104	Brian Doyle	.05
105	Aurelio Rodriguez	.05
106	Doug Bird	.05
107	Mike Griffin	.05
108	Tim Lollar	.05
109	Willie Randolph	.05
110	Steve Garvey	.35
111	Reggie Smith	.05
112	Don Sutton	.15
113	Burt Hooton	.05
114	Davey Lopes	.05
115	Dusty Baker	.10
116	Tom Lasorda	.10
117	Bill Russell	.05
118	Jerry Reuss	.05

119 Terry Forster	.05
120 Robert Welch	
1st: "Bob" on back	.35
2nd: "Robert" on back	.05
121 Don Stanhouse	.05
122 Rick Monday	.05
123 Derrel Thomas	.05
124 Joe Ferguson	.05
125 Rick Sutcliffe	.05
126 Ron Cey	.10
127 Dave Goltz	.05
128 Jay Johnstone	.05
129 Steve Yeager	.05
130 Gary Weiss	.05
131 Mike Scioscia	.05
132 Vic Davalillo	.05
133 Doug Rau	.05
134 Pepe Frias	.05
135 Mickey Hatcher	.05
136 Steve Howe	.05
137 Robert Castillo	.05
138 Gary Thomasson	.05
139 Rudy Law	.05
140 Fernando Valenzuela	1.00
141 Manny Mota	.05
142 Gary Carter	.35
143 Steve Rogers	.10
144 Warren Cromartie	.05
145 Andre Dawson	.15
146 Larry Parrish	.05
147 Rowland Office	.05
148 Ellis Valentine	.05
149 Dick Williams	.05
150 Bill Gullickson	.05
151 Elias Sosa	.05
152 John Tamargo	.05
153 Chris Speier	.05
154 Ron LeFlore	.05
155 Rodney Scott	.05
156 Stan Bahnsen	.05
157 Bill Lee	.05
158 Fred Norman	.05
159 Woodie Fryman	.05
160 Dave Palmer	.05

161 Jerry White	.05
162 Roberto Ramos	.05
163 John D'Acquisto	.05
164 Tommy Hutton	.05
165 Charlie Lea	.05
166 Scott Sanderson	.05
167 Ken Macha	.05
168 Tony Bernazard	.05
169 Jim Palmer	.25
170 Steve Stone	.05
171 Mike Flanagan	.05
172 Al Bumbry	.05
173 Doug DeCinces	.05
174 Scott McGregor	.05
175 Mark Belanger	.05
176 Tim Stoddard	.05
177 Rick Dempsey	.05
178 Earl Weaver	.10
179 Tippy Martinez	.05
180 Dennis Martinez	.05
181 Sammy Stewart	.05
182 Rich Dauer	.05
183 Lee May	.05
184 Eddie Murray	.20
185 Benny Ayala	.05
186 John Lowenstein	.05
187 Gary Roenicke	.05
188 Ken Singleton	.10
189 Dan Graham	.05
190 Terry Crowley	.05
191 Kiko Garcia	.05
192 Dave Ford	.05
193 Mark Corey	.05
194 Lenn Sakata	.05
195 Doug DeCinces	.05
196 Johnny Bench	.25
197 Dave Concepcion	.10
198 Ray Knight	.05
199 Ken Griffey	.10
200 Tom Seaver	.25
201 Dave Collins	.05
202 George Foster	
1st: No. on back "216"	.35
2nd: No. on back "202"	.05

203	Junior Kennedy	.05
204	Frank Pastore	.05
205	Dan Driessen	.05
206	Hector Cruz	.05
207	Paul Moskau	.05
208	Charlie Leibrandt	.05
209	Harry Spilman	.05
210	Joe Price	.05
211	Tom Hume	.05
212	Joe Nolan	.05
213	Doug Bair	.05
214	Mario Soto	.10
215	Bill Bonham	.05
216	George Foster	.20
217	Paul Householder	.05
218	Ron Oester	.05
219	Sam Mejias	.05
220	Sheldon Burnside	.05
221	Carl Yastrzemski	.50
222	Jim Rice	.35
223	Fred Lynn	.25
224	Carlton Fisk	.10
225	Rick Burleson	.05
226	Dennis Eckersley	.05
227	Butch Hobson	.05
228	Tom Burgmeier	.05
229	Garry Hancock	.05
230	Don Zimmer	.05
231	Steve Renko	.05
232	Dwight Evans	.05
233	Mike Torrez	.05
234	Bob Stanley	.05
235	Jim Dwyer	.05
236	Dave Stapleton	.05
237	Glenn Hoffman	.05
238	Jerry Remy	.05
239	Dick Drago	.05
240	Bill Campbell	.05
241	Tony Perez	.10
242	Phil Niekro	.05
243	Dale Murphy	.50
244	Bob Horner	.20
245	Jeff Burroughs	.05
246	Rick Camp	.05
247	Bob Cox	.05
248	Bruce Benedict	.05
249	Gene Garber	.05
250	Jerry Royster	.05
251	Gary Matthews	.05
252	Chris Chambliss	.10
253	Luis Gomez	.05
254	Bill Nahorodny	.05
255	Doyle Alexander	.05
256	Brian Asselstine	.05
257	Biff Pocoroba	.05
258	Mike Lum	.05
259	Charlie Spikes	.05
260	Glenn Hubbard	.05
261	Tommy Boggs	.05
262	Al Hrabosky	.05
263	Rick Matula	.05
264	Preston Hanna	.05
265	Larry Bradford	.05
266	Rafael Ramirez	.05
267	Larry McWilliams	.05
268	Rod Carew	.50
269	Bobby Grich	.05
270	Carney Lansford	.10
271	Don Baylor	.10
272	Joe Rudi	.05
273	Dan Ford	.05
274	Jim Fregosi	.05
275	Dave Frost	.05
276	Frank Tanana	.05
277	Dickie Thon	.10
278	Jason Thompson	.05
279	Rick Miller	.05
280	Bert Campaneris	.05
281	Tom Donohue	.05
282	Brian Downing	.05
283	Fred Patek	.05
284	Bruce Kison	.05
285	Dave LaRoche	.05
286	Don Aase	.05
287	Jim Barr	.05
288	Alfredo Martinez	.05
289	Larry Harlow	.05
290	Andy Hassler	.05

291	Dave Kingman	.10
292	Bill Buckner	.10
293	Rick Reuschel	.05
294	Bruce Sutter	.15
295	Jerry Martin	.05
296	Scot Thompson	.05
297	Ivan De Jesus	.05
298	Steve Dillard	.05
299	Dick Tidrow	.05
300	Randy Martz	.05
301	Lenny Randle	.05
302	Lynn McGlothen	.05
303	Cliff Johnson	.05
304	Tim Blackwell	.05
305	Dennis Lamp	.05
306	Bill Caudill	.05
307	Carlos Lezcano	.05
308	Jim Tracy	.05
309	Doug Capilla	.05
310	Willie Hernandez	.05
311	Mike Vail	.05
312	Mike Krukow	.05
313	Barry Foote	.05
314	Larry Biittner	.05
315	Mike Tyson	.05
316	Lee Mazzilli	.05
317	John Stearns	.05
318	Alex Trevino	.05
319	Craig Swan	.05
320	Frank Taveras	.05
321	Steve Henderson	.05
322	Neil Allen	.05
323	Mark Bomback	.05
324	Mike Jorgensen	.05
325	Joe Torre	.05
326	Elliott Maddox	.05
327	Pete Falcone	.05
328	Ray Burris	.05
329	Claudell Washington	.05
330	Doug Flynn	.05
331	Joel Youngblood	.05
332	Bill Almon	.05
333	Tom Hausman	.05
334	Pat Zachry	.05
335	Jeff Reardon	.05
336	Wally Backman	.05
337	Dan Norman	.05
338	Jerry Morales	.05
339	Ed Farmer	.05
340	Bob Molinaro	.05
341	Todd Cruz	.05
342	Britt Burns	.10
343	Kevin Bell	.05
344	Tony LaRussa	.05
345	Steve Trout	.05
346	Harold Baines	.10
347	Richard Wortham	.05
348	Wayne Nordhagen	.05
349	Mike Squires	.05
350	Lamar Johnson	.05
351	Rickey Henderson	.30
352	Francisco Barrios	.05
353	Thad Bosley	.05
354	Chet Lemon	.05
355	Bruce Kimm	.05
356	Richard Dotson	.05
357	Jim Morrison	.05
358	Mike Proly	.05
359	Greg Pryor	.05
360	Dave Parker	.20
361	Omar Moreno	.05
362	Kent Tekulve	.05
363	Willie Stargell	.25
364	Phil Garner	.05
365	Ed Ott	.05
366	Don Robinson	.05
367	Chuck Tanner	.05
368	Jim Rooker	.05
369	Dale Berra	.05
370	Jim Bibby	.05
371	Steve Nicosia	.05
372	Mike Easler	.10
373	Bill Robinson	.05
374	Lee Lacy	.05
375	John Candelaria	.05
376	Manny Sanguillen	.05
377	Rick Rhoden	.05
378	Grant Jackson	.05

379 Tom Foli	.05
380 Rod Scurry	.05
381 Bill Madlock	.10
382 Kurt Bevacqua	
1st: "P" on cap backwards	.35
2nd: "P" on cap correct	.05
383 Bert Blyleven	.05
384 Eddie Solomon	.05
385 Enrique Romo	.05
386 John Milner	.05
387 Mike Hargrove	.05
388 Jorge Orta	.05
389 Toby Harrah	.05
390 Tom Veryzer	.05
391 Miguel Dilone	.05
392 Dan Spillner	.05
393 Jack Brohamer	.05
394 Wayne Garland	.05
395 Sid Monge	.05
396 Rick Waits	.05
397 Joe Charboneau	.05
398 Gary Alexander	.05
399 Jerry Dybzinski	.05
400 Mike Stanton	.05
401 Mike Paxton	.05
402 Gary Gray	.05
403 Rick Manning	.05
404 Bo Diaz	.05
405 Ron Hassey	.05
406 Ross Grimsley	.05
407 Victor Cruz	.05
408 Len Barker	.05
409 Bob Bailor	.05
410 Otto Velez	.05
411 Ernie Whitt	.05
412 Jim Clancy	.05
413 Barry Bonnell	.05
414 Dave Stieb	.10
415 Damaso Garcia	.05
416 John Mayberry	.05
417 Roy Howell	.05
418 Dan Ainge	.05
419 Jesse Jefferson	.05
420 Joey McLaughlin	.05

421 Lloyd Moseby	.05
422 Al Woods	.05
423 Garth Iorg	.05
424 Doug Ault	.05
425 Ken Schrom	.05
426 Mike Willis	.05
427 Steve Braun	.05
428 Bob Davis	.05
429 Jerry Garvin	.05
430 Alfredo Griffin	.05
431 Bob Mattick	.05
432 Vida Blue	.10
433 Jack Clark	.10
434 Willie McCovey	.25
435 Mike Ivie	.05
436 Darrell Evans	
1st: "Darrel"	.35
2nd: "Darrell"	.05
437 Terry Whitfield	.05
438 Rennie Stennett	.05
439 John Montefusco	.05
440 Jim Wohlford	.05
441 Bill North	.05
442 Milt May	.05
443 Max Venable	.05
444 Ed Whitson	.05
445 Al Holland	.05
446 Randy Moffitt	.05
447 Bob Knepper	.05
448 Gary Lavelle	.05
449 Greg Minton	.05
450 Johnnie LeMaster	.05
451 Larry Herndon	.05
452 Rich Murray	.05
453 Joe Pettini	.05
454 Allen Ripley	.05
455 Dennis Littlejohn	.05
456 Tom Griffin	.05
457 Alan Hargesheimer	.05
458 Joe Strain	.05
459 Steve Kemp	.05
460 Sparky Anderson	.10
461 Alan Trammell	.05
462 Mark Fidrych	.05

463	Lou Whitaker	.05
464	Dave Rozema	.05
465	Milt Wilcox	.05
466	Champ Summers	.05
467	Lance Parrish	.05
468	Dan Petry	.05
469	Pat Underwood	.05
470	Rick Peters	.05
471	Al Cowens	.05
472	John Wockenfuss	.05
473	Tom Brookens	.05
474	Richie Hebner	.05
475	Jack Morris	.05
476	Jim Lentine	.05
477	Bruce Robbins	.05
478	Mark Wagner	.05
479	Tim Corcoran	.05
480	Stan Papi	
	1st: "Pitcher" on front	.35
	2nd: "Shortstop" on front	.05
481	Kirk Gibson	.25
482	Dan Schatzeder	.05
483	Aurelio Lopez	
	1st: "Outfield" on front, No. "32" on back	.35
	2nd: "Series Starter" on front, No. "483" on back	.05
484	Dave Winfield	.25
485	Rollie Fingers	.15
486	Gene Richards	.05
487	Randy Jones	.05
488	Ozzie Smith	.10
489	Gene Tenace	.05
490	Bill Fahey	.05
491	John Curtis	.05
492	Dave Cash	.05
493	Tim Flannery	
	1st: Photo batting right	.35
	2nd: Photo batting left	.05
494	Jerry Mumphrey	.05
495	Bob Shirley	.05
496	Steve Mura	.05
497	Eric Rasmussen	.05
498	Broderick Perkins	.05

499	Barry Evans	.05
500	Chuck Baker	.05
501	Luis Salazar	.05
502	Gary Lucas	.05
503	Mike Armstrong	.05
504	Jerry Turner	.05
505	Dennis Kinney	.05
506	Willie Montanez	.05
507	Gorman Thomas	.10
508	Ben Oglivie	.05
509	Larry Hisle	.05
510	Sal Bando	.05
511	Robin Yount	.35
512	Mike Caldwell	.05
513	Sixto Lezcano	.05
514	Billy Travers	
	1st: "Jerry Augustine" front & back	.35
	2nd: "Billy Travers" front & back	.05
515	Paul Molitor	.10
516	Moose Haas	.05
517	Bill Castro	.05
518	Jim Slaton	.05
519	Lary Sorensen	.05
520	Bob McClure	.05
521	Charlie Moore	.05
522	Jim Gantner	.05
523	Reggie Cleveland	.05
524	Don Money	.05
525	Billy Travers	.05
526	Buck Martinez	.05
527	Dick Davis	.05
528	Ted Simmons	.10
529	Garry Templeton	.10
530	Ken Reitz	.05
531	Tony Scott	.05
532	Ken Oberkfell	.05
533	Bob Sykes	.05
534	Keith Smith	.05
535	John Littlefield	.05
536	Jim Kaat	.10
537	Bob Forsch	.05
538	Mike Phillips	.05

539	Tito Landrum	.05
540	Leon Durham	.10
541	Terry Kennedy	.10
542	George Hendrick	.10
543	Dane Iorg	.05
544	Mark Littell	.05
545	Keith Hernandez	.20
546	Silvio Martinez	.05
547	Don Hood	
	1st: "Pete Vuckovich" front & back	.35
	2nd: "Don Hood" front & back	.05
548	Bobby Bonds	.05
549	Mike Ramsey	.05
550	Tom Herr	.05
551	Roy Smalley	.05
552	Jerry Koosman	.05
553	Ken Landreaux	.05
554	John Castino	.05
555	Doug Corbett	.05
556	Bombo Rivera	.05
557	Ron Jackson	.05
558	Butch Wynegar	.05
559	Hosken Powell	.05
560	Pete Redfern	.05
561	Roger Erickson	.05
562	Glenn Adams	.05
563	Rick Sofield	.05
564	Geoff Zahn	.05
565	Pete Mackanin	.05
566	Mike Cubbage	.05
567	Darrell Jackson	.05
568	Dave Edwards	.05
569	Rob Wilfong	.05
570	Sal Butera	.05
571	Jose Morales	.05
572	Rick Langford	.05
573	Mike Norris	.05
574	Rickey Henderson	.25
575	Tony Armas	.10
576	Dave Revering	.05
577	Jeff Newman	.05
578	Bob Lacey	.05
579	Brian Kingman	.05
580	Mitchell Page	.05
581	Billy Martin	.05
582	Rob Picciolo	.05
583	Mike Heath	.05
584	Mickey Klutts	.05
585	Orlando Gonzalez	.05
586	Mike Davis	.05
587	Wayne Gross	.05
588	Matt Keough	.05
589	Steve McCatty	.05
590	Dwayne Murphy	.05
591	Mario Guerrero	.05
592	Dave McKay	.05
593	Jim Essian	.05
594	Dave Heaverlo	.05
595	Maury Wills	.05
596	Juan Beniquez	.05
597	Rodney Craig	.05
598	Jim Anderson	.05
599	Floyd Bannister	.05
600	Bruce Bochte	.05
601	Julio Cruz	.05
602	Ted Cox	.05
603	Dan Meyer	.05
604	Larry Cox	.05
605	Bill Stein	.05
606	Steve Garvey	.25
607	Dave Roberts	.05
608	Leon Roberts	.05
609	Reggie Walton	.05
610	Dave Edler	.05
611	Larry Milbourne	.05
612	Kim Allen	.05
613	Mario Mendoza	.05
614	Tom Paciorek	.05
615	Glenn Abbott	.05
616	Joe Simpson	.05
617	Mickey Rivers	.05
618	Jim Kern	.05
619	Jim Sundberg	.05
620	Richie Zisk	.05
621	Jon Matlack	.05
622	Ferguson Jenkins	.10

623	Pat Corrales	.05
624	Ed Figueroa	.05
625	Buddy Bell	.05
626	Al Oliver	.20
627	Doc Medich	.05
628	Bump Wills	.05
629	Rusty Staub	.05
630	Pat Putnam	.05
631	John Grubb	.05
632	Danny Darwin	.05
633	Ken Clay	.05
634	Jim Norris	.05
635	John Butcher	.05
636	Dave Roberts	.05
637	Billy Sample	.05
638	Carl Yastrzemski	.50
639	Cecil Cooper	.15

640 Mike Schmidt
    1st: "Third Base" on front   .50
    2nd: "1980 Home Run King" on
front   .25

641 Checklist (Phillies/Royals)
    1st: "No. 41" on back "Hal
McRae"   .35
    2nd: "No. 41" on back "Hal
McRae Double Threat"   .10

642 Checklist (Astros/Yankees)   .05

643 Checklist (Expos/Dodgers)   .05

644 Checklist (Reds/Orioles)
    1st: "No. 202" on front "George
Foster"   .50
    2nd: "No. 202" on front "George
Foster, Slugger"   .25

645 Schmidt, Rose, Bowa
    1st: no No. on back   1.00
    2nd: No. "645" on back   .50

646 Checklist (Braves/Red Sox)   .05

647 Checklist (Cubs/Angels)   .05

648 Checklist (Mets/White Sox)   .05

649 Checklist (Indians/Pirates)   .05

650 Reggie Jackson
    "Mr. Baseball"
    1st: "No. 79" on back   .75
    2nd: "No. 650" on back   .50

651 Checklist (Giants/Blue Jays)   .05

652 Checklist (Tigers/Padres)
    1st: "Card 483" listed on
front   .35
    2nd: "Card 483" deleted from
front   .10

653 Willie Wilson
    "Most Hits, Most Runs"
    1st: "No. 29" on back   .35
    2nd: "No. 653" on back   .10

654 Checklist (Brewers/Cardinals)
    1st "Card 514" listed on front as
"Jerry Augustine." Card 574
listed on front as "Pete
Vuckovich"   .35
    2nd: Card 514 listed on front as
"Billy Travers." Card 547 listed on
front as "Don Hood"   .10

655 George Brett ".390 Average"
    1st: "No. 28" on back   1.00
    2nd: "No. 655" on back   .50

656 Checklist (Twins/Oakland A's)   .05

657 Tug McGraw
    "Game Saver"
    1st: "No. 7" on back   .35
    2nd: "No. 657" on back   .10

658 Checklist (Rangers/Mariners)   .05

659 Checklist (Misc.)
    1st: "Willie Wilson, Most Hits,
Most Runs" on front   .35
    2nd: Changed to "Amos Otis,
Series Starter   .10

660 Steve Carlton
    "Golden Arm"
    1st: "No. 6" on back   .75
    2nd: "No. 660" on back   .35

FLEER—1982

(2¹/₂″ × 3¹/₂″, Numbered 1–660, Color) Mint Condition

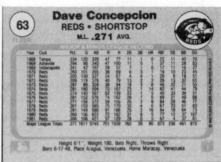

Complete Set	$17.00	
1 Dusty Baker	.05	
2 Robert Castillo	.05	
3 Ron Cey	.10	
4 Terry Forster	.05	
5 Steve Garvey	.25	
6 Dave Goltz	.05	
7 Pedro Guerrero	.10	
8 Bert Hooton	.05	
9 Steve Howe	.05	
10 Jay Johnstone	.05	
11 Ken Landreaux	.05	
12 Davey Lopes	.05	
13 Mike Marshall	.50	
14 Bobby Mitchell	.05	
15 Rick Monday	.05	
16 Tom Niedenfuer	.05	
17 Ted Power	.05	
18 Jerry Reuss	.05	
19 Ron Roenicke	.05	
20 Bill Russell	.05	
21 Steve Sax	.20	
22 Mike Scioscia	.05	
23 Reggie Smith	.05	
24 Dave Stewart	.05	
25 Rick Sutcliffe	.05	
26 Derrel Thomas	.05	
27 Fernando Valenzuela	.35	
28 Bob Welch	.05	
29 Steve Yeager	.05	
30 Bobby Brown	.05	
31 Rick Cerone	.05	
32 Ron Davis	.05	
33 Bucky Dent	.05	
34 Barry Foote	.05	
35 George Frazier	.05	
36 Oscar Gamble	.05	
37 Rich Gossage	.10	

38	Ron Guidry	.15
39	Reggie Jackson	.50
40	Tommy John	.10
41	Rudy May	.05
42	Larry Milbourne	.05
43	Jerry Mumphrey	.05
44	Bobby Murcer	.05
45	Gene Nelson	.05
46	Graig Nettles	.05
47	Johnny Oates	.05
48	Lou Piniella	.05
49	Willie Randolph	.05
50	Rick Reuschel	.05
51	Dave Revering	.05
52	Dave Righetti	.35
53	Aurelio Rodriquez	.05
54	Bob Watson	.05
55	Dennis Werth	.05
56	Dave Winfield	.15
57	Johnny Bench	.35
58	Bruce Berenyi	.05
59	Larry Biittner	.05
60	Scott Brown	.05
61	Dave Collins	.05
62	Geoff Combe	.05
63	Dave Concepcion	.10
64	Dan Driessen	.10
65	Joe Edelen	.05
66	George Foster	.25
67	Ken Griffey	.10
68	Paul Householder	.05
69	Tom Hume	.05
70	Junior Kennedy	.05
71	Ray Knight	.05
72	Mike LaCoss	.05
73	Rafael Landestoy	.05
74	Charlie Leibrandt	.05
75	Sam Mejias	.05
76	Paul Moskau	.05
77	Joe Nolan	.05
78	Mike O'Berry	.05
79	Ron Oester	.05
80	Frank Pastore	.05
81	Joe Price	.05

82	Tom Seaver	.25
83	Mario Soto	.05
84	Mike Vail	.05
85	Tony Armas	.10
86	Shooty Babitt	.05
87	Dave Beard	.05
88	Rick Bosetti	.05
89	Keith Drumright	.05
90	Wayne Gross	.05
91	Mike Heath	.05
92	Rickey Henderson	.20
93	Cliff Johnson	.05
94	Jeff Jones	.05
95	Matt Keough	.05
96	Brian Kingman	.05
97	Mickey Klutts	.05
98	Rick Langford	.05
99	Steve McCatty	.05
100	Dave McKay	.05
101	Dwayne Murphy	.05
102	Jeff Newman	.05
103	Mike Norris	.05
104	Bob Owchinko	.05
105	Mitchell Page	.05
106	Rob Picciolo	.05
107	Jim Spencer	.05
108	Fred Stanley	.05
109	Tom Underwood	.05
110	Joaquin Andujar	.05
111	Steve Braun	.05
112	Bob Forsch	.05
113	George Hendrick	.10
114	Keith Hernandez	.15
115	Tom Herr	.05
116	Dane Iorg	.05
117	Jim Kaat	.05
118	Tito Landrum	.05
119	Sixto Lezcano	.05
120	Mark Littell	.05
121	John Martin	.05
122	Silvio Martinez	.05
123	Ken Oberkfell	.05
124	Darrell Porter	.05
125	Mike Ramsey	.05

126 Orlando Sanchez	.05	
127 Bob Shirley	.05	
128 Lary Sorensen	.05	
129 Bruce Sutter	.10	
130 Bob Sykes	.05	
131 Garry Templeton	.10	
132 Gene Tenace	.05	
133 Jerry Augustine	.05	
134 Sal Bando	.05	
135 Mark Brouhard	.05	
136 Mike Caldwell	.05	
137 Reggie Cleveland	.05	
138 Cecil Cooper	.10	
139 Jamie Easterly	.05	
140 Marshall Edwards	.05	
141 Rollie Fingers	.15	
142 Jim Gantner	.05	
143 Moose Haas	.05	
144 Larry Hisle	.05	
145 Roy Howell	.05	
146 Rickey Keeton	.05	
147 Randy Lerch	.05	
148 Paul Molitor	.10	
149 Don Money	.05	
150 Charlie Moore	.05	
151 Ben Oglivie	.05	
152 Ted Simmons	.05	
153 Jim Slaton	.05	
154 Gorman Thomas	.05	
155 Robin Yount	.25	
156 Pete Vuckovich	.10	
157 Benny Ayala	.05	
158 Mark Belanger	.05	
159 Al Bumbry	.05	
160 Terry Crowley	.05	
161 Rich Dauer	.05	
162 Doug DeCinces	.05	
163 Rick Dempsey	.05	
164 Jim Dwyer	.05	
165 Mike Flanagan	.05	
166 Dave Ford	.05	
167 Dan Graham	.05	
168 Wayne Krenchicki	.05	
169 John Lowenstein	.05	

170 Dennis Martinez	.05
171 Tippy Martinez	.05
172 Scott McGregor	.05
173 Jose Morales	.05
174 Eddie Murray	.20
175 Jim Palmer	.25
176 Cal Ripken, Jr.	1.00
177 Gary Roenicke	.05
178 Lenn Sakata	.05
179 Ken Singleton	.10
180 Sammy Stewart	.05
181 Tim Stoddard	.05
182 Steve Stone	.05
183 Stan Bahnsen	.05
184 Ray Burris	.05
185 Gary Carter	.25
186 Warren Cromartie	.10
187 Andre Dawson	.20
188 Terry Francona	.05
189 Woodie Fryman	.05
190 Bill Gullickson	.05
191 Grant Jackson	.05
192 Wallace Johnson	.05
193 Charlie Lea	.05
194 Bill Lee	.05
195 Jerry Manuel	.05
196 Brad Mills	.05
197 John Milner	.05
198 Rowland Office	.05
199 David Palmer	.05
200 Larry Parrish	.05
201 Mike Phillips	.05
202 Tim Raines	.50
203 Bobby Ramos	.05
204 Jeff Reardon	.05
205 Scott Rogers	.10
206 Scott Sanderson	.05
207 Rodney Scott	.05
208 Elias Sosa	.05
209 Chris Speier	.05
210 Tim Wallach	.05
211 Jerry White	.05
212 Alan Ashby	.05
213 Cesar Cedeno	.05

214	Jose Cruz	.05	
215	Kiko Garcia	.05	
216	Phil Garner	.05	
217	Danny Heep	.05	
218	Art Howe	.05	
219	Bob Knepper	.05	
220	Frank LaCorte	.05	
221	Joe Niekro	.05	
222	Joe Pittman	.05	
223	Terry Puhl	.05	
224	Luis Pujols	.05	
225	Craig Reynolds	.05	
226	J. R. Richard	.10	
227	Dave Roberts	.05	
228	Vern Ruhle	.05	
229	Nolan Ryan	.25	
230	Joe Sambito	.05	
231	Tony Scott	.05	
232	Dave Smith	.05	
233	Harry Spilman	.05	
234	Don Sutton	.15	
235	Dickie Thon	.10	
236	Denny Walling	.05	
237	Gary Woods	.05	
238	Luis Aguayo	.05	
239	Ramon Aviles	.05	
240	Bob Boone	.05	
241	Larry Bowa	.05	
242	Warren Brusstar	.05	
243	Steve Carlton	.35	
244	Larry Christenson	.05	
245	Dick Davis	.05	
246	Greg Gross	.05	
247	Sparky Lyle	.05	
248	Garry Maddox	.05	
249	Gary Matthews	.05	
250	Bake McBride	.05	
251	Tug McGraw	.05	
252	Keith Moreland	.05	
253	Dickie Noles	.05	
254	Mike Proly	.05	
255	Ron Reed	.05	
256	Pete Rose	.75	
257	Dick Ruthven	.05	
258	Mike Schmidt	.35	
259	Lonnie Smith	.10	
260	Manny Trillo	.05	
261	Del Unser	.05	
262	George Vukovich	.05	
263	Tom Brookens	.05	
264	George Cappuzzello	.05	
265	Marty Castillo	.05	
266	Al Cowens	.05	
267	Kirk Gibson	.25	
268	Richie Hebner	.05	
269	Ron Jackson	.05	
270	Lynn Jones	.05	
271	Steve Kemp	.05	
272	Rick Leach	.05	
273	Aurelio Lopez	.05	
274	Jack Morris	.05	
275	Kevin Saucier	.05	
276	Lance Parrish	.05	
277	Rick Peters	.05	
278	Dan Petry	.05	
279	David Rozema	.05	
280	Stan Papi	.05	
281	Dan Schatzeder	.05	
282	Champ Summers	.05	
283	Alan Trammell	.05	
284	Lou Whitaker	.05	
285	Milt Wilcox	.05	
286	John Wockenfuss	.05	
287	Gary Allenson	.05	
288	Tom Burgmeier	.05	
289	Bill Campbell	.05	
290	Mark Clear	.05	
291	Steve Crawford	.05	
292	Dennis Eckersley	.05	
293	Dwight Evans	.05	
294	Rich Gedman	.05	
295	Garry Hancock	.05	
296	Glenn Hoffman	.05	
297	Bruce Hurst	.05	
298	Carney Lansford	.10	
299	Rick Miller	.05	
300	Reid Nichols	.05	
301	Bob Ojeda	.05	

302	Tony Perez	.10	347	Jerry Koosman		.05
303	Chuck Rainey	.05	348	Rusty Kuntz		.05
304	Jerry Remy	.05	349	Dennis Lamp		.05
305	Jim Rice	.35	350	Ron LeFlore		.05
306	Joe Rudi	.05	351	Chet Lemon		.05
307	Bob Stanley	.05	352	Greg Luzinski		.10
308	Dave Stapleton	.05	353	Bob Molinaro		.05
309	Frank Tanana	.05	354	Jim Morrison		.05
310	Mike Torrez	.05	355	Wayne Nordhagen		.05
311	John Tudor	.05	356	Greg Pryor		.05
312	Carl Yastrzemski	.35	357	Mike Squires		.05
313	Buddy Bell	.05	358	Steve Trout		.05
314	Steve Comer	.05	359	Alan Bannister		.05
315	Danny Darwin	.05	360	Len Barker		.05
316	John Ellis	.05	361	Bert Blyleven		.05
317	John Grubb	.05	362	Joe Charboneau		.05
318	Rick Honeycutt	.05	363	John Denny		.05
319	Charlie Hough	.05	364	Bo Diaz		.05
320	Ferguson Jenkins	.10	365	Miguel Dilone		.05
321	John Henry Johnson	.05	366	Jerry Dybzinski		.05
322	Jim Kern	.05	367	Wayne Garland		.05
323	Jon Matlack	.05	368	Mike Hargrove		.05
324	Doc Medich	.05	369	Toby Harrah		.05
325	Mario Mendoza	.05	370	Ron Hassey		.05
326	Al Oliver	.20	371	Von Hayes		.05
327	Pat Putnam	.05	372	Pat Kelly		.05
328	Mickey Rivers	.05	373	Duane Kuiper		.05
329	Leon Roberts	.05	374	Rick Manning		.05
330	Billy Sample	.05	375	Sid Monge		.05
331	Bill Stein	.05	376	Jorge Orta		.05
332	Jim Sundberg	.05	377	Dave Rosello		.05
333	Mark Wagner	.05	378	Dan Spillner		.05
334	Bump Wills	.05	379	Mike Stanton		.05
335	Bill Almon	.05	380	Andre Thornton		.05
336	Harold Baines	.05	381	Tom Veryzer		.05
337	Ross Baumgarten	.05	382	Rick Waits		.05
338	Tony Bernazard	.05	383	Doyle Alexander		.05
339	Britt Burns	.10	384	Vida Blue		.10
340	Richard Dotson	.05	385	Fred Breining		.05
341	Jim Essian	.05	386	Enos Cabell		.05
342	Ed Farmer	.05	387	Jack Clark		.10
343	Carlton Fisk	.10	388	Darrell Evans		.05
344	Kevin Hickey	.05	389	Tom Griffin		.05
345	LaMarr Hoyt	.15	390	Larry Herndon		.05
346	Lamar Johnson	.05	391	Al Holland		.05

392	Gary Lavelle	.05	437	Glenn Hubbard	.05
393	Johnnie LeMaster	.05	438	Al Hrabosky	.05
394	Jerry Martin	.05	439	Rufino Linares	.05
395	Milt May	.05	440	Rick Mahler	.05
396	Greg Minton	.05	441	Ed Miller	.05
397	Joe Morgan	.10	442	John Montefusco	.05
398	Joe Pettini	.05	443	Dale Murphy	.35
399	Allen Ripley	.05	444	Phil Niekro	.10
400	Billy Smith	.05	445	Gaylord Perry	.15
401	Rennie Stennett	.05	446	Biff Pocoroba	.05
402	Ed Whitson	.05	447	Rafael Ramirez	.05
403	Jim Wohlford	.05	448	Jerry Royster	.05
404	Willie Aikens	.05	449	Claudell Washington	.05
405	George Brett	.35	450	Don Aase	.05
406	Ken Brett	.05	451	Don Baylor	.05
407	Dave Chalk	.05	452	Juan Beniquez	.05
408	Rich Gale	.05	453	Rick Burleson	.05
409	Cesar Geronimo	.05	454	Bert Campaneris	.05
410	Larry Gura	.05	455	Rod Carew	.35
411	Clint Hurdle	.05	456	Bob Clark	.05
412	Mike Jones	.05	457	Brian Downing	.05
413	Dennis Leonard	.05	458	Dan Ford	.05
414	Renie Martin	.05	459	Ken Forsch	.05
415	Lee May	.05	460	Dave Frost	.05
416	Hal McRae	.05	461	Bobby Grich	.05
417	Darryl Motley	.05	462	Larry Harlow	.05
418	Rance Mulliniks	.05	463	John Harris	.05
419	Amos Otis	.05	464	Andy Hassler	.05
420	Ken Phelps	.05	465	Butch Hobson	.05
421	Jamie Quirk	.05	466	Jesse Johnson	.05
422	Dan Quisenberry	.15	467	Bruce Kison	.05
423	Paul Splittorff	.05	468	Fred Lynn	.25
424	U. L. Washington	.05	469	Angel Moreno	.05
425	John Wathan	.05	470	Ed Ott	.05
426	Frank White	.05	471	Fred Patek	.05
427	Willie Wilson	.15	472	Steve Renko	.05
428	Brian Asselstine	.05	473	Mike Witt	.05
429	Bruce Benedict	.05	474	Geoff Zahn	.05
430	Tom Boggs	.05	475	Gary Alexander	.05
431	Larry Bradford	.05	476	Dale Berra	.05
432	Rick Camp	.05	477	Kurt Bevacqua	.05
433	Chris Chambliss	.10	478	Jim Bibby	.05
434	Gene Garber	.05	479	John Candelaria	.05
435	Preston Hanna	.05	480	Victor Cruz	.05
436	Bob Horner	.25	481	Mike Easler	.10

482	Tim Foli	.05	**527**	Ron Hodges	.05
483	Lee Lacy	.05	**528**	Randy Jones	.05
484	Vance Law	.05	**529**	Mike Jorgensen	.05
485	Bill Madlock	.15	**530**	Dave Kingman	.10
486	Willie Montanez	.05	**531**	Ed Lynch	.05
487	Omar Moreno	.05	**532**	Mike Marshall	.05
488	Steve Nicosia	.05	**533**	Lee Mazzilli	.05
489	Dave Parker	.20	**534**	Dyar Miller	.05
490	Tony Pena	.05	**535**	Mike Scott	.05
491	Pascual Perez	.05	**536**	Rusty Staub	.05
492	Johnny Ray	.35	**537**	John Stearns	.05
493	Rick Rhoden	.05	**538**	Craig Swan	.05
494	Bill Robinson	.05	**539**	Frank Taveras	.05
495	Don Robinson	.05	**540**	Alex Trevino	.05
496	Enrique Romo	.05	**541**	Ellis Valentine	.05
497	Rod Scurry	.05	**542**	Mookie Wilson	.15
498	Eddie Solomon	.04	**543**	Joel Youngblood	.05
499	Willie Stargell	.25	**544**	Pat Zachry	.05
500	Kent Tekulve	.05	**545**	Glenn Adams	.05
501	Jason Thompson	.05	**546**	Fernando Arroyo	.05
502	Glenn Abbot	.05	**547**	John Verhoeven	.05
503	Jim Anderson	.05	**548**	Sal Butera	.05
504	Floyd Bannister	.05	**549**	John Castino	.05
505	Bruce Bochte	.05	**550**	Don Cooper	.05
506	Jeff Burroughs	.05	**551**	Doug Corbett	.05
507	Bryan Clark	.05	**552**	Dave Engle	.05
508	Ken Clay	.05	**553**	Roger Erickson	.05
509	Julio Cruz	.05	**554**	Danny Goodwin	.05
510	Dick Drago	.05	**555**	Darrell Jackson	.05
511	Gary Gray	.05	**556**	Pete Mackanin	.05
512	Dan Meyer	.05	**557**	Jack O'Connor	.05
513	Jerry Narron	.05	**558**	Hosken Powell	.05
514	Tom Paciorek	.05	**559**	Pete Redfern	.05
515	Casey Parsons	.05	**560**	Roy Smalley	.05
516	Lenny Randle	.05	**561**	Chuck Baker	.05
517	Shane Rawley	.05	**562**	Gary Ward	.05
518	Joe Simpson	.05	**563**	Rob Wilfong	.05
519	Richie Zisk	.05	**564**	Al Williams	.05
520	Neil Allen	.05	**565**	Butch Wynegar	.05
521	Bob Bailor	.05	**566**	Randy Bass	.05
522	Hubie Brooks	.05	**567**	Juan Bonilla	.05
523	Mike Cubbage	.05	**568**	Danny Boone	.05
524	Pete Falcone	.05	**569**	John Curtis	.05
525	Doug Flynn	.05	**570**	Juan Eichelberger	.05
526	Tom Hausman	.05	**571**	Barry Evans	.05

572 Tim Flannery	.05
573 Ruppert Jones	.05
574 Terry Kennedy	.10
575 Joe Lefebvre	.05
576 John Littlefield	.05
577 Gary Lucas	.05
578 Steve Mura	.05
579 Broderick Perkins	.05
580 Gene Richards	.05
581 Luis Salazar	.05
582 Ozzie Smith	.10
583 John Urrea	.05
584 Chris Welsh	.05
585 Rick Wise	.05
586 Doug Bird	.05
587 Tim Blackwell	.05
588 Bobby Bonds	.05
589 Bill Buckner	.10
590 Bill Caudill	.05
591 Hector Cruz	.05
592 Jody Davis	.05
593 Ivan De Jesus	.05
594 Steve Dillard	.05
595 Leon Durham	.10
596 Rawly Eastwick	.05
597 Steve Henderson	.05
598 Mike Krukow	.05
599 Mike Lum	.05
600 Randy Martz	.05
601 Jerry Morales	.05
602 Ken Reitz	.05
603 Lee Smith	.05
604 Dick Tidrow	.05
605 Jim Tracy	.05
606 Mike Tyson	.05
607 Ty Waller	.05
608 Danny Ainge	.05
609 Jorge Bell	.05
610 Mark Bomback	.05
611 Barry Bonnell	.05
612 Jim Clancey	.05
613 Damaso Garcia	.05
614 Jerry Garvin	.05
615 Alfredo Griffin	.05
616 Garth Iorg	.05

617 Luis Leal	.05
618 Ken Macha	.05
619 John Mayberry	.05
620 Joey McLaughlin	.05
621 Lloyd Moseby	.05
622 Dave Stieb	.10
623 Jackson Todd	.05
624 Willie Upshaw	.05
625 Otto Velez	.05
626 Ernie Whitt	.05
627 Al Woods	.05
628 All-Star Game	.10
629 All-Star Infielders	.10
630 Big Red Machine	.10
631 Bruce Sutter	.10
632 Steve Carlton	.15
633 Carl Yastrzemski	.35
634 Dynamic Duo	.20
635 West Meets East	.25
636 Fernando Valenzuela	.35
637 Mike Schmidt	.35
638 N. L. All-Stars	.15
639 Perfect Game	.10
640 Pete & Re-Pete	1.00
641 Phillies Finest	.25
642 Red Sox Reunion	.20
643 Rickey Henderson	.20
644 Rollie Fingers	.20
645 Tom Seaver	.20
646 Yankee Powerhouse	.20
647 Checklist (Dodgers/Yankees)	.05
648 Checklist (Reds/A's)	.05
649 Checklist (Cardinals/Brewers)	.05
650 Checklist (Expos/Orioles)	.05
651 Checklist (Astros/Phillies)	.05
652 Checklist (Tigers/Red Sox)	.05
653 Checklist (Rangers/White Sox)	.05
654 Checklist (Giants/Indians)	.05
655 Checklist (Royals/Braves)	.05
656 Checklist (Angels/Pirates)	.05
657 Checklist (Mariners/Mets)	.05
658 Checklist (Twins/Padres)	.05
659 Checklist (Cubs/Blue Jays)	.05
660 Checklist	.05

FLEER—1983

($3^{1}/_{2}$" × $2^{1}/_{2}$", Numbered 1–646, Color) Mint Condition

	Complete Set	$15.00	
	Complete Set	$15.00		
1	Joaquin Andujar	.04
2	Doug Bair	.04
3	Steve Braun	.04
4	Glenn Brummer	.04
5	Bob Forsch	.04
6	David Green	.40
7	George Hendrick	.10
8	Keith Hernandez	.10
9	Tom Herr	.05
10	Dane Iorg	.04
11	Jim Kaat	.10
12	Jeff Lahti	.04
13	Tito Landrum	.04
14	Dave LaPoint	.04
15	Willie McGee	.75
16	Steve Mura	.04
17	Ken Oberkfell	.04
18	Darrell Porter	.04
19	Mike Ramsey	.04
20	Gene Roof	.04
21	Lonnie Smith	.10
22	Ozzie Smith	.10
23	John Stuper	.04
24	Bruce Sutter	.10
25	Gene Tenace	.04
26	Jerry Augustine	.04
27	Dwight Bernard	.04
28	Mark Brouhard	.04
29	Mike Caldwell	.04
30	Cecil Cooper	.10
31	Jamie Easterly	.04
32	Marshall Edwards	.04
33	Rollie Fingers	.15
34	Jim Gantner	.04
35	Moose Haas	.04

36	Roy Howell	.04
37	Peter Ladd	.04
38	Bob McClure	.04
39	Doc Medich	.04
40	Paul Molitor	.10
41	Don Money	.04
42	Charlie Moore	.04
43	Ben Oglivie	.04
44	Ed Romero	.04
45	Ted Simmons	.10
46	Jim Slaton	.04
47	Don Sutton	.10
48	Gorman Thomas	.10
49	Pete Vuckovich	.10
50	Ned Yost	.04
51	Robin Yount	.20
52	Benny Ayala	.04
53	Bob Bonner	.04
54	Al Bumbry	.04
55	Terry Crowley	.04
56	Storm Davis	.04
57	Rich Dauer	.04
58	Rick Dempsey	.04
59	Jim Dwyer	.04
60	Mike Flanagan	.04
61	Dan Ford	.04
62	Glenn Gulliver	.04
63	John Lowenstein	.04
64	Dennis Martinez	.04
65	Tippy Martinez	.04
66	Scott McGregor	.04
67	Eddie Murray	.15
68	Joe Nolan	.04
69	Jim Palmer	.25
70	Cal Ripken, Jr.	.25
71	Gary Roenicke	.04
72	Lenn Sakata	.04
73	Ken Singleton	.04
74	Sammy Stewart	.04
75	Tim Stoddard	.04
76	Don Aase	.04
77	Don Baylor	.10
78	Juan Beniquez	.04
79	Bob Boone	.04

80	Rick Burleson	.04
81	Rod Carew	.25
82	Bobby Clark	.04
83	Doug Corbett	.04
84	John Curtis	.04
85	Doug DeCinces	.04
86	Brian Downing	.04
87	Joe Ferguson	.04
88	Tim Foli	.04
89	Ken Forsch	.04
90	Dave Goltz	.04
91	Bobby Grich	.04
92	Andy Hassler	.04
93	Reggie Jackson	.35
94	Ron Jackson	.04
95	Tommy John	.10
96	Bruce Kison	.04
97	Fred Lynn	.15
98	Ed Ott	.05
99	Steve Renko	.04
100	Luis Sanchez	.04
101	Rob Wilfong	.04
102	Mike Witt	.04
103	Geoff Zahn	.04
104	Willie Aikens	.04
105	Mike Armstrong	.04
106	Vida Blue	.10
107	Bud Black	.04
108	George Brett	.25
109	Bill Castro	.04
110	Onix Concepcion	.04
111	Dave Frost	.04
112	Cesar Geronimo	.04
113	Larry Gura	.04
114	Steve Hammond	.04
115	Don Hood	.04
116	Dennis Leonard	.04
117	Jerry Martin	.04
118	Lee May	.04
119	Hal McRae	.04
120	Amos Otis	.04
121	Greg Pryor	.04
122	Dan Quisenberry	.04
123	Don Slaught	.04

124	Paul Splittorff	.04	168	Sid Monge	.04
125	U. L. Washington	.04	169	Ron Reed	.04
126	John Wathan	.04	170	Bill Robinson	.04
127	Frank White	.04	171	Pete Rose	.50
128	Willie Wilson	.10	172	Dick Ruthven	.04
129	Steve Bedrosian	.04	173	Mike Schmidt	.35
130	Bruce Benedict	.04	174	Manny Trillo	.04
131	Tommy Boggs	.04	175	Ozzie Virgil	.04
132	Brett Butler	.04	176	George Vukovich	.04
133	Rick Camp	.04	177	Gary Allenson	.04
134	Chris Chambliss	.10	178	Luis Aponte	.04
135	Ken Dayley	.04	179	Wade Boggs	1.50
136	Gene Garber	.04	180	Tom Burgmeier	.04
137	Terry Harper	.04	181	Mike Clear	.04
138	Bob Horner	.20	182	Dennis Eckersley	.04
139	Glenn Hubbard	.04	183	Dwight Evans	.04
140	Rufino Linares	.04	184	Rich Gedman	.04
141	Rick Mahler	.04	185	Glenn Hoffman	.04
142	Dale Murphy	.25	186	Bruce Hurst	.04
143	Phil Niekro	.10	187	Carney Lansford	.04
144	Pascual Perez	.04	188	Rick Miller	.04
145	Biff Pocoroba	.04	189	Reid Nichols	.04
146	Rafael Ramirez	.04	190	Bob Ojeda	.04
147	Jerry Royster	.04	191	Tony Perez	.04
148	Ken Smith	.04	192	Chuck Rainey	.04
149	Bob Walk	.04	193	Jerry Remy	.04
150	Claudell Washington	.04	194	Jim Rice	.25
151	Bob Watson	.04	195	Bob Stanley	.04
152	Larry Whisenton	.04	196	Dave Stapleton	.04
153	Porfirio Altamirano	.04	197	Mike Torrez	.04
154	Marty Bystrom	.04	198	John Tudor	.04
155	Steve Carlton	.25	199	Julio Valdez	.04
156	Larry Christenson	.04	200	Carl Yastrzemski	.25
157	Ivan De Jesus	.04	201	Dusty Baker	.04
158	John Denny	.04	202	Joe Beckwith	.04
159	Bob Dernier	.04	203	Greg Brock	.15
160	Bo Diaz	.04	204	Ron Cey	.10
161	Ed Farmer	.04	205	Terry Forster	.05
162	Greg Gross	.04	206	Steve Garvey	.25
163	Mike Krukow	.04	207	Pedro Guerrero	.10
164	Garry Maddox	.04	208	Burt Hooton	.04
165	Gary Matthews	.04	209	Steve Howe	.04
166	Tug McGraw	.04	210	Ken Landreaux	.04
167	Bob Molinaro	.04	211	Mike Marshall	.15

212	Candy Maldonado	.04	256	Jack Clark	.10
213	Rick Monday	.04	257	Chili Davis	.04
214	Tom Niedenfuer	.04	258	Darrell Evans	.04
215	Jorge Orta	.04	259	Alan Fowlkes	.04
216	Jerry Reuss	.04	260	Rich Gale	.04
217	Ron Roenicke	.04	261	Atlee Hammaker	.04
218	Vicente Romo	.04	262	Al Holland	.04
219	Bill Russell	.04	263	Duane Kuiper	.04
220	Steve Sax	.10	264	Bill Laskey	.04
221	Mike Scioscia	.04	265	Gary Lavelle	.04
222	Dave Stewart	.04	266	Johnnie LeMaster	.04
223	Derrel Thomas	.04	267	Renie Martin	.04
224	Fernando Valenzuela	.25	268	Milt May	.04
225	Bob Welch	.04	269	Greg Minton	.04
226	Ricky Wright	.04	270	Joe Morgan	.10
227	Steve Yeager	.04	271	Tom O'Malley	.04
228	Bill Almon	.04	272	Reggie Smith	.04
229	Harold Baines	.04	273	Guy Sularz	.04
230	Salome Barojas	.04	274	Champ Summers	.04
231	Tony Bernazard	.04	275	Max Venable	.04
232	Britt Burns	.04	276	Jim Wohlford	.04
233	Richard Dotson	.04	277	Ray Burris	.04
234	Ernesto Escarrega	.04	278	Gary Carter	.20
235	Carlton Fisk	.10	279	Warren Cromartie	.04
236	Jerry Hairston	.04	280	Andre Dawson	.10
237	Kevin Hickey	.04	281	Terry Francona	.04
238	LaMarr Hoyt	.15	282	Doug Flynn	.04
239	Steve Kemp	.04	283	Woodie Fryman	.04
240	Jim Kern	.04	284	Bill Gullickson	.04
241	Ron Kittle	2.00	285	Wallace Johnson	.04
242	Jerry Koosman	.04	286	Charlie Lea	.04
243	Dennis Lamp	.04	287	Randy Lerch	.04
244	Rudy Law	.04	288	Brad Mills	.04
245	Vance Law	.04	289	Dan Norman	.04
246	Ron LeFlore	.04	290	Al Oliver	.10
247	Greg Luzinski	.10	291	David Palmer	.04
248	Tom Paciorek	.04	292	Tim Raines	.10
249	Aurelio Rodriguez	.04	293	Jeff Reardon	.04
250	Mike Squires	.04	294	Steve Rogers	.10
251	Steve Trout	.04	295	Scott Sanderson	.04
252	Jim Barr	.04	296	Dan Schatzeder	.04
253	Dave Bergman	.04	297	Bryn Smith	.04
254	Fred Breining	.04	298	Chris Speier	.04
255	Bob Brenly	.04	299	Tim Wallach	.04

300	Jerry White	.04	344	Alan Trammell		.04
301	Joel Youngblood	.04	345	Jerry Turner		.04
302	Ross Baumgarten	.04	346	Jerry Ujdur		.04
303	Dale Berra	.04	347	Pat Underwood		.04
304	John Candelaria	.04	348	Lou Whitaker		.04
305	Dick Davis	.04	349	Milt Wilcox		.04
306	Mike Easler	.04	350	Glenn Wilson		.15
307	Richie Hebner	.04	351	John Wockenfuss		.04
308	Lee Lacy	.04	352	Kurt Bevacqua		.04
309	Bill Madlock	.10	353	Juan Bonilla		.04
310	Larry McWilliams	.04	354	Floyd Chiffer		.04
311	John Milner	.04	355	Luis De Leon		.04
312	Omar Moreno	.04	356	Dave Dravecky		.04
313	Jim Morrison	.04	357	Dave Edwards		.04
314	Steve Nicosia	.04	358	Juan Eichelberger		.04
315	Dave Parker	.20	359	Tim Flannery		.04
316	Tony Pena	.04	360	Tony Gwynn		.04
317	Johnny Ray	.04	361	Ruppert Jones		.04
318	Rick Rhoden	.04	362	Terry Kennedy		.10
319	Don Robinson	.04	363	Joe Lefebvre		.04
320	Enrique Romo	.04	364	Sixto Lezcano		.04
321	Manny Sarmiento	.04	365	Tim Lollar		.04
322	Rod Scurry	.04	366	Gary Lucas		.04
323	Jim Smith	.04	367	John Montefusco		.04
324	Willie Stargell	.25	368	Broderick Perkins		.04
325	Jason Thompson	.04	369	Joe Pittman		.04
326	Kent Tekulve	.04	370	Gene Richards		.04
327	Tom Brookens	.04	371	Luis Salazar		.04
328	Enos Cabell	.04	372	Eric Show		.04
329	Kirk Gibson	.10	373	Garry Templeton		.10
330	Larry Herndon	.04	374	Chris Welsh		.04
331	Mike Ivie	.04	375	Alan Wiggins		.04
332	Howard Johnson	.04	376	Rick Cerone		.04
333	Lynn Jones	.04	377	Dave Collins		.04
334	Rick Leach	.04	378	Roger Erickson		.04
335	Chet Lemon	.04	379	George Frazier		.04
336	Jack Morris	.04	380	Oscar Gamble		.04
337	Lance Parrish	.04	381	Goose Gossage		.10
338	Larry Pashnick	.04	382	Ken Griffey		.04
339	Dan Petry	.04	383	Ron Guidry		.15
340	Dave Rozema	.04	384	Dave LaRoche		.04
341	Dave Rucker	.04	385	Rudy May		.04
342	Elias Sosa	.04	386	John Mayberry		.04
343	Dave Tobik	.04	387	Lee Mazzilli		.04

388 Mike Morgan	.04
389 Jerry Mumphrey	.04
390 Bobby Murcer	.04
391 Graig Nettles	.04
392 Lou Piniella	.04
393 Willie Randolph	.04
394 Shane Rawley	.04
395 Dave Righetti	.15
396 Andre Robertson	.04
397 Roy Smalley	.04
398 Dave Winfield	.20
399 Butch Wynegar	.04
400 Chris Bando	.04
401 Alan Bannister	.04
402 Len Barker	.04
403 Tom Brennan	.04
404 Carmelo Castillo	.04
405 Miguel Dilone	.04
406 Jerry Dybzinski	.04
407 Mike Fischlin	.04
408 Ed Glynn	.04
409 Mke Hargrove	.04
410 Toby Harrah	.04
411 Ron Hassey	.04
412 Von Hayes	.04
413 Rick Manning	.04
414 Bake McBride	.04
415 Larry Milbourne	.04
416 Bill Nahorodny	.04
417 Jack Perconte	.04
418 Lary Sorensen	.04
419 Dan Spillner	.04
420 Rick Sutcliffe	.04
421 Andre Thornton	.04
422 Rick Waits	.04
423 Eddie Whitson	.04
424 Jesse Barfield	.04
425 Barry Bonnell	.04
426 Jim Clancy	.04
427 Damaso Garcia	.04
428 Jerry Garvin	.04
429 Alfredo Griffin	.04
430 Garth Iorg	.04
431 Roy Lee Jackson	.04

432 Luis Leal	.04
433 Buck Martinez	.04
434 Joey McLaughlin	.04
435 Lloyd Moseby	.04
436 Rance Mulliniks	.04
437 Dale Murray	.04
438 Wayne Nordhagen	.04
439 Gene Petralli	.04
440 Hosken Powell	.04
441 Dave Stieb	.04
442 Willie Upshaw	.04
443 Ernie Whitt	.04
444 Al Woods	.04
445 Alan Ashby	.04
446 Jose Cruz	.04
447 Kiko Garcia	.04
448 Phil Garner	.04
449 Danny Heep	.04
450 Art Howe	.04
451 Bob Knepper	.04
452 Alan Knicely	.04
453 Ray Knight	.04
454 Frank LaCorte	.04
455 Mike LaCoss	.04
456 Randy Moffitt	.04
457 Joe Niekro	.04
458 Terry Puhl	.04
459 Luis Pujols	.04
460 Craig Reynolds	.04
461 Bert Roberge	.04
462 Vern Ruhle	.04
463 Nolan Ryan	.25
464 Joe Sambito	.04
465 Tony Scott	.04
466 Dave Smith	.04
467 Harry Spilman	.04
468 Dickie Thon	.04
469 Denny Walling	.04
470 Larry Andersen	.04
471 Floyd Bannister	.04
472 Jim Beattie	.04
473 Bruce Bochte	.04
474 Manny Castillo	.04
475 Bill Caudill	.04

476	Bryan Clark	.04	520	Cliff Johnson		.04
477	Al Cowens	.04	521	Matt Keough		.04
478	Julio Cruz	.04	522	Brian Kingman		.04
479	Todd Cruz	.04	523	Rick Langford		.04
480	Gary Gray	.04	524	Davey Lopes		.04
481	Dave Henderson	.04	525	Steve McCatty		.04
482	Mike Moore	.04	526	Dave McKay		.04
483	Gaylord Perry	.20	527	Dan Meyer		.04
484	Dave Revering	.04	528	Dwayne Murphy		.04
485	Joe Simpson	.04	529	Jeff Newman		.04
486	Mike Stanton	.04	530	Mike Norris		.04
487	Rick Sweet	.04	531	Bob Owchinko		.04
488	Ed Vandeberg	.04	532	Joe Rudi		.04
489	Richie Zisk	.04	533	Jimmy Sexton		.04
490	Doug Bird	.04	534	Fred Stanley		.04
491	Larry Bowa	.10	535	Tom Underwood		.04
492	Bill Buckner	.04	536	Neil Allen		.04
493	Bill Campbell	.04	537	Wally Backman		.04
494	Jody Davis	.04	538	Bob Bailor		.04
495	Leon Durham	.10	539	Hubie Brooks		.04
496	Steve Henderson	.04	540	Carlos Diaz		.04
497	Willie Hernandez	.04	541	Pete Falcone		.04
498	Ferguson Jenkins	.10	542	George Foster		.04
499	Jay Johnstone	.04	543	Ron Gardenhire		.04
500	Junior Kennedy	.04	544	Brian Giles		.04
501	Randy Martz	.04	545	Ron Hodges		.04
502	Jerry Morales	.04	546	Randy Jones		.04
503	Keith Moreland	.04	547	Mike Jorgensen		.04
504	Dickie Noles	.04	548	Dave Kingman		.04
505	Mike Proly	.04	549	Ed Lynch		.04
506	Allen Ripley	.04	550	Jesse Orosco		.04
507	Ryne Sandberg	.04	551	Rick Ownbey		.04
508	Lee Smith	.04	552	Charlie Puleo		.04
509	Pat Tabler	.04	553	Gary Rajsich		.04
510	Dick Tidrow	.04	554	Mike Scott		.04
511	Bump Wills	.04	555	Rusty Staub		.04
512	Gary Woods	.04	556	John Stearns		.04
513	Tony Armas	.04	557	Craig Swan		.04
514	Dave Beard	.04	558	Ellis Valentine		.04
515	Jeff Burroughs	.04	559	Tom Veryzer		.04
516	John D'Acquisto	.04	560	Mookie Wilson		.04
517	Wayne Gross	.04	561	Pat Zachry		.04
518	Mike Heath	.04	562	Buddy Bell		.04
519	Rickey Henderson	.15	563	John Butcher		.04

564 Steve Comer	.04	608 Bobby Castillo	.04
565 Danny Darwin	.04	609 John Castino	.04
566 Bucky Dent	.04	610 Ron Davis	.04
567 John Grubb	.04	611 Lenny Faedo	.04
568 Rick Honeycutt	.04	612 Terry Felton	.04
569 Dave Hostetler	.04	613 Gary Gaetti	.04
570 Charlie Hough	.04	614 Mickey Hatcher	.04
571 Lamar Johnson	.04	615 Brad Havens	.04
572 Jon Matlack	.04	616 Kent Hrbek	.10
573 Paul Mirabella	.04	617 Randy Johnson	.04
574 Larry Parrish	.04	618 Tim Laudner	.04
575 Mike Richardt	.04	619 Jeff Little	.04
576 Mickey Rivers	.04	620 Bob Mitchell	.04
577 Billy Sample	.04	621 Jack O'Connor	.04
578 Dave Schmidt	.04	622 John Pacella	.04
579 Bill Stein	.04	623 Pete Redfern	.04
580 Jim Sundberg	.04	624 Jesus Vega	.04
581 Frank Tanana	.04	625 Frank Viola	.04
582 Mark Wagner	.04	626 Ron Washington	.04
583 George Wright	.04	627 Gary Ward	.04
584 Johnny Bench	.25	628 Al Williams	.04
585 Bruce Berenyi	.04	629 Red Sox All-Stars	.20
586 Larry Biittner	.04	630 300 Career Wins	.15
587 Cesar Cedeno	.04	631 Pride of Venezuela, Concepcion	
588 Dave Concepcion	.04	and Trillo	.10
589 Dan Driessen	.04	632 All-Star Infielders	.10
590 Greg Harris	.04	633 Mr. Vet and Mr. Rookie	.10
591 Ben Hayes	.04	634 Fountain of Youth	.15
592 Paul Householder	.04	635 Big Chiefs	.10
593 Tom Hume	.04	636 "Smith Bros."	.10
594 Wayne Krenchicki	.04	637 Base Stealers' Threat	.10
595 Rafael Landestoy	.04	638 All-Star Catchers	.10
596 Charlie Leibrandt	.04	639 The Silver Shoe	.15
597 Eddie Milner	.04	640 Home Run Threats	.15
598 Ron Oester	.04	641 Two Teams, Same Day	.10
599 Frank Pastore	.04	642 Last Perfect Game	.10
600 Joe Price	.04	643 Bud Black	.10
601 Tom Seaver	.20	644 Vida Blue	.10
602 Bob Shirley	.04	645 Speed	.10
603 Mario Soto	.04	646 Power	.10
604 Alex Trevino	.04	Cardinals, 1-25	.04
605 Mike Vail	.04	Brewers, 26-51	.04
606 Duane Walker	.04	Orioles, 52-75	.04
607 Tom Brunansky	.04	Angels, 76-103	.04

Royals, 104-128	.04	Indians, 400-423	.04
Braves, 129-152	.04	Blue Jays, 424-444	.04
Phillies, 153-176	.04	Astros, 445-469	.04
Red Sox, 177-200	.04	Mariners, 470-489	.04
Dodgers, 201-227	.04	Cubs, 490-512	.04
White Sox, 228-251	.04	A's, 513-535	.04
Giants, 252-276	.04	Mets, 536-561	.04
Expos, 277-301	.04	Rangers, 562-583	.04
Pirates, 302-326	.04	Reds, 584-606	.04
Tigers, 327-351	.04	Twins, 607-628	.04
Padres, 352-375	.04	Special Cards, 629-646	.04
Yankees, 376-399	.04	Checklist, 647-660	.04

FLEER—1984

(3½″ × 2½″, Numbered 1–660, Color) Mint Condition

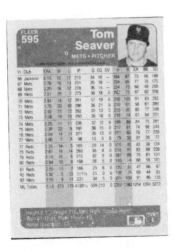

Complete Set	$12.00	
1 Mike Boddicker	.10	
2 Al Bumbry	.03	
3 Todd Cruz	.03	
4 Rich Dauer	.03	
5 Storm Davis	.03	
6 Rick Dempsey	.03	
7 Jim Dwyer	.03	
8 Mike Flanagan	.03	
9 Dan Ford	.03	
10 John Lowenstein	.03	
11 Dennis Martinez	.03	
12 Tippy Martinez	.03	
13 Scott McGregor	.03	
14 Eddie Murray	.25	
15 Joe Nolan	.03	
16 Jim Palmer	.10	
17 Cal Ripken, Jr.	.25	
18 Gary Roenicke	.03	
19 Lenn Sakata	.03	
20 John Shelby	.03	
21 Ken Singleton	.03	
22 Sammy Stewart	.03	
23 Tim Stoddard	.03	
24 Marty Bystrom	.03	
25 Steve Carlton	.25	
26 Ivan De Jesus	.03	
27 John Denny	.03	
28 Bob Dernier	.03	
29 Bo Diaz	.03	
30 Kiko Garcia	.03	
31 Greg Gross	.03	
32 Kevin Gross	.03	
33 Von Hayes	.03	
34 Willie Hernandez	.03	
35 Al Holland	.03	
36 Charles Hudson	.03	
37 Joe Lefebvre	.03	

38	Sixto Lezcano	.03
39	Garry Maddox	.03
40	Gary Matthews	.03
41	Len Matuszek	.03
42	Tug McGraw	.03
43	Joe Morgan	.10
44	Tony Perez	.03
45	Ron Reed	.03
46	Pete Rose	.50
47	Juan Samuel	.03
48	Mike Schmidt	.30
49	Ozzie Virgil	.03
50	Juan Agosto	.03
51	Harold Baines	.03
52	Floyd Bannister	.03
53	Salome Barojas	.03
54	Britt Burns	.05
55	Julio Cruz	.03
56	Richard Dotson	.03
57	Jerry Dybzinski	.03
58	Carlton Fisk	.05
59	Scott Fletcher	.03
60	Jerry Hairston	.03
61	Kevin Hickey	.03
62	Marc Hill	.03
63	LaMarr Hoyt	.05
64	Ron Kittle	.50
65	Jerry Koosman	.03
66	Dennis Lamp	.03
67	Rudy Law	.03
68	Vance Law	.03
69	Greg Luzinski	.05
70	Tom Paciorek	.03
71	Mike Squires	.03
72	Dick Tidrow	.03
73	Greg Walker	.03
74	Glenn Abbott	.03
75	Howard Bailey	.03
76	Doug Bair	.03
77	Juan Berenguer	.03
78	Tom Brookens	.03
79	Enos Cabell	.03
80	Kirk Gibson	.05
81	John Grubb	.03

82	Larry Herndon	.03
83	Wayne Krenchicki	.03
84	Rick Leach	.03
85	Chet Lemon	.03
86	Aurelio Lopez	.03
87	Jack Morris	.05
88	Lance Parrish	.03
89	Dan Petry	.03
90	Dave Rozema	.03
91	Alan Trammell	.03
92	Lou Whitaker	.05
93	Milt Wilcox	.03
94	Glenn Wilson	.05
95	John Wockenfuss	.03
96	Dusty Baker	.03
97	Joe Beckwith	.03
98	Greg Brock	.03
99	Jack Fimple	.03
100	Pedro Guerrero	.20
101	Rick Honeycutt	.03
102	Burt Hooton	.03
103	Steve Howe	.03
104	Ken Landreaux	.03
105	Mike Marshall	.05
106	Rick Monday	.03
107	Jose Morales	.03
108	Tom Niedenfuer	.03
109	Alejandro Pena	.03
110	Jerry Reuss	.03
111	Bill Russell	.03
112	Steve Sax	.10
113	Mike Scioscia	.03
114	Derrel Thomas	.03
115	Fernando Valenzuela	.20
116	Bob Welch	.03
117	Steve Yeager	.03
118	Pat Zachry	.03
119	Don Baylor	.05
120	Bert Campaneris	.03
121	Rick Cerone	.03
122	Ray Fontenot	.05
123	George Frazier	.03
124	Oscar Gamble	.03
125	Goose Gossage	.05

126	Ken Griffey	.03	170	Len Barker	.03
127	Ron Guidry	.10	171	Steve Bedrosian	.03
128	Jay Howell	.03	172	Bruce Benedict	.03
129	Steve Kemp	.03	173	Brett Butler	.03
130	Matt Keough	.03	174	Rick Camp	.03
131	Don Mattingly	.05	175	Chris Chambliss	.03
132	John Montefusco	.03	176	Ken Dayley	.03
133	Omar Moreno	.03	177	Pete Falcone	.03
134	Dale Murray	.03	178	Terry Forster	.03
135	Graig Nettles	.03	179	Gene Garber	.03
136	Lou Piniella	.03	180	Terry Harper	.03
137	Willie Randolph	.03	181	Bob Horner	.15
138	Shane Rawley	.03	182	Glenn Hubbard	.03
139	Dave Righetti	.10	183	Randy Johnson	.03
140	Andre Robertson	.03	184	Craig McMurtry	.10
141	Bob Shirley	.03	185	Donnie Moore	.03
142	Roy Smalley	.03	186	Dale Murphy	.25
143	Dave Winfield	.15	187	Phil Niekro	.05
144	Butch Wynegar	.03	188	Pascual Perez	.03
145	Jim Acker	.03	189	Biff Pocoroba	.03
146	Doyle Alexander	.03	190	Rafael Ramirez	.03
147	Jesse Barfield	.03	191	Jerry Royster	.03
148	Jorge Bell	.03	192	Claudell Washington	.03
149	Barry Bonnell	.03	193	Bob Watson	.03
150	Jim Clancy	.03	194	Jerry Augustine	.03
151	Dave Collins	.03	195	Mark Brouhard	.03
152	Tony Fernandez	.03	196	Mike Caldwell	.03
153	Damaso Garcia	.03	197	Tom Candiotti	.03
154	Dave Geisel	.03	198	Cecil Cooper	.10
155	Jim Gott	.03	199	Rollie Fingers	.05
156	Alfredo Griffin	.03	200	Jim Gantner	.03
157	Garth Iorg	.03	201	Bob Gibson	.03
158	Roy Lee Jackson	.03	202	Moose Haas	.03
159	Cliff Johnson	.03	203	Roy Howell	.03
160	Luis Leal	.03	204	Pete Ladd	.03
161	Buck Martinez	.03	205	Rick Manning	.03
162	Joey McLaughlin	.03	206	Bob McClure	.03
163	Randy Moffitt	.03	207	Paul Molitor	.10
164	Lloyd Moseby	.03	208	Don Money	.03
165	Rance Mulliniks	.03	209	Charlie Moore	.03
166	Jorge Orta	.03	210	Ben Oglivie	.03
167	Dave Stieb	.10	211	Chuck Porter	.03
168	Willie Upshaw	.03	212	Ed Romero	.03
169	Ernie Whitt	.03	213	Ted Simmons	.05

214	Jim Slaton	.03	
215	Don Sutton	.05	
216	Tom Tellmann	.03	
217	Pete Vuckovich	.05	
218	Ned Yost	.03	
219	Robin Yount	.25	
220	Alan Ashby	.03	
221	Kevin Bass	.03	
222	Jose Cruz	.03	
223	Bill Dawley	.03	
224	Frank Di Pino	.03	
225	Bill Doran	.03	
226	Phil Garner	.03	
227	Art Howe	.03	
228	Bob Knepper	.03	
229	Ray Knight	.03	
230	Frank LaCorte	.03	
231	Mike LaCoss	.03	
232	Mike Madden	.03	
233	Jerry Mumphrey	.03	
234	Joe Niekro	.03	
235	Terry Puhl	.03	
236	Luis Pujols	.03	
237	Craig Reynolds	.03	
238	Vern Ruhle	.03	
239	Nolan Ryan	.15	
240	Mike Scott	.03	
241	Tony Scott	.03	
242	Dave Smith	.03	
243	Dickie Thon	.05	
244	Denny Walling	.03	
245	Dale Berra	.03	
246	Jim Bibby	.03	
247	John Candelaria	.03	
248	Jose DeLeon	.25	
249	Mike Easler	.05	
250	Cecilio Guante	.03	
251	Richie Hebner	.03	
252	Lee Lacy	.03	
253	Bill Madlock	.10	
254	Milt May	.03	
255	Lee Mazzilli	.03	
256	Larry McWilliams	.03	
257	Jim Morrison	.03	
258	Dave Parker	.10	
259	Tony Pena	.03	
260	Johnny Ray	.05	
261	Rick Rhoden	.03	
262	Don Robinson	.03	
263	Manny Sarmiento	.03	
264	Rod Scurry	.03	
265	Kent Tekulve	.03	
266	Gene Tenace	.03	
267	Jason Thompson	.03	
268	Lee Tunnell	.03	
269	Marvell Wynne	.10	
270	Ray Burris	.03	
271	Gary Carter	.15	
272	Warren Cromartie	.03	
273	Andre Dawson	.15	
274	Doug Flynn	.03	
275	Terry Francona	.03	
276	Bill Gullickson	.03	
277	Bob James	.03	
278	Charlie Lea	.03	
279	Bryan Little	.03	
280	Al Oliver	.10	
281	Tim Raines	.15	
282	Bobby Ramos	.03	
283	Jeff Reardon	.03	
284	Steve Rogers	.10	
285	Scott Sanderson	.03	
286	Dan Schatzeder	.03	
287	Bryn Smith	.03	
288	Chris Speier	.03	
289	Manny Trillo	.03	
290	Mike Vail	.03	
291	Tim Wallach	.03	
292	Chris Welsh	.03	
293	Jim Wohlford	.03	
294	Kurt Bevacqua	.03	
295	Juan Bonilla	.03	
296	Bobby Brown	.03	
297	Luis DeLeon	.03	
298	Dave Dravecky	.03	
299	Tim Flannery	.03	
300	Steve Garvey	.25	
301	Tony Gwynn	.03	

302 Andy Hawkins	.03
303 Ruppert Jones	.03
304 Terry Kennedy	.03
305 Tim Lollar	.03
306 Gary Lucas	.03
307 Kevin McReynolds	.03
308 Sid Monge	.03
309 Mario Ramirez	.03
310 Gene Reynolds	.03
311 Luis Salazar	.03
312 Eric Show	.03
313 Elias Sosa	.03
314 Garry Templeton	.05
315 Mark Thurmond	.03
316 Ed Whitson	.03
317 Alan Wiggins	.03
318 Neil Allen	.03
319 Joaquin Andujar	.03
320 Steve Braun	.03
321 Glenn Brummer	.03
322 Bob Forsch	.03
323 David Green	.10
324 George Hendrick	.10
325 Tom Herr	.03
326 Dane Iorg	.03
327 Jeff Lahti	.03
328 Dave LaPoint	.03
329 Willie McGee	.20
330 Ken Oberkfell	.03
331 Darrell Porter	.03
332 Jamie Quirk	.03
333 Mike Ramsey	.03
334 Floyd Rayford	.03
335 Lonnie Smith	.05
336 Ozzie Smith	.05
337 John Stuper	.03
338 Bruce Sutter	.05
339 Andy Van Slyke	.05
340 Dave Von Ohlen	.03
341 Willie Aikens	.03
342 Mike Armstrong	.03
343 Bud Black	.03
344 George Brett	.25
345 Onix Concepcion	.03

346 Keith Creel	.03
347 Larry Gura	.03
348 Don Hood	.03
349 Dennis Leonard	.03
350 Hal McRae	.03
351 Amos Otis	.03
352 Gaylord Perry	.10
353 Greg Pryor	.03
354 Dan Quisenberry	.10
355 Steve Renko	.03
356 Leon Roberts	.03
357 Pat Sheridan	.03
358 Joe Simpson	.03
359 Don Slaught	.03
360 Paul Splittorff	.03
361 U. L. Washington	.03
362 John Wathan	.03
363 Frank White	.03
364 Willie Wilson	.10
365 Jim Barr	.03
366 Dave Bergman	.03
367 Fred Breining	.03
368 Bob Brenly	.03
369 Jack Clark	.10
370 Chili Davis	.03
371 Mark Davis	.03
372 Darrell Evans	.03
373 Atlee Hammaker	.03
374 Mike Krukow	.03
375 Duane Kuiper	.03
376 Bill Laskey	.03
377 Gary Lavelle	.03
378 Johnnie LeMaster	.03
379 Jeff Leonard	.03
380 Randy Lerch	.03
381 Renie Martin	.03
382 Andy McGaffigan	.03
383 Greg Minton	.03
384 Tom O'Malley	.03
385 Max Venable	.03
386 Brad Wellman	.03
387 Joel Youngblood	.03
388 Gary Allenson	.03
389 Luis Aponte	.03

390	Tony Armas	.03	434	Wayne Tolleson	.03
391	Doug Bird	.03	435	George Wright	.03
392	Wade Boggs	.50	436	Bill Almon	.03
393	Dennis Boyd	.03	437	Keith Atherton	.03
394	Mike Brown	.03	438	Dave Beard	.03
395	Mark Clear	.03	439	Tom Burgmeier	.03
396	Dennis Eckersley	.03	440	Jeff Burroughs	.03
397	Dwight Evans	.03	441	Chris Codiroli	.03
398	Rich Gedman	.03	442	Tim Conroy	.03
399	Glenn Hoffman	.03	443	Mike Davis	.03
400	Bruce Hurst	.03	444	Wayne Gross	.03
401	John Henry Johnson	.03	445	Garry Hancock	.03
402	Ed Jurak	.03	446	Mike Heath	.03
403	Rick Miller	.03	447	Rickey Henderson	.20
404	Jeff Newman	.03	448	Don Hill	.03
405	Reid Nichols	.03	449	Bob Kearney	.03
406	Bob Ojeda	.03	450	Bill Krueger	.03
407	Jerry Remy	.03	451	Rick Langford	.03
408	Jim Rice	.25	452	Carney Lansford	.03
409	Bob Stanley	.03	453	Davey Lopes	.03
410	Dave Stapleton	.03	454	Steve McCatty	.03
411	John Tudor	.03	455	Dan Meyer	.03
412	Carl Yastrzemski	.25	456	Dwayne Murphy	.03
413	Buddy Bell	.05	457	Mike Norris	.03
414	Larry Biittner	.03	458	Ricky Peters	.03
415	John Butcher	.03	459	Tony Phillips	.03
416	Danny Darwin	.03	460	Tom Underwood	.03
417	Bucky Dent	.03	461	Mike Warren	.03
418	Dave Hostetler	.03	462	Johnny Bench	.25
419	Charlie Hough	.03	463	Bruce Berenyi	.03
420	Bobby Johnson	.03	464	Dann Bilardello	.03
421	Odell Jones	.03	465	Cesar Cedeno	.03
422	John Matlack	.03	466	Dave Concepcion	.03
423	Pete O'Brien	.03	467	Dan Driessen	.03
424	Larry Parrish	.03	468	Nick Esasky	.03
425	Mickey Rivers	.03	469	Rich Gale	.03
426	Billy Sample	.03	470	Ben Hayes	.03
427	Dave Schmidt	.03	471	Paul Householder	.03
428	Mike Smithson	.03	472	Tom Hume	.03
429	Bill Stein	.03	473	Alan Knicely	.03
430	Dave Stewart	.03	474	Eddie Milner	.03
431	Jim Sundberg	.03	475	Ron Oester	.03
432	Frank Tanana	.03	476	Kelly Paris	.03
433	Dave Tobik	.03	477	Frank Pastore	.03

478	Ted Power	.03	522	Tommy John	.05
479	Joe Price	.03	523	Bruce Kison	.03
480	Charlie Puleo	.03	524	Steve Lubratich	.03
481	Gary Redus	.03	525	Fred Lynn	.10
482	Bill Scherrer	.03	526	Gary Pettis	.03
483	Mario Soto	.03	527	Luis Sanchez	.03
484	Alex Trevino	.03	528	Daryl Sconiers	.03
485	Duane Walker	.03	529	Ellis Valentine	.03
486	Larry Bowa	.03	530	Rob Wilfong	.03
487	Warren Brusstar	.03	531	Mike Witt	.03
488	Bill Buckner	.03	532	Geoff Zahn	.03
489	Bill Campbell	.03	533	Bud Anderson	.03
490	Ron Cey	.03	534	Chris Bando	.03
491	Jody Davis	.03	535	Alan Bannister	.03
492	Leon Durham	.03	536	Bert Blyleven	.03
493	Mel Hall	.20	537	Tom Brennan	.03
494	Ferguson Jenkins	.05	538	Jamie Easterly	.03
495	Jay Johnstone	.03	539	Juan Eichelberger	.03
496	Craig Lefferts	.03	540	Jim Essian	.03
497	Carmelo Martinez	.03	541	Mike Fischlin	.03
498	Jerry Morales	.03	542	Julio Franco	.03
499	Keith Moreland	.03	543	Mike Hargrove	.03
500	Dickie Noles	.03	544	Toby Harrah	.03
501	Mike Proly	.03	545	Ron Hassey	.03
502	Chuck Rainey	.03	546	Neal Heaton	.03
503	Dick Ruthven	.03	547	Bake McBride	.03
504	Ryne Sandberg	.03	548	Broderick Perkins	.03
505	Lee Smith	.05	549	Lary Sorensen	.03
506	Steve Trout	.03	550	Dan Spillner	.03
507	Gary Woods	.03	551	Rick Sutcliffe	.03
508	Juan Beniquez	.03	552	Pat Tabler	.03
509	Bob Boone	.03	553	Gorman Thomas	.05
510	Rick Burleson	.03	554	Andre Thornton	.03
511	Rod Carew	.25	555	George Vukovich	.03
512	Bobby Clark	.03	556	Darrell Brown	.03
513	John Curtis	.03	557	Tom Brunansky	.03
514	Doug DeCinces	.05	558	Randy Bush	.03
515	Brian Downing	.03	559	Bobby Castillo	.03
516	Tim Foli	.03	560	John Castino	.03
517	Ken Forsch	.03	561	Ron Davis	.03
518	Bobby Grich	.03	562	Dave Engle	.03
519	Andy Hassler	.03	563	Lenny Faedo	.03
520	Reggie Jackson	.25	564	Pete Filson	.03
521	Ron Jackson	.03	565	Gary Gaetti	.03

566 Mickey Hatcher	.03
567 Kent Hrbek	.15
568 Rusty Kuntz	.03
569 Tim Laudner	.03
570 Rick Lysander	.03
571 Bobby Mitchell	.03
572 Ken Schrom	.03
573 Ray Smith	.03
574 Tim Teufel	.03
575 Frank Viola	.03
576 Gary Ward	.03
577 Ron Washington	.03
578 Len Whitehouse	.03
579 Al Williams	.03
580 Bob Bailor	.03
581 Mark Bradley	.03
582 Hubie Brooks	.03
583 Carlos Diaz	.03
584 George Foster	.05
585 Brian Giles	.03
586 Danny Heep	.03
587 Keith Hernandez	.05
588 Ron Hodges	.03
589 Scott Holman	.03
590 Dave Kingman	.03
591 Ed Lynch	.03
592 Jose Oquendo	.03
593 Jesse Orosco	.03
594 Junior Ortiz	.03
595 Tom Seaver	.20
596 Doug Sisk	.03
597 Rusty Staub	.03
598 John Stearns	.03
599 Darryl Strawberry	2.00
600 Craig Swan	.03
601 Walt Terrell	.03
602 Mike Torrez	.03
603 Mookie Wilson	.03
604 Jamie Allen	.03
605 Jim Beattie	.03
606 Tony Bernazard	.03
607 Manny Castillo	.03
608 Bill Caudill	.03
609 Bryan Clark	.03

610 Al Cowens	.03
611 Dave Henderson	.03
612 Steve Henderson	.03
613 Orlando Mercado	.03
614 Mike Moore	.03
615 Ricky Nelson	.03
616 Spike Owen	.03
617 Pat Putnam	.03
618 Ron Roenicke	.03
619 Mike Stanton	.03
620 Bob Stoddard	.03
621 Rick Sweet	.03
622 Roy Thomas	.03
623 Ed Vande Berg	.03
624 Matt Young	.03
625 Richie Zisk	.03
626 Fred Lynn—'83 All-Star Game Record Breaker	.05
627 Manny Trillo—'83 All-Star Game Record Breaker	.05
628 Steve Garvey—N.L. Iron Man	.10
629 Rod Carew—A.L. Batting Runner-Up	.10
630 Wade Boggs—A.L. Batting Champion	.10
631 Tim Raines—Letting Go of the Raines	.10
632 Al Oliver—Double Trouble	.10
633 Steve Sax—All-Star Second Base	.10
634 Dickie Thon—All-Star Shortstop	.05
635 Quisenberry & Martinez—Ace Firemen	.10
636 Perez, Rose & Morgan—Reds Reunited	.10
637 Parrish & Boone—Backstop Stars	.10
638 Brett & Perry—The Pine Tar Incident, 7/24/83	.10
639 Forsch, Warren & Righetti—1983 No-Hitters	.10
640 Bench & Yaz—Retiring Superstars	.10

641 Gaylord Perry—Going Out in
Style .05
642 Steve Carlton—300 Club &
Strikeout Record .10
643 Altobelli & Owens—World Series
Managers .05
644 Rick Dempsey—World Series
MVP .10
645 Mike Boddicker—World Series
Rookie Winner .10
646 Scott McGregor—World Series
Clincher .10
647 Orioles/Royals Checklist .03
648 Phillies/Giants Checklist .03
649 White Sox/Red Sox Checklist .03
650 Tigers/Rangers Checklist .03
651 Dodgers/A's Checklist .03
652 Yankees/Reds Checklist .03
653 Blue Jays/Cubs Checklist .03
654 Braves/Angels Checklist .03
655 Brewers/Indians Checklist .03
656 Astros/Twins Checklist .03
657 Pirates/Mets Checklist .03
658 Expos/Mariners Checklist .03
659 Padres/Special Cards Checklist .03
660 Cardinals/Baseball Card
Checklist .03

DONRUSS—1981

(2½″ × 3½″, Numbered 1–600, Color) Mint Condition

BOB KNEPPER PITCHER

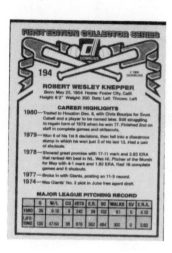

Complete Set	$24.00	
(1st print)		
Complete Set	$18.00	
(2nd print)		
1 Ozzie Smith	.15	
2 Rollie Fingers	.15	
3 Rick Wise	.05	
4 Gene Richards	.05	
5 Alan Trammell	.05	
6 Tom Brookens	.05	
7 Duffy Dyer		
1st: with decimal point	.35	
2nd: no decimal point	.05	
8 Mark Fidrych	.05	
9 Dave Rozema	.05	
10 Ricky Peters	.05	
11 Mike Schmidt	.50	

12 Willie Stargell	.25
13 Tim Foli	.05
14 Manny Sanguillen	.05
15 Grant Jackson	.05
16 Eddie Solomon	.05
17 Omar Moreno	.05
18 Joe Morgan	.15
19 Rafael Landestoy	.05
20 Bruce Bochy	.05
21 Joe Sambito	.05
22 Manny Trillo	.05
23 Dave Smith	.05
24 Terry Puhl	.05
25 Bump Wills	.05
26 John Ellis	
1st: Danny Walton's picture	.35
2nd: John Ellis' picture	.05

27 Jim Kern	.05
28 Richie Zisk	.05
29 John Mayberry	.05
30 Bob Davis	.05
31 Jackson Todd	.05
32 Al Woods	.05
33 Steve Carlton	.35
34 Lee Mazzilli	.05
35 John Stearns	.05
36 Roy Jackson	.05
37 Mike Scott	.05
38 Lamar Johnson	.05
39 Kevin Bell	.05
40 Ed Farmer	.05
41 Ross Baumgarten	.05
42 Leo Sutherland	.05
43 Dan Meyer	.05
44 Ron Reed	.05
45 Mario Mendoza	.05
46 Rick Honeycutt	.05
47 Glen Abbott	.05
48 Leon Roberts	.05
49 Rod Carew	.50
50 Bert Campaneris	.05
51 Tom Donohue	
1st: "Donahue"	.35
2nd: "Donohue"	.05
52 Dave Frost	.05
53 Ed Halicki	.05
54 Dan Ford	.05
55 Garry Maddox	.05
56 Steve Garvey	
1st: 25 HR's	.50
2nd: 21 HR's	.25
57 Bill Russell	.05
58 Don Sutton	.10
59 Reggie Smith	.05
60 Rick Monday	.05
61 Ray Knight	.05
62 Johnny Bench	.35
63 Mario Soto	.05
64 Doug Bair	.05
65 George Foster	.25
66 Jeff Burroughs	.05

67 Keith Hernandez	.25
68 Tom Herr	.05
69 Bob Forsch	.05
70 John Fulgham	.05
71 Bobby Bonds	
1st: "986 HR's"	.35
2nd: "326 HR's"	.10
72 Rennie Stennett	.05
73 Joe Strain	.05
74 Ed Whitson	.05
75 Tom Griffin	.05
76 Billy North	.05
77 Gene Garber	.05
78 Mike Hargrove	.05
79 Dave Rosello	.05
80 Ron Hassey	.05
81 Sid Monge	.05
82 Joe Charboneau	
1st: "For some reason"	.35
2nd: Phrase deleted	.10
83 Cecil Cooper	.15
84 Sal Bando	.05
85 Moose Haas	.05
86 Mike Caldwell	.05
87 Larry Hisle	
1st: "28 RBI's in '77"	.35
2nd: "28 HR's in '77"	.05
88 Luis Gomez	.05
89 Larry Parrish	.05
90 Gary Carter	.25
91 Bill Gullickson	.05
92 Fred Norman	.05
93 Tommy Hutton	.05
94 Carl Yastrzemski	
1st: "83 Runs"	.75
2nd: "93 Runs"	.50
95 Glenn Hoffman	.05
96 Dennis Eckersley	.05
97 Tom Burgmeier	
1st: "Throws right"	.35
2nd: "Throws left"	.05
98 Win Remmerswaal	.05
99 Bob Horner	.25
100 George Brett	.35

101 Dave Chalk	.05
102 Dennis Leonard	.05
103 Renie Martin	.05
104 Amos Otis	.05
105 Graig Nettles	.10
106 Eric Soderholm	.05
107 Tommy John	.10
108 Tom Underwood	.05
109 Lou Piniella	.05
110 Mickey Klutts	.05
111 Bobby Murcer	.05
112 Eddie Murray	.25
113 Rick Dempsey	.05
114 Scott McGregor	.05
115 Ken Singleton	.10
116 Gary Roenicke	.05
117 Dave Revering	.05
118 Mike Norris	.05
119 Rickey Henderson	.25
120 Mike Heath	.05
121 Dave Cash	.05
122 Randy Jones	.05
123 Eric Rasmussen	.05
124 Jerry Mumphrey	.05
125 Richie Hebner	.05
126 Mark Wagner	.05
127 Jack Morris	.05
128 Dan Petry	.05
129 Bruce Robbins	.05
130 Champ Summers	.05
131 Pete Rose	
1st: ". . . career highlights, see card 251."	1.00
2nd: ". . . career highlights, see card 371."	.75
132 Willie Stargell	.50
133 Ed Ott	.05
134 Jim Bibby	.05
135 Bert Blyleven	.05
136 Dave Parker	.20
137 Bill Robinson	.05
138 Enos Cabell	.05
139 Dave Bergman	.05
140 J. R. Richard	.10

141 Ken Forsch	.05
142 Larry Bowa	.05
143 Frank LaCorte	.05
144 Dennis Walling	.05
145 Buddy Bell	.05
146 Ferguson Jenkins	.10
147 Danny Darwin	.05
148 John Grubb	.05
149 Alfredo Griffin	.05
150 Jerry Garvin	.05
151 Paul Mirabella	.05
152 Rick Bosetti	.05
153 Dick Ruthven	.05
154 Frank Taveras	.05
155 Craig Swan	.05
156 Jeff Reardon	.05
157 Steve Henderson	.05
158 Jim Morrison	.05
159 Glenn Borgmann	.05
160 LaMarr Hoyt	.25
161 Rich Wortham	.05
162 Thad Bosley	.05
163 Julio Cruz	.05
164 Del Unser	
1st: Triples omitted	.35
2nd: Triples included	.05
165 Jim Anderson	.05
166 Jim Beattie	.05
167 Shane Rawley	.05
168 Joe Simpson	.05
169 Rod Carew	.50
170 Fred Patek	.05
171 Frank Tanana	.05
172 Alfredo Martinez	.05
173 Chris Knapp	.05
174 Joe Rudi	.05
175 Greg Luzinski	.10
176 Steve Garvey	.35
177 Joe Ferguson	.05
178 Bob Welch	.05
179 Dusty Baker	.05
180 Rudy Law	.05
181 Dave Concepcion	.05
182 Johnny Bench	.25

183 Mike LaCoss	.05	
184 Ken Griffey	.05	
185 Dave Collins	.05	
186 Brian Asselstine	.05	
187 Garry Templeton	.10	
188 Mike Phillips	.05	
189 Pete Vuckovich	.10	
190 John Urrea	.05	
191 Tony Scott	.05	
192 Darrell Evans	.05	
193 Milt May	.05	
194 Bob Knepper	.05	
195 Randy Moffitt	.05	
196 Larry Herndon	.05	
197 Rick Camp	.05	
198 Andre Thornton	.05	
199 Tom Veryzer	.05	
200 Gary Alexander	.05	
201 Rick Waits	.05	
202 Rick Manning	.05	
203 Paul Molitor	.20	
204 Jim Gantner	.05	
205 Paul Mitchell	.05	
206 Reggie Cleveland	.05	
207 Sixto Lezcano	.05	
208 Bruce Benedict	.05	
209 Rodney Scott	.05	
210 John Tamargo	.05	
211 Bill Lee	.05	
212 Andre Dawson	.20	
213 Rowland Office	.05	
214 Carl Yastrzemski	.50	
215 Jerry Remy	.05	
216 Mike Torrez	.05	
217 Skip Lockwood	.05	
218 Fred Lynn	.35	
219 Chris Chambliss	.05	
220 Willie Aikens	.05	
221 John Wathan	.05	
222 Dan Quisenberry	.10	
223 Willie Wilson	.15	
224 Clint Hurdle	.05	
225 Bob Watson	.10	
226 Jim Spencer	.05	

227 Ron Guidry	.25	
228 Reggie Jackson	.50	
229 Oscar Gamble	.05	
230 Jeff Cox	.05	
231 Luis Tiant	.05	
232 Rich Dauer	.05	
233 Dan Graham	.05	
234 Mike Flanagan	.05	
235 John Lowenstein	.05	
236 Benny Ayala	.05	
237 Wayne Gross	.05	
238 Rick Langford	.05	
239 Tony Armas	.10	
240 Bob Lacey		
1st: "Lacy"	.35	
2nd: "Lacey"	.05	
241 Gene Tenace	.05	
242 Bob Shirley	.05	
243 Gary Lucas	.05	
244 Jerry Turner	.05	
245 John Wockenfuss	.05	
246 Stan Papi	.05	
247 Milt Wilcox	.05	
248 Dan Schatzeder	.05	
249 Steve Kemp	.05	
250 Jim Lentine	.05	
251 Pete Rose	.75	
252 Bill Madlock	.20	
253 Dale Berra	.05	
254 Kent Tekulve	.05	
255 Enrique Romo	.05	
256 Mike Easler	.10	
257 Chuck Tanner	.05	
258 Art Howe	.05	
259 Alan Ashby	.05	
260 Nolan Ryan	.25	
261 Vern Ruhle		
1st: Ken Forsch's picture	.35	
2nd: Vern Ruhle's picture	.05	
262 Bob Boone	.05	
263 Cesar Cedeno	.05	
264 Jeff Leonard	.05	
265 Pat Putnam	.05	
266 Jon Matlack	.05	

267 Dave Rajsich	.05
268 Bill Sample	.05
269 Damaso Garcia	.05
270 Tom Buskey	.05
271 Joey McLaughlin	.05
272 Barry Bonnell	.05
273 Tug McGraw	.05
274 Mike Jorgensen	.05
275 Pat Zachry	.05
276 Neil Allen	.05
277 Joel Youngblood	.05
278 Greg Pryor	.05
279 Britt Burns	.10
280 Rich Dotson	.05
281 Chet Lemon	.05
282 Rusty Kuntz	.05
283 Ted Cox	.05
284 Sparky Lyle	.05
285 Larry Cox	.05
286 Floyd Bannister	.05
287 Byron McLaughlin	.05
288 Rodney Craig	.05
289 Bobby Grich	.05
290 Dickie Thon	.10
291 Mark Clear	.05
292 Dave Lemanczyk	.05
293 Jason Thompson	.05
294 Rick Miller	.05
295 Lonnie Smith	.10
296 Ron Cey	.10
297 Steve Yeager	.05
298 Bobby Castillo	.05
299 Manny Mota	.05
300 Jay Johnstone	.05
301 Dan Driessen	.05
302 Joe Nolan	.05
303 Paul Householder	.05
304 Harry Spilman	.05
305 Cesar Geronimo	.05
306 Gary Matthews	
1st: "Mathews"	.35
2nd: "Matthews"	.05
307 Ken Reitz	.05
308 Ted Simmons	.10

309 John Littlefield	.05
310 George Frazier	.05
311 Dane Iorg	.05
312 Mike Ivie	.05
313 Dennis Littlejohn	.05
314 Gary Lavelle	.05
315 Jack Clark	.10
316 Jim Wohlford	.05
317 Rick Matula	.05
318 Toby Harrah	.05
319 Duane Kuiper	
1st: "Dwane"	.35
2nd: "Duane"	.05
320 Len Barker	.05
321 Victor Cruz	.05
322 Dell Alston	.05
323 Robin Yount	.35
324 Charlie Moore	.05
325 Lary Sorensen	.05
326 Gorman Thomas	
1st: "30 HR mark for 4th straight year."	.35
2nd: ". . . 3rd straight year."	.10
327 Bob Rogers	.05
328 Phil Niekro	.10
329 Chris Speier	.05
330 Steve Rogers	
1st: "Rogers"	.35
2nd: "Rogers"	.10
331 Woodie Fryman	.05
332 Warren Cromartie	.05
333 Jerry White	.05
334 Tony Perez	.10
335 Carlton Fisk	.15
336 Dick Drago	.05
337 Steve Renko	.05
338 Jim Rice	.35
339 Jerry Royster	.05
340 Frank White	.05
341 Jamie Quirk	.05
342 Paul Splittorff	
1st: "Spittorff"	.35
2nd: "Splittorff"	.10

343	Marty Pattin	.05	383	Jose Cruz	.05
344	Pete LaCock	.05	384	Bill Virdon	.05
345	Willie Randolph	.05	385	Jim Sundberg	.05
346	Rick Cerone	.05	386	Doc Medich	.05
347	Rich Gossage	.10	387	Al Oliver	.20
348	Reggie Jackson	.50	388	Jim Norris	.05
349	Ruppert Jones	.05	389	Bob Bailor	.05
350	Dave McKay	.05	390	Ernie Whitt	.05
351	Yogi Berra	.10	391	Otto Velez	.05
352	Doug DeCinces	.10	392	Roy Howell	.05
353	Jim Palmer	.35	393	Bob Walk	.05
354	Tippy Martinez	.05	394	Doug Flynn	.05
355	Al Bumbry	.05	395	Pete Falcone	.05
356	Earl Weaver	.10	396	Tom Hausman	.05
357	Rob Picciolo		397	Elliott Maddox	.05
	1st: "Bob"	.35	398	Mike Squires	.05
	2nd: "Rob"	.05	399	Marvis Foley	.05
358	Matt Keough	.05	400	Steve Trout	.05
359	Dwayne Murphy	.05	401	Wayne Nordhagen	.05
360	Brian Kingman	.05	402	Tony LaRussa	.05
361	Bill Fahey	.05	403	Bruce Bochte	.05
362	Steve Mura	.05	404	Bake McBride	.05
363	Dennis Kinney	.05	405	Jerry Narron	.05
364	Dave Winfield	.35	406	Rob Dressler	.05
365	Lou Whitaker	.05	407	Dave Heaverlo	.05
366	Lance Parrish	.05	408	Tom Paciorek	.05
367	Tim Corcoran	.05	409	Carney Lansford	.10
368	Pat Underwood	.05	410	Brian Downing	.05
369	Al Cowens	.05	411	Don Aase	.05
370	Sparky Anderson	.10	412	Jim Barr	.05
371	Pete Rose	.75	413	Don Baylor	.10
372	Phil Garner	.05	414	Jim Fregosi	.05
373	Steve Nicosia	.05	415	Dallas Green	.05
374	John Candelaria	.05	416	Dave Lopes	.05
375	Don Robinson	.05	417	Jerry Reuss	.05
376	Lee Lacy	.05	418	Rick Sutcliffe	.05
377	John Milner	.05	419	Derrel Thomas	.05
378	Craig Reynolds	.05	420	Tommy Lasorda	.10
379	Luis Pujols		421	Charles Leibrandt	.05
	1st: "Pujois"	.35	422	Tom Seaver	.35
	2nd: "Pujols"	.05	423	Ron Oester	.05
380	Joe Niekro	.05	424	Junior Kennedy	.05
381	Joaquin Andujar	.05	425	Tom Seaver	.35
382	Keith Moreland	.05	426	Bobby Cox	.05

427 Leon Durham	.10	
428 Terry Kennedy	.10	
429 Silvio Martinez	.05	
430 George Hendrick	.10	
431 Red Schoendienst	.05	
432 John LeMaster	.05	
433 Vida Blue	.10	
434 John Montefusco	.05	
435 Terry Whitfield	.05	
436 Dave Bristol	.05	
437 Dale Murphy	.35	
438 Jerry Dybzinski	.05	
439 Jorge Orta	.05	
440 Wayne Garland	.05	
441 Miguel Dilone	.05	
442 Dave Garcia	.05	
443 Don Money	.05	
444 Buck Martinez		
1st: Uniform number backward	.35	
2nd: Corrected	.05	
445 Jerry Augustine	.05	
446 Ben Oglivie	.05	
447 Jim Slaton	.05	
448 Doyle Alexander	.05	
449 Tony Bernazard	.05	
450 Scott Sanderson	.05	
451 Dave Palmer	.05	
452 Stan Bahnsen	.05	
453 Dick Williams	.05	
454 Rick Burleson	.05	
455 Gary Allenson	.05	
456 Bob Stanley	.05	
457 John Tudor		
1st: "Career Record of 9.7"	.35	
2nd: "Career Record of 9–7"	.05	
458 Dwight Evans	.05	
459 Glenn Hubbard	.05	
460 U. L. Washington	.05	
461 Larry Gura	.05	
462 Rich Gale	.05	
463 Hal McRae	.05	
464 Jim Frey	.05	

465 Bucky Dent	.05	
466 Dennis Werth	.05	
467 Ron Davis	.05	
468 Reggie Jackson	.50	
469 Bobby Brown	.05	
470 Mike Davis	.05	
471 Gaylord Perry	.20	
472 Mark Belanger	.05	
473 Jim Palmer	.20	
474 Sammy Stewart	.05	
475 Tim Stoddard	.05	
476 Steve Stone	.05	
477 Jeff Newman	.05	
478 Steve McCatty	.05	
479 Billy Martin	.10	
480 Mitchell Page	.05	
481 Cy Young—'80	.10	
482 Bill Buckner	.10	
483 Ivan De Jesus		
1st: "702 Lifetime" Hits	.35	
2nd: "642 Lifetime" Hits	.05	
484 Cliff Johnson	.05	
485 Lenny Randle	.05	
486 Larry Milbourne	.05	
487 Roy Smalley	.05	
488 John Castino	.05	
489 Ron Jackson	.05	
490 Dave Roberts		
1st: "with Rangers"	.35	
2nd: "with Astros"	.05	
491 A.L.—M.V.P.—'80	.05	
492 Mike Cubbage	.05	
493 Rob Wilfong	.05	
494 Danny Goodwin	.05	
495 Jose Morales	.05	
496 Mickey Rivers	.05	
497 Mike Edwards	.05	
498 Mike Sadek	.05	
499 Lenn Sakata	.05	
500 Gene Michael	.05	
501 Dave Roberts	.05	
502 Steve Dillard	.05	
503 Jim Essian	.05	
504 Rance Mulliniks	.05	

505 Darrell Porter	.05	
506 Joe Torre	.05	
507 Terry Crowley	.05	
508 Bill Travers	.05	
509 Nelson Norman	.05	
510 Bob McClure	.05	
511 Steve Howe	.05	
512 Dave Rader	.05	
513 Mike Kelleher	.05	
514 Kiko Garcia	.05	
515 Larry Biittner	.05	
516 Willie Norwood		
1st: "with Twins"	.35	
2nd: "with Mariners"	.05	
517 Bo Diaz	.05	
518 Juan Beniquez	.05	
519 Scott Thompson	.05	
520 Jim Tracy	.05	
521 Carlos Lezcano	.05	
522 Joe Amalfitano	.05	
523 Preston Hanna	.05	
524 Ray Burris		
1st: "with Cubs"	.35	
2nd: "with Mets"	.05	
525 Broderick Perkins	.05	
526 Mickey Hatcher	.05	
527 John Goryl	.05	
528 Dick Davis	.05	
529 Butch Wynegar	.05	
530 Sal Butera	.05	
531 Jerry Koosman	.05	
532 Geoff Zahn		
1st: "with Twins"	.35	
2nd: "with Angels"	.05	
533 Dennis Martinez	.05	
534 Gary Thomasson	.05	
535 Steve Macko	.05	
536 Jim Kaat	.10	
537 Best Hitters	.35	
538 Tim Raines	1.25	
539 Keith Smith	.05	
540 Ken Macha	.05	
541 Burt Hooton	.05	
542 Butch Hobson	.05	

543 Bill Stein	.05	
544 Dave Stapleton	.05	
545 Bob Pate	.05	
546 Doug Corbett	.05	
547 Darrell Jackson	.05	
548 Pete Redfern	.05	
549 Roger Erickson	.05	
550 Al Hrabosky	.05	
551 Dick Tidrow	.05	
552 Dave Ford	.05	
553 Dave Kingman	.10	
554 Mike Vail		
1st: "with Cubs"	.35	
2nd: "with Reds"	.05	
555 Jerry Martin		
1st: "with Cubs"	.35	
2nd: "with Giants"	.05	
556 Jesus Figueroa		
1st: "with Cubs"	.35	
2nd: "with Giants"	.05	
557 Don Stanhouse	.05	
558 Barry Foote	.05	
559 Tim Blackwell	.05	
560 Bruce Sutter	.10	
561 Rick Reuschel	.05	
562 Lynn McGlothen	.05	
563 Bob Owchinko		
1st: "with Indians"	.35	
2nd: "with Pirates"	.05	
564 John Verhoeven	.05	
565 Ken Landreaux	.05	
566 Glenn Adams		
1st: "Glen"	.35	
2nd: "Glenn"	.05	
567 Hosken Powell	.05	
568 Dick Noles	.05	
569 Danny Ainge	.05	
570 Bobby Mattick	.05	
571 Joe Lefebvre	.05	
572 Bobby Clark	.05	
573 Dennis Lamp	.05	
574 Randy Lerch	.05	
575 Mookie Wilson	.10	
576 Ron LeFlore	.05	

577 Jim Dwyer	.05
578 Bill Castro	.05
579 Greg Minton	.05
580 Mark Littell	.05
581 Andy Hassler	.05
582 Dave Stieb	.10
583 Ken Oberkfell	.05
584 Larry Bradford	.05
585 Fred Stanley	.05
586 Bill Caudill	.05
587 Doug Capilla	.05
588 George Riley	.05
589 Willie Hernandez	.05
590 N.L.—M.V.P.—'80	.15
591 Cy Young	.10
592 Rick Sofield	.05

593 Bombo Rivera	.05
594 Gary Ward	.05
595 Dave Edwards	
1st: "with Twins"	.35
2nd: "with Padres"	.05
596 Mike Proly	.05
597 Tommy Boggs	.05
598 Greg Gross	.05
599 Elias Sosa	.05
600 Pat Kelly	
Checklist #1	.05
Checklist #2	.05
Checklist #3	.05
Checklist #4	.05
Checklist #5	.05

DONRUSS—1982

(2¹/₂″ × 3¹/₂″, Numbered 1–660, Color) Mint Condition

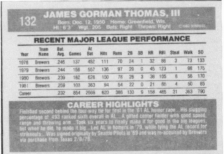

Complete Set	$17.00	**17** Dave Kingman	.10
1 Pete Rose	.50	**18** Dave Winfield	.20
2 Gary Carter	.25	**19** Mike Norris	.05
3 Steve Garvey	.25	**20** Carlton Fisk	.10
4 Vida Blue	.10	**21** Ozzie Smith	.10
5 Alan Trammell	.05	**22** Roy Smalley	.05
6 Len Barker	.05	**23** Buddy Bell	.05
7 Dwight Evans	.05	**24** Ken Singleton	.10
8 Rod Carew	.35	**25** John Mayberry	.05
9 George Hendrick	.10	**26** Gorman Thomas	.05
10 Phil Niekro	.10	**27** Earl Weaver	.10
11 Richie Zisk	.05	**28** Rollie Fingers	.10
12 Dave Parker	.20	**29** Sparky Anderson	.10
13 Nolan Ryan	.20	**30** Dennis Eckersley	.05
14 Ivan De Jesus	.05	**31** Dave Winfield	.20
15 George Brett	.35	**32** Burt Hooton	.05
16 Tom Seaver	.25	**33** Rick Waits	.05

34	George Brett	.25	78	Paul Molitor	.10
35	Steve McCatty	.05	79	Dennis Martinez	.05
36	Steve Rogers	.10	80	Jim Slaton	.05
37	Bill Stein	.05	81	Champ Summers	.05
38	Steve Renko	.05	82	Carney Lansford	.10
39	Mike Squires	.05	83	Barry Foote	.05
40	George Hendrick	.10	84	Steve Garvey	.35
41	Bob Knepper	.05	85	Rick Manning	.05
42	Steve Carlton	.35	86	John Wathan	.05
43	Larry Biittner	.05	87	Brian Kingman	.05
44	Chris Welsh	.05	88	Andre Dawson	.10
45	Steve Nicosia	.05	89	Jim Kern	.05
46	Jack Clark	.10	90	Bobby Grich	.05
47	Chris Chambliss	.10	91	Bob Forsch	.05
48	Ivan De Jesus	.05	92	Art Howe	.05
49	Lee Mazzilli	.05	93	Marty Bystrom	.05
50	Julio Cruz	.05	94	Ozzie Smith	.10
51	Pete Redfern	.05	95	Dave Parker	.15
52	Dave Stieb	.10	96	Doyle Alexander	.05
53	Doug Corbett	.05	97	Al Hrabosky	.05
54	Jorge Bell	.05	98	Frank Taveras	.05
55	Joe Simpson	.05	99	Tim Blackwell	.05
56	Rusty Staub	.05	100	Floyd Bannister	.05
57	Hector Cruz	.05	101	Alfredo Griffin	.05
58	Claudell Washington	.05	102	Dave Engle	.05
59	Enrique Romo	.05	103	Mario Soto	.05
60	Gary Lavelle	.05	104	Ross Baumgarten	.05
61	Tim Flannery	.05	105	Ken Singleton	.10
62	Joe Nolan	.05	106	Ted Simmons	.10
63	Larry Bowa	.05	107	Jack Morris	.05
64	Sixto Lezcano	.05	108	Bob Watson	.10
65	Joe Sambito	.05	109	Dwight Evans	.05
66	Bruce Kison	.05	110	Tom Lasorda	.10
67	Wayne Nordhagen	.05	111	Bert Blyleven	.05
68	Woodie Fryman	.05	112	Dan Quisenberry	.10
69	Billy Sample	.05	113	Rickey Henderson	.20
70	Amos Otis	.05	114	Gary Carter	.20
71	Matt Keough	.05	115	Brian Downing	.05
72	Toby Harrah	.05	116	Al Oliver	.15
73	Dave Righetti	.35	117	LaMarr Hoyt	.25
74	Carl Yastrzemski	.35	118	Cesar Cedeno	.05
75	Bob Welch	.05	119	Keith Moreland	.05
76	Alan Trammell	.05	120	Bob Shirley	.05
77	Rick Dempsey	.05	121	Terry Kennedy	.10

122	Frank Pastore	.05	166	Dane Iorg	.05
123	Gene Garber	.05	167	Joe Niekro	.05
124	Tony Pena	.05	168	Pete Rose	.75
125	Allen Ripley	.05	169	Dave Collins	.05
126	Randy Martz	.05	170	Rick Wise	.05
127	Richie Zisk	.05	171	Jim Bibby	.05
128	Mike Scott	.05	172	Larry Herndon	.05
129	Lloyd Moseby	.05	173	Bob Horner	.20
130	Rob Wilfong	.05	174	Steve Dillard	.05
131	Tim Stoddard	.05	175	Mookie Wilson	.10
132	Gorman Thomas	.10	176	Dan Meyer	.05
133	Dan Petry	.05	177	Fernando Arroyo	.05
134	Bob Stanley	.05	178	Jackson Todd	.05
135	Lou Piniella	.05	179	Darrell Jackson	.05
136	Pedro Guerrero	.10	180	Al Woods	.05
137	Len Barker	.05	181	Jim Anderson	.05
138	Rich Gale	.05	182	Dave Kingman	.10
139	Wayne Gross	.05	183	Steve Henderson	.05
140	Tim Wallach	.05	184	Brian Asselstine	.05
141	Gene Mauch	.05	185	Rod Scurry	.05
142	Doc Medich	.05	186	Fred Breining	.05
143	Tony Bernazard	.05	187	Danny Boone	.05
144	Bill Virdon	.05	188	Junior Kennedy	.05
145	John Littlefield	.05	189	Sparky Lyle	.05
146	Dave Bergman	.05	190	Whitey Herzog	.05
147	Dick Davis	.05	191	Dave Smith	.05
148	Tom Seaver	.25	192	Ed Ott	.05
149	Matt Sinatro	.05	193	Greg Luzinski	.10
150	Chuck Tanner	.05	194	Bill Lee	.05
151	Leon Durham	.10	195	Don Zimmer	.05
152	Gene Tenace	.05	196	Hal McRae	.05
153	Al Bumbry	.05	197	Mike Norris	.05
154	Mark Brouhard	.05	198	Duane Kuiper	.05
155	Rick Peters	.05	199	Rick Cerone	.05
156	Jerry Remy	.05	200	Jim Rice	.25
157	Rick Reuschel	.05	201	Steve Yeager	.05
158	Steve Howe	.05	202	Tom Brookens	.05
159	Alan Bannister	.05	203	Jose Morales	.05
160	U. L. Washington	.05	204	Roy Howell	.05
161	Rick Langford	.05	205	Tippy Martinez	.05
162	Bill Gullickson	.05	206	Moose Haas	.05
163	Mark Wagner	.05	207	Al Cowens	.05
164	Geoff Zahn	.05	208	Dave Stapleton	.05
165	Ron LeFlore	.05	209	Bucky Dent	.05

210 Ron Cey	.10	254 Pat Zachry	.05
211 Jorge Orta	.05	255 Luis Leal	.05
212 Jamie Quirk	.05	256 John Castino	.05
213 Jeff Jones	.05	257 Rich Dauer	.05
214 Tim Raines	.35	258 Cecil Cooper	.15
215 Jon Matlack	.05	259 Dave Rozema	.05
216 Rod Carew	.35	260 John Tudor	.05
217 Jim Kaat	.05	261 Jerry Mumphrey	.05
218 Joe Pittman	.05	262 Jay Johnstone	.05
219 Larry Christenson	.05	263 Bo Diaz	.05
220 Juan Bonilla	.05	264 Dennis Leonard	.05
221 Mike Easler	.10	265 Jim Spencer	.05
222 Vida Blue	.05	266 John Milner	.05
223 Rick Camp	.05	267 Don Aase	.05
224 Mike Jorgensen	.05	268 Jim Sundberg	.05
225 Jody Davis	.05	269 Lamar Johnson	.05
226 Mike Parrott	.05	270 Frank LaCorte	.05
227 Jim Clancy	.05	271 Barry Evans	.05
228 Hosken Powell	.05	272 Enos Cabell	.05
229 Tom Hume	.05	273 Del Unser	.05
230 Britt Burns	.10	274 George Foster	.20
231 Jim Palmer	.20	275 Brett Butler	.05
232 Bob Rogers	.05	276 Lee Lacy	.05
233 Milt Wilcox	.05	277 Ken Reitz	.05
234 Dave Revering	.05	278 Keith Hernandez	.20
235 Mike Torrez	.05	279 Doug DeCinces	.05
236 Robert Castillo	.05	280 Charlie Moore	.05
237 Von Hayes	.05	281 Lance Parrish	.05
238 Renie Martin	.05	282 Ralph Houk	.05
239 Dwayne Murphy	.05	283 Rich Gossage	.10
240 Rodney Scott	.05	284 Jerry Reuss	.05
241 Fred Patek	.05	285 Mike Stanton	.05
242 Mickey Rivers	.05	286 Frank White	.05
243 Steve Trout	.05	287 Bob Owchinko	.05
244 Jose Cruz	.05	288 Scott Sanderson	.05
245 Manny Trillo	.05	289 Bump Wills	.05
246 Lary Sorensen	.05	290 Dave Frost	.05
247 Dave Edwards	.05	291 Chet Lemon	.05
248 Dan Driessen	.10	292 Tito Landrum	.05
249 Tommy Boggs	.05	293 Vern Ruhle	.05
250 Dale Berra	.05	294 Mike Schmidt	.35
251 Ed Whitson	.05	295 Sam Mejias	.05
252 Lee Smith	.05	296 Gary Lucas	.05
253 Tom Paciorek	.05	297 John Candelaria	.05

298	Jerry Martin	.05	**342**	Rick Burleson	.05
299	Dale Murphy	.25	**343**	John Martin	.05
300	Mike Lum	.05	**344**	Craig Reynolds	.05
301	Tom Hausman	.05	**345**	Mike Proly	.05
302	Glenn Abbott	.05	**346**	Ruppert Jones	.05
303	Roger Erickson	.05	**347**	Omar Moreno	.05
304	Otto Velez	.05	**348**	Greg Minton	.05
305	Danny Goodwin	.05	**349**	Rick Mahler	.05
306	John Mayberry	.05	**350**	Alex Trevino	.05
307	Lenny Randle	.05	**351**	Mike Krukow	.05
308	Bob Bailor	.05	**352**	Shane Rawley	.05
309	Jerry Morales	.05	**353**	Garth Iorg	.05
310	Rufino Linares	.05	**354**	Pete Mackanin	.05
311	Kent Tekulve	.05	**355**	Paul Moskau	.05
312	Joe Morgan	.15	**356**	Richard Dotson	.05
313	John Urrea	.05	**357**	Steve Stone	.05
314	Paul Householder	.05	**358**	Larry Hisle	.05
315	Garry Maddox	.05	**359**	Aurelio Lopez	.05
316	Mike Ramsey	.05	**360**	Oscar Gamble	.05
317	Alan Ashby	.05	**361**	Tom Burgmeier	.05
318	Bob Clark	.05	**362**	Terry Forster	.05
319	Tony LaRussa	.05	**363**	Joe Charboneau	.05
320	Charlie Lea	.05	**364**	Ken Brett	.05
321	Danny Darwin	.05	**365**	Tony Armas	.10
322	Cesar Geronimo	.05	**366**	Chris Speier	.05
323	Tom Underwood	.05	**367**	Fred Lynn	.20
324	Andre Thornton	.05	**368**	Buddy Bell	.05
325	Rudy May	.05	**369**	Jim Essian	.05
326	Frank Tanana	.05	**370**	Terry Puhl	.05
327	Davey Lopes	.05	**371**	Greg Gross	.05
328	Richie Hebner	.05	**372**	Bruce Sutter	.10
329	Mike Flanagan	.05	**373**	Joe Lefebvre	.05
330	Mike Caldwell	.05	**374**	Ray Knight	.05
331	Scott McGregor	.05	**375**	Bruce Benedict	.05
332	Jerry Augustine	.05	**376**	Tim Foli	.05
333	Stan Papi	.05	**377**	Al Holland	.05
334	Rick Miller	.05	**378**	Ken Kravec	.05
335	Graig Nettles	.05	**379**	Jeff Burroughs	.05
336	Dusty Baker	.05	**380**	Pete Falcone	.05
337	Dave Garcia	.05	**381**	Ernie Whitt	.05
338	Larry Gura	.05	**382**	Brad Havens	.05
339	Cliff Johnson	.05	**383**	Terry Crowley	.05
340	Warren Cromartie	.05	**384**	Don Money	.05
341	Steve Comer	.05	**385**	Dan Schatzeder	.05

386	Gary Allenson	.05	430	Jerry Garvin	.05
387	Yogi Berra	.10	431	Glenn Adams	.05
388	Ken Landreaux	.05	432	Barry Bonnell	.05
389	Mike Hargrove	.05	433	Jerry Narron	.05
390	Darryl Motley	.05	434	John Stearns	.05
391	Dave McKay	.05	435	Mike Tyson	.05
392	Stan Bahnsen	.05	436	Glenn Hubbard	.05
393	Ken Forsch	.05	437	Eddie Solomon	.05
394	Mario Mendoza	.05	438	Jeff Leonard	.05
395	Jim Morrison	.05	439	Randy Bass	.05
396	Mike Ivie	.05	440	Mike LaCoss	.05
397	Broderick Perkins	.05	441	Gary Matthews	.05
398	Darrell Evans	.05	442	Mark Littell	.05
399	Ron Reed	.05	443	Don Sutton	.10
400	Johnny Bench	.20	444	John Harris	.05
401	Steve Bedrosian	.05	445	Vada Pinson	.05
402	Bill Robinson	.05	446	Elias Sosa	.05
403	Bill Buckner	.10	447	Charlie Hough	.05
404	Ken Oberkfell	.05	448	Willie Wilson	.10
405	Cal Ripken, Jr.	1.00	449	Fred Stanley	.05
406	Jim Gantner	.05	450	Tom Veryzer	.05
407	Kirk Gibson	.10	451	Ron Davis	.05
408	Tony Perez	.10	452	Mark Clear	.05
409	Tommy John	.10	453	Bill Russell	.05
410	Dave Stewart	.05	454	Lou Whitaker	.05
411	Dan Spillner	.05	455	Dan Graham	.05
412	Willie Aikens	.05	456	Reggie Cleveland	.05
413	Mike Heath	.05	457	Sammy Stewart	.05
414	Ray Burris	.05	458	Pete Vuckovich	.10
415	Leon Roberts	.05	459	John Wockenfuss	.05
416	Mike Witt	.05	460	Glenn Hoffman	.05
417	Bob Molinaro	.05	461	Willie Randolph	.05
418	Steve Braun	.05	462	Fernando Valenzuela	.50
419	Nolan Ryan	.25	463	Ron Hassey	.05
420	Tug McGraw	.05	464	Paul Splittorff	.05
421	Dave Concepcion	.10	465	Ron Picciolo	.05
422	Juan Eichelberger	.05	466	Larry Parrish	.05
423	Rick Rhoden	.05	467	Johnny Grubb	.05
424	Frank Robinson	.05	468	Dan Ford	.05
425	Eddie Miller	.05	469	Silvio Martinez	.05
426	Bill Caudill	.05	470	Kiko Garcia	.05
427	Doug Flynn	.05	471	Bob Boone	.05
428	Larry Andersen	.05	472	Luis Salazar	.05
429	Al Williams	.05	473	Randy Niemann	.05

474 Tom Griffin	.05	
475 Phil Niekro	.10	
476 Hubie Brooks	.05	
477 Dick Tidrow	.05	
478 Jim Beattie	.05	
479 Damaso Garcia	.05	
480 Mickey Hatcher	.05	
481 Joe Price	.05	
482 Ed Farmer	.05	
483 Eddie Murray	.20	
484 Ben Oglivie	.05	
485 Kevin Saucier	.05	
486 Bobby Murcer	.05	
487 Bill Campbell	.05	
488 Reggie Smith	.05	
489 Wayne Garland	.05	
490 Jim Wright	.05	
491 Billy Martin	.10	
492 Jim Fanning	.05	
493 Don Baylor	.10	
494 Rick Honeycutt	.05	
495 Carlton Fisk	.10	
496 Denny Walling	.05	
497 Bake McBride	.05	
498 Darrell Porter	.05	
499 Gene Richards	.05	
500 Ron Oester	.05	
501 Ken Dayley	.05	
502 Jason Thompson	.05	
503 Milt May	.05	
504 Doug Bird	.05	
505 Bruce Bochte	.05	
506 Neil Allen	.05	
507 Joey McLaughlin	.05	
508 Butch Wynegar	.05	
509 Gary Roenicke	.05	
510 Robin Yount	.25	
511 Dave Tobik	.05	
512 Rich Gedman	.05	
513 Gene Nelson	.05	
514 Rick Monday	.05	
515 Miguel Dilone	.05	
516 Clint Hurdle	.05	
517 Jeff Newman	.05	

518 Grant Jackson	.05
519 Andy Hassler	.05
520 Pat Putnam	.05
521 Greg Pryor	.05
522 Tony Scott	.05
523 Steve Mura	.05
524 Johnnie LeMaster	.05
525 Dick Ruthven	.05
526 John McNamara	.05
527 Larry McWilliams	.05
528 Johnny Ray	.10
529 Pat Tabler	.05
530 Tom Herr	.05
531 San Diego Chicken	.75
532 Sal Butera	.05
533 Mike Griffin	.05
534 Kelvin Moore	.05
535 Reggie Jackson	.30
536 Ed Romero	.05
537 Derrel Thomas	.05
538 Mike O'Berry	.05
539 Jack O'Connor	.05
540 Bob Ojeda	.05
541 Roy Lee Jackson	.05
542 Lynn Jones	.05
543 Gaylord Perry	.15
544 Phil Garner	.05
545 Garry Templeton	.10
546 Rafael Ramirez	.05
547 Jeff Reardon	.05
548 Ron Guidry	.10
549 Tim Laudner	.05
550 John Henry Johnson	.05
551 Chris Bando	.05
552 Bobby Brown	.05
553 Larry Bradford	.05
554 Scot Fletcher	.05
555 Jerry Royster	.05
556 Shooty Babitt	.05
557 Kent Hrbek	.15
558 Guidry & John	.20
559 Mark Bomback	.05
560 Julio Valdez	.05
561 Buck Martinez	.05

562 Mike Marshall	.10
563 Rennie Stennett	.05
564 Steve Crawford	.05
565 Bob Babcock	.05
566 Johnny Podres	.05
567 Paul Serna	.05
568 Harold Baines	.10
569 Dave LaRoche	.05
570 Lee May	.05
571 Gary Ward	.05
572 John Denny	.05
573 Roy Smalley	.05
574 Bob Brenly	.05
575 Jackson & Winfield	.20
576 Luis Pujols	.05
577 Butch Hobson	.05
578 Harvey Kuenn	.05
579 Cal Ripken	1.00
580 Juan Berenguer	.05
581 Benny Ayala	.05
582 Vance Law	.05
583 Rick Leach	.05
584 George Frazier	.05
585 Rose & Schmidt	.35
586 Joe Rudi	.05
587 Juan Beniquez	.05
588 Luis De Leon	.05
589 Craig Swan	.05
590 Dave Chalk	.05
591 Billy Gardner	.05
592 Sal Bando	.05
593 Bert Campaneris	.05
594 Steve Kemp	.05
595 Randy Lerch	.05
596 Bryan Clark	.05
597 David Ford	.05
598 Mike Scioscia	.05
599 John Lowenstein	.05
600 Rene Lachemann	.05
601 Mick Kelleher	.05
602 Ron Jackson	.05
603 Jerry Koosman	.05
604 Dave Goltz	.05
605 Ellis Valentine	.05

606 Lonnie Smith	.10
607 Joaquin Andujar	.05
608 Garry Hancock	.05
609 Jerry Turner	.05
610 Bob Bonner	.05
611 Jim Dwyer	.05
612 Terry Bulling	.05
613 Joel Youngblood	.05
614 Larry Milbourne	.05
615 Gene Roof	.05
616 Keith Drumright	.05
617 Dave Rosello	.05
618 Rickey Keeton	.05
619 Dennis Lamp	.05
620 Sid Monge	.05
621 Jerry White	.05
622 Luis Aguayo	.05
623 Jamie Easterly	.05
624 Steve Sax	.10
625 Dave Roberts	.05
626 Rick Bosetti	.05
627 Terry Francona	.05
628 Seaver & Bench	.35
629 Paul Mirabella	.05
630 Rance Mulliniks	.05
631 Kevin Hickey	.05
632 Reid Nichols	.05
633 Dave Giesel	.05
634 Ken Griffey	.05
635 Bob Lemon	.10
636 Orlando Sanchez	.05
637 Bill Almon	.05
638 Danny Ainge	.05
639 Willie Stargell	.20
640 Bob Sykes	.05
641 Ed Lynch	.05
642 John Ellis	.05
643 Ferguson Jenkins	.10
644 Lenn Sakata	.05
645 Julio Gonzalez	.05
646 Jesse Orosco	.05
647 Jerry Dybzinski	.05
648 Tommy Davis	.05
649 Ron Gardenhire	.05

650 Felipe Alou	.05	
651 Harvey Haddix	.05	
652 Willie Upshaw	.05	
653 Bill Madlock	.10	
654 Checklist	.05	
655 Checklist	.05	

656 Checklist	.05
657 Checklist	.05
658 Checklist	.05
659 Checklist	.05
660 Checklist	.05

DONRUSS—1983

(2½″ × 3½″, Numbered 1–653, Color) Mint Condition

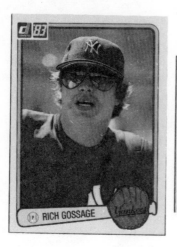

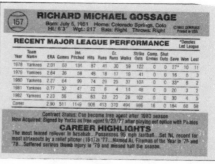

	Complete Set	$15.00			
1	Fernando Valenzuela	.35	17	Ron Guidry	.20
2	Rollie Fingers	.15	18	Steve Rogers	.15
3	Reggie Jackson	.25	19	Kent Hrbek	.15
4	Jim Palmer	.20	20	Keith Hernandez	.15
5	Jack Morris	.04	21	Floyd Bannister	.10
6	George Foster	.10	22	Johnny Bench	.20
7	Jim Sundberg	.04	23	Britt Burns	.04
8	Willie Stargell	.25	24	Joe Morgan	.15
9	Dave Stieb	.04	25	Carl Yastrzemski	.25
10	Joe Niekro	.04	26	Terry Kennedy	.10
11	Rickey Henderson	.20	27	Gary Roenicke	.04
12	Dale Murphy	.20	28	Dwight Bernard	.04
13	Toby Harrah	.04	29	Pat Underwood	.04
14	Bill Buckner	.10	30	Gary Allenson	.04
15	Willie Wilson	.20	31	Ron Guidry	.15
16	Steve Carlton	.25	32	Burt Hooton	.04
			33	Chris Bando	.04

34 Vida Blue	.10
35 Rickey Henderson	.15
36 Ray Burris	.04
37 John Butcher	.04
38 Don Aase	.04
39 Jerry Koosman	.04
40 Bruce Sutter	.10
41 Jose Cruz	.04
42 Pete Rose	.75
43 Cesar Cedeno	.04
44 Floyd Chiffer	.04
45 Larry McWilliams	.04
46 Alan Fowlkes	.04
47 Dale Murphy	.20
48 Doug Bird	.04
49 Hubie Brooks	.04
50 Floyd Bannister	.04
51 Jack O'Connor	.04
52 Steve Senteney	.04
53 Gary Gaetti	.04
54 Damaso Garcia	.04
55 Gene Nelson	.04
56 Mookie Wilson	.04
57 Allen Ripley	.04
58 Bob Horner	.20
59 Tony Pena	.04
60 Gary Lavelle	.04
61 Tim Lollar	.04
62 Frank Pastore	.04
63 Garry Maddox	.04
64 Bob Forsch	.04
65 Harry Spilman	.04
66 Geoff Zahn	.04
67 Salome Barojas	.04
68 David Palmer	.04
69 Charlie Hough	.04
70 Dan Quisenberry	.10
71 Tony Armas	.04
72 Rick Sutcliffe	.04
73 Steve Balboni	.04
74 Jerry Remy	.04
75 Mike Scioscia	.04
76 John Wockenfuss	.05
77 Jim Palmer	.25
78 Rollie Fingers	.15
79 Joe Nolan	.04
80 Pete Vuckovich	.04
81 Rick Leach	.04
82 Rick Miller	.04
83 Graig Nettles	.04
84 Ron Cey	.10
85 Miguel Dilone	.04
86 John Wathan	.04
87 Kelvin Moore	.04
88 Bryn Smith	.04
89 Dave Hostetler	.04
90 Rod Carew	.25
91 Lonnie Smith	.04
92 Bob Knepper	.04
93 Marty Bystrom	.04
94 Chris Welsh	.04
95 Jason Thompson	.04
96 Tom O'Malley	.04
97 Phil Niekro	.10
98 Neil Allen	.04
99 Bill Buckner	.10
100 Ed Vandeberg	.04
101 Jim Clancy	.04
102 Robert Castillo	.04
103 Bruce Berenyi	.04
104 Carlton Fisk	.10
105 Mike Flanagan	.04
106 Cecil Cooper	.10
107 Jack Morris	.04
108 Mike Morgan	.04
109 Luis Aponte	.04
110 Pedro Guerrero	.10
111 Len Barker	.04
112 Willie Wilson	.10
113 Dave Beard	.04
114 Mike Gates	.04
115 Reggie Jackson	.35
116 George Wright	.04
117 Vance Law	.04
118 Nolan Ryan	.25
119 Mike Krukow	.04
120 Ozzie Smith	.04
121 Broderick Perkins	.04

122	Tom Seaver	.30
123	Chris Chambliss	.10
124	Chuck Tanner	.04
125	Johnnie LeMaster	.04
126	Mel Hall	.25
127	Bruce Bochte	.04
128	Charlie Puleo	.04
129	Luis Leal	.04
130	John Pacella	.04
131	Glenn Gulliver	.04
132	Don Money	.04
133	Dave Rozema	.04
134	Bruce Hurst	.04
135	Rudy May	.04
136	Tom Lasorda	.10
137	Dan Spillner	.04
138	Jerry Martin	.04
139	Mike Norris	.04
140	Al Oliver	.10
141	Daryl Sconiers	.04
142	Lamar Johnson	.04
143	Harold Baines	.04
144	Alan Ashby	.04
145	Garry Templeton	.10
146	Al Holland	.04
147	Bo Diaz	.04
148	Dave Concepcion	.10
149	Rick Camp	.04
150	Jim Morrison	.04
151	Randy Martz	.04
152	Keith Hernandez	.10
153	John Lowenstein	.04
154	Mike Caldwell	.04
155	Milt Wilcox	.04
156	Rich Gedman	.04
157	Rich Gossage	.10
158	Jerry Reuss	.04
159	Ron Hassey	.04
160	Larry Gura	.04
161	Dwayne Murphy	.04
162	Woodie Fryman	.04
163	Steve Comer	.04
164	Ken Forsch	.04
165	Dennis Lamp	.04
166	David Green	.04
167	Terry Puhl	.04
168	Mike Schmidt	.35
169	Eddie Milner	.04
170	John Curtis	.04
171	Don Robinson	.04
172	Richard Gale	.04
173	Steve Bedrosian	.04
174	Willie Hernandez	.04
175	Ron Gardenhire	.04
176	Jim Beattie	.04
177	Tim Laudner	.04
178	Buck Martinez	.04
179	Kent Hrbek	.10
180	Alfredo Griffin	.04
181	Larry Andersen	.04
182	Pete Falcone	.04
183	Jody Davis	.04
184	Glenn Hubbard	.04
185	Dale Berra	.04
186	Greg Minton	.04
187	Gary Lucas	.04
188	Dave Van Gorder	.04
189	Bob Dernier	.04
190	Willie McGee	.50
191	Dickie Thon	.04
192	Bob Boone	.04
193	Britt Burns	.04
194	Jeff Reardon	.04
195	Jon Matlack	.04
196	Don Slaught	.04
197	Fred Stanley	.04
198	Rick Manning	.04
199	Dave Righetti	.15
200	Dave Stapleton	.04
201	Steve Yeager	.04
202	Enos Cabell	.04
203	Sammy Stewart	.04
204	Moose Haas	.04
205	Lenn Sakata	.04
206	Charlie Moore	.04
207	Alan Trammell	.04
208	Jim Rice	.25
209	Roy Smalley	.04

210 Bill Russell	.04	
211 Andre Thornton	.04	
212 Willie Aikens	.04	
213 Dave McKay	.04	
214 Tim Blackwell	.04	
215 Buddy Bell	.04	
216 Doug DeCinces	.04	
217 Tom Herr	.04	
218 Frank LaCorte	.04	
219 Steve Carlton	.35	
220 Terry Kennedy	.10	
221 Mike Easler	.04	
222 Jack Clark	.10	
223 Gene Garber	.04	
224 Scott Holman	.04	
225 Mike Proly	.04	
226 Terry Bulling	.04	
227 Jerry Garvin	.04	
228 Ron Davis	.04	
229 Tom Hume	.04	
230 Marc Hill	.04	
231 Dennis Martinez	.04	
232 Jim Gantner	.04	
233 Larry Pashnick	.04	
234 Dave Collins	.04	
235 Tom Burgmeier	.04	
236 Ken Landreaux	.04	
237 John Denny	.04	
238 Hal McRae	.04	
239 Matt Keough	.04	
240 Doug Flynn	.04	
241 Fred Lynn	.15	
242 Billy Sample	.04	
243 Tom Paciorek	.04	
244 Joe Sambito	.04	
245 Sid Monge	.04	
246 Ken Oberkfell	.04	
247 Joe Pittman	.04	
248 Mario Soto	.04	
249 Claudell Washington	.04	
250 Rick Rhoden	.04	
251 Darrell Evans	.04	
252 Steve Henderson	.04	
253 Manny Castillo	.04	
254 Craig Swan	.04
255 Joey McLaughlin	.04
256 Pete Redfern	.04
257 Ken Singleton	.04
258 Robin Yount	.20
259 Elias Sosa	.04
260 Bob Ojeda	.04
261 Bobby Murcer	.04
262 Candy Maldonado	.04
263 Rick Waits	.04
264 Greg Pryor	.04
265 Bob Owchinko	.04
266 Chris Speier	.04
267 Bruce Kison	.04
268 Mark Wagner	.04
269 Steve Kemp	.04
270 Phil Garner	.04
271 Gene Richards	.04
272 Renie Martin	.04
273 Dave Roberts	.04
274 Dan Driessen	.04
275 Rufino Linares	.04
276 Lee Lacy	.04
277 Ryne Sandberg	.20
278 Darrell Porter	.04
279 Cal Ripken	.25
280 Jamie Easterly	.04
281 Bill Fahey	.04
282 Glenn Hoffman	.04
283 Willie Randolph	.04
284 Fernando Valenzuela	.25
285 Alan Bannister	.04
286 Paul Splittorff	.04
287 Joe Rudi	.04
288 Bil Gullickson	.04
289 Danny Darwin	.04
290 Andy Hassler	.04
291 Ernesto Escarrega	.04
292 Steve Mura	.04
293 Tony Scott	.04
294 Manny Trillo	.04
295 Greg Harris	.04
296 Luis DeLeon	.04
297 Kent Tekulve	.04

298	Atlee Hammaker	.04
299	Bruce Benedict	.04
300	Fergie Jenkins	.10
301	Dave Kingman	.10
302	Bill Caudill	.04
303	John Castino	.04
304	Ernie Whitt	.04
305	Randy Johnson	.04
306	Garth Iorg	.04
307	Gaylord Perry	.20
308	Ed Lynch	.04
309	Keith Moreland	.04
310	Rafael Ramirez	.04
311	Bill Madlock	.10
312	Milt May	.04
313	John Montefusco	.04
314	Wayne Krenchicki	.04
315	George Vukovich	.04
316	Joaquin Andujar	.04
317	Craig Reynolds	.04
318	Rick Burleson	.04
319	Richard Dotson	.04
320	Steve Rogers	.10
321	Dave Schmidt	.04
322	Bud Black	.04
323	Jeff Burroughs	.04
324	Von Hayes	.04
325	Butch Wynegar	.04
326	Carl Yastrzemski	.50
327	Ron Roenicke	.04
328	Howard Johnson	.04
329	Rick Dempsey	.04
330	Jim Slaton	.04
331	Benny Ayala	.04
332	Ted Simmons	.10
333	Lou Whitaker	.04
334	Chuck Rainey	.04
335	Lou Piniella	.04
336	Steve Sax	.10
337	Toby Harrah	.05
338	George Brett	.50
339	Davey Lopes	.04
340	Gary Carter	.20
341	John Grubb	.04
342	Tim Foli	.04

343	Jim Kaat	.10
344	Mike LaCoss	.04
345	Larry Christenson	.04
346	Juan Bonilla	.04
347	Omar Moreno	.04
348	Charles Davis	.04
349	Tommy Boggs	.04
350	Rusty Staub	.04
351	Bump Wills	.04
352	Rick Sweet	.04
353	Jim Gott	.04
354	Terry Felton	.04
355	Jim Kern	.04
356	Bill Almon	.04
357	Tippy Martinez	.04
358	Roy Howell	.04
359	Dan Petry	.04
360	Jerry Mumphrey	.04
361	Mark Clear	.04
362	Mike Marshall	.15
363	Lary Sorensen	.04
364	Amos Otis	.04
365	Rick Langford	.04
366	Brad Mills	.04
367	Brian Downing	.04
368	Mike Richardt	.04
369	Aurelio Rodriguez	.04
370	Dave Smith	.04
371	Tug McGraw	.04
372	Doug Bair	.04
373	Ruppert Jones	.04
374	Alex Trevino	.04
375	Ken Dayley	.04
376	Rod Scurry	.04
377	Bob Brenly	.04
378	Scot Thompson	.04
379	Julio Cruz	.04
380	John Stearns	.04
381	Dale Murray	.04
382	Frank Viola	.04
383	Al Bumbry	.04
384	Ben Oglivie	.04
385	Dave Tobik	.04
386	Bob Stanley	.04
387	Andre Robertson	.04

388 Jorge Orta	.04	**433** Mike Stanton	.04
389 Ed Whitson	.04	**434** Jesse Orosco	.04
390 Don Hood	.04	**435** Larry Bowa	.10
391 Tom Underwood	.04	**436** Biff Pocoroba	.04
392 Tim Wallach	.04	**437** Johnny Ray	.04
393 Steve Renko	.04	**438** Joe Morgan	.15
394 Mickey Rivers	.04	**439** Eric Show	.04
395 Greg Luzinski	.10	**440** Larry Biittner	.04
396 Art Howe	.04	**441** Greg Gross	.04
397 Alan Wiggins	.04	**442** Gene Tenace	.04
398 Jim Barr	.04	**443** Danny Heep	.04
399 Ivan De Jesus	.04	**444** Bobby Clark	.04
400 Tom Lawless	.04	**445** Kevin Hickey	.04
401 Bob Walk	.04	**446** Scott Sanderson	.04
402 Jimmy Smith	.04	**447** Frank Tanana	.04
403 Lee Smith	.04	**448** Cesar Geronimo	.04
404 George Hendrick	.10	**449** Jimmy Sexton	.04
405 Eddie Murray	.20	**450** Mike Hargrove	.04
406 Marshall Edwards	.04	**451** Doyle Alexander	.04
407 Lance Parrish	.04	**452** Dwight Evans	.04
408 Carney Lansford	.04	**453** Terry Forster	.04
409 Dave Winfield	.20	**454** Tom Brookens	.04
410 Bob Welch	.04	**455** Rich Dauer	.04
411 Larry Milbourne	.04	**456** Rob Picciolo	.04
412 Dennis Leonard	.04	**457** Terry Crowley	.04
413 Dan Meyer	.04	**458** Ned Yost	.04
414 Charlie Lea	.04	**459** Kirk Gibson	.10
415 Rick Honeycutt	.04	**460** Reid Nichols	.04
416 Mike Witt	.04	**461** Oscar Gamble	.04
417 Steve Trout	.04	**462** Dusty Baker	.04
418 Glenn Brummer	.04	**463** Jack Perconte	.04
419 Denny Walling	.04	**464** Frank White	.04
420 Gary Matthews	.04	**465** Mickey Klutts	.04
421 Charlie Leibrandt	.04	**466** Warren Cromartie	.04
422 Juan Eichelberger	.04	**467** Larry Parrish	.04
423 Matt Guante	.04	**468** Bobby Grich	.04
424 Bill Laskey	.04	**469** Dane Iorg	.04
425 Jerry Royster	.04	**470** Joe Niekro	.04
426 Dickie Noles	.04	**471** Ed Farmer	.04
427 George Foster	.20	**472** Tim Flannery	.04
428 Mike Moore	.04	**473** Dave Parker	.20
429 Gary Ward	.04	**474** Jeff Leonard	.04
430 Barry Bonnell	.04	**475** Al Hrabosky	.04
431 Ron Washington	.04	**476** Ron Hodges	.04
432 Rance Mulliniks	.04	**477** Leon Durham	.10

478 Jim Essian	.04	
479 Roy Lee Jackson	.04	
480 Brad Havens	.04	
481 Joe Price	.04	
482 Tony Bernazard	.04	
483 Scott McGregor	.04	
484 Paul Molitor	.10	
485 Mike Ivie	.04	
486 Ken Griffey	.10	
487 Dennis Eckersley	.04	
488 Steve Garvey	.35	
489 Mike Fischlin	.04	
490 U. L. Washington	.04	
491 Steve McCatty	.04	
492 Roy Johnson	.04	
493 Don Baylor	.10	
494 Bobby Johnson	.04	
495 Mike Squires	.04	
496 Bert Roberge	.04	
497 Dick Ruthven	.04	
498 Tito Landrum	.04	
499 Sixto Lezcano	.04	
500 Johnny Bench	.25	
501 Larry Whisenton	.04	
502 Manny Sarmiento	.04	
503 Fred Breining	.04	
504 Bill Campbell	.04	
505 Todd Cruz	.04	
506 Bob Bailor	.04	
507 Dave Stieb	.04	
508 Al Williams	.04	
509 Dan Ford	.04	
510 Gorman Thomas	.10	
511 Chet Lemon	.04	
512 Mike Torrez	.04	
513 Shane Rawley	.04	
514 Mark Belanger	.04	
515 Rodney Craig	.04	
516 Onix Concepcion	.04	
517 Mike Heath	.04	
518 Andre Dawson	.10	
519 Luis Sanchez	.04	
520 Terry Bogener	.04	
521 Rudy Law	.04	

522 Ray Knight	.04
523 Joe Lefebvre	.04
524 Jim Wohlford	.04
525 Julio Franco	.04
526 Ron Oester	.04
527 Rick Mahler	.04
528 Steve Nicosia	.04
529 Junior Kennedy	.04
530 Whitey Herzog	.04
531 Don Sutton	.10
532 Mark Brouhard	.04
533 Sparky Anderson	.10
534 Roger LaFrancois	.04
535 George Frazier	.04
536 Tom Niedenfuer	.04
537 Ed Glynn	.04
538 Lee May	.04
539 Bob Kearney	.04
540 Tim Raines	.15
541 Paul Mirabella	.04
542 Luis Tiant	.04
543 Ron LeFlore	.04
544 Dave LaPoint	.04
545 Randy Moffitt	.04
546 Luis Aguayo	.04
547 Brad Lesley	.04
548 Luis Salazar	.04
549 John Candelaria	.04
550 Dave Bergman	.04
551 Bob Watson	.10
552 Pat Tabler	.04
553 Brent Gaff	.04
554 Al Cowens	.04
555 Tom Brunansky	.04
556 Lloyd Moseby	.04
557 Pascual Perez	.04
558 Willie Upshaw	.04
559 Richie Zisk	.04
560 Pat Zachry	.04
561 Jay Johnstone	.04
562 Carlos Diaz	.04
563 John Tudor	.04
564 Frank Robinson	.04
565 Dave Edwards	.04

566 Paul Householder	.04	610 Willie Stargell	.25
567 Ron Reed	.04	611 Reggie Smith	.04
568 Mike Ramsey	.04	612 Rob Wilfong	.04
569 Kiko Garcia	.04	613 Niekro Brothers	.10
570 Tommy John	.10	614 Lee Elia	.04
571 Tony LaRussa	.04	615 Mickey Hatcher	.04
572 Joel Youngblood	.04	616 Jerry Hairston	.04
573 Wayne Tolleson	.04	617 John Martin	.04
574 Keith Creel	.04	618 Wally Backman	.04
575 Billy Martin	.10	619 Storm Davis	.04
576 Jerry Dybzinski	.04	620 Alan Knicely	.04
577 Rick Cerone	.04	621 John Stuper	.04
578 Tony Perez	.10	622 Matt Sinatro	.04
579 Greg Brock	.10	623 Gene Petralli	.04
580 Glen Wilson	.25	624 Duane Walker	.04
581 Tim Stoddard	.04	625 Dick Williams	.04
582 Bob McClure	.04	626 Pat Corrales	.04
583 Jim Dwyer	.04	627 Vern Ruhle	.04
584 Ed Romero	.04	628 Joe Torre	.04
585 Larry Herndon	.04	629 Anthony Johnson	.04
586 Wade Boggs	1.00	630 Steve Howe	.04
587 Jay Howell	.04	631 Gary Woods	.04
588 Dave Stewart	.04	632 LaMarr Hoyt	.15
589 Bert Blyleven	.04	633 Steve Swisher	.04
590 Dick Howser	.04	634 Terry Leach	.04
591 Wayne Gross	.04	635 Jeff Newman	.04
592 Terry Francona	.04	636 Brett Butler	.04
593 Don Werner	.04	637 Gary Gray	.04
594 Bill Stein	.04	638 Lee Mazzilli	.04
595 Jesse Barfield	.04	639 Ron Jackson	.04
596 Bobby Molinaro	.04	640 Juan Beniquez	.04
597 Mike Vail	.04	641 Dave Rucker	.04
598 Tony Gwynn	.15	642 Luis Pujols	.04
599 Gary Rajsich	.04	643 Rick Monday	.04
600 Jerry Udjur	.04	644 Hosken Powell	.04
601 Cliff Johnson	.04	645 The Chicken	.10
602 Jerry White	.04	646 Dave Engle	.04
603 Bryan Clark	.04	647 Dick Davis	.04
604 Joe Ferguson	.04	648 Blue/Robinson/Morgan	.10
605 Guy Sularz	.04	649 Al Chambers	.04
606 Ozzie Virgil	.04	650 Jesus Vega	.04
607 Terry Harper	.04	651 Jeff Jones	.04
608 Harvey Kuenn	.04	652 Marvis Foley	.04
609 Jim Sundberg	.04	653 Ty Cobb	.25

DONRUSS—1984

(3½″ × 2½″, Numbered 1–651, Color) Mint Condition

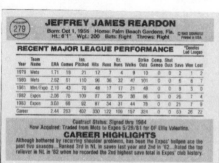

	Complete Set	$12.00			
1	Robin Yount	.25	19	Jim Clancy	.03
2	Dave Concepcion	.03	20	Bill Madlock	.10
3	Dwayne Murphy	.03	21	Larry Parrish	.03
4	John Castino	.03	22	Eddie Murray	.25
5	Leon Durham	.05	23	Mike Schmidt	.50
6	Rusty Staub	.03	24	Pedro Guerrero	.20
7	Jack Clark	.05	25	Andre Thornton	.03
8	Dave Dravecky	.03	26	Wade Boggs	.50
9	Al Oliver	.10	27	Joel Skinner	.03
10	Dave Righetti	.10	28	Tommy Dunbar	.03
11	Hal McRae	.03	29	Mike Stenhouse	.03
12	Ray Knight	.03	30	Ron Darling	.20
13	Bruce Sutter	.05	31	Dion James	.03
14	Bob Horner	.15	32	Tony Fernandez	.03
15	Lance Parrish	.03	33	Angel Salazar	.03
16	Matt Young	.03	34	Kevin McReynolds	.50
17	Fred Lynn	.15	35	Dick Schofield	.03
18	Ron Kittle	.25	36	Brad Komminsk	.03
			37	Tim Teufel	.03

38	Doug Frobel	.03
39	Greg Gagne	.03
40	Mike Fuentes	.03
41	Joe Carter	.03
42	Mike Brown	.03
43	Mike Jeffcoat	.03
44	Sid Fernandez	.03
45	Brian Dayett	.03
46	Chris Smith	.03
47	Eddie Murray	.25
48	Robin Yount	.25
49	Lance Parrish	.03
50	Jim Rice	.25
51	Dave Winfield	.15
52	Fernando Valenzuela	.15
53	George Brett	.25
54	Rickey Henderson	.25
55	Gary Carter	.15
56	Buddy Bell	.05
57	Reggie Jackson	.25
58	Harold Baines	.05
59	Ozzie Smith	.05
60	Nolan Ryan	.15
61	Pete Rose	.50
62	Ron Oester	.03
63	Steve Garvey	.25
64	Jason Thompson	.03
65	Jack Clark	.10
66	Dale Murphy	.25
67	Leon Durham	.05
68	Darryl Strawberry	2.00
69	Richie Zisk	.03
70	Kent Hrbek	.15
71	Dave Stieb	.05
72	Ken Schrom	.03
73	George Bell	.03
74	John Moses	.03
75	Ed Lynch	.03
76	Chuck Rainey	.03
77	Biff Pocoroba	.03
78	Cecilio Guante	.03
79	Jim Barr	.03
80	Kurt Bevacqua	.03
81	Tom Foley	.03
82	Joe Lefebvre	.03
83	Andy Van Slyke	.03
84	Bob Lillis	.03
85	Rick Adams	.03
86	Jerry Hairston	.03
87	Bob James	.03
88	Joe Altobelli	.03
89	Ed Romero	.03
90	John Grubb	.03
91	John H. Johnson	.03
92	Juan Espino	.03
93	Candy Maldonado	.03
94	Andre Thornton	.03
95	Onix Concepcion	.03
96	Don Hill	.03
97	Andre Dawson	.10
98	Frank Tanana	.03
99	Curt Wilkerson	.03
100	Larry Gura	.03
101	Dwayne Murphy	.03
102	Tom Brennan	.03
103	Dave Righetti	.10
104	Steve Sax	.10
105	Dan Petry	.03
106	Cal Ripken	.25
107	Paul Molitor	.10
108	Fred Lynn	.10
109	Neil Allen	.03
110	Joe Niekro	.03
111	Steve Carlton	.25
112	Terry Kennedy	.05
113	Bill Madlock	.10
114	Chili Davis	.03
115	Jim Gantner	.03
116	Tom Seaver	.15
117	Bill Buckner	.05
118	Bill Caudill	.03
119	Jim Clancy	.03
120	John Castino	.03
121	Dave Concepcion	.03
122	Greg Luzinski	.05
123	Mike Boddicker	.05
124	Pete Ladd	.03
125	Juan Berenguer	.03

126 John Montefusco	.03	
127 Ed Jurak	.03	
128 Tom Niedenfuer	.03	
129 Bert Blyleven	.03	
130 Bud Black	.03	
131 Gorman Heimueller	.03	
132 Dan Schatzeder	.03	
133 Ron Jackson	.03	
134 Tom Henke	.03	
135 Kevin Hickey	.03	
136 Mike Scott	.03	
137 Bo Diaz	.03	
138 Glenn Brummer	.03	
139 Sid Monge	.03	
140 Rich Gale	.03	
141 Brett Butler	.03	
142 Brian Harper	.03	
143 John Rabb	.03	
144 Gary Woods	.03	
145 Pat Putnam	.03	
146 Jim Acker	.03	
147 Mickey Hatcher	.03	
148 Todd Cruz	.03	
149 Tom Tellmann	.03	
150 John Wockenfuss	.03	
151 Wade Boggs	.50	
152 Don Baylor	.05	
153 Bob Welch	.03	
154 Alan Bannister	.03	
155 Willie Aikens	.03	
156 Jeff Burroughs	.03	
157 Bryan Little	.03	
158 Bob Boone	.03	
159 Dave Hostetler	.03	
160 Jerry Dybzinski	.03	
161 Mike Madden	.03	
162 Luis DeLeon	.03	
163 Willie Hernandez	.03	
164 Frank Pastore	.03	
165 Rick Camp	.03	
166 Lee Mazzilli	.03	
167 Scott Thompson	.03	
168 Bob Forsch	.03	
169 Mike Flanagan	.03	

170 Rick Manning	.03
171 Chet Lemon	.03
172 Jerry Remy	.03
173 Ron Guidry	.10
174 Pedro Guerrero	.15
175 Willie Wilson	.10
176 Carney Lansford	.03
177 Al Oliver	.10
178 Jim Sundberg	.03
179 Bobby Grich	.03
180 Rich Dotson	.03
181 Joaquin Andujar	.03
182 Jose Cruz	.03
183 Mike Schmidt	.25
184 Gary Redus	.03
185 Garry Templeton	.05
186 Tony Pena	.03
187 Greg Minton	.03
188 Phil Niekro	.05
189 Ferguson Jenkins	.05
190 Mookie Wilson	.03
191 Jim Beattie	.03
192 Gary Ward	.03
193 Jesse Barfield	.03
194 Pete Filson	.03
195 Roy Lee Jackson	.03
196 Rick Sweet	.03
197 Jesse Orosco	.03
198 Steve Lake	.03
199 Ken Dayley	.03
200 Manny Sarmiento	.03
201 Mark Davis	.03
202 Tim Flannery	.03
203 Bill Scherrer	.03
204 Al Holland	.03
205 Dave Von Ohlen	.03
206 Mike LaCoss	.03
207 Juan Beniquez	.03
208 Juan Agosto	.03
209 Bobby Ramos	.03
210 Al Bumbry	.03
211 Mark Brouhard	.03
212 Howard Bailey	.03
213 Bruce Hurst	.03

214	Bob Shirley	.03
215	Pat Zachry	.03
216	Julio Franco	.03
217	Mike Armstrong	.03
218	Dave Beard	.03
219	Steve Rogers	.10
220	John Butcher	.03
221	Mike Smithson	.03
222	Frank White	.03
223	Mike Heath	.03
224	Chris Bando	.03
225	Roy Smalley	.03
226	Dusty Baker	.03
227	Lou Whitaker	.03
228	John Lowenstein	.03
229	Ben Oglivie	.03
230	Doug DeCinces	.05
231	Lonnie Smith	.05
232	Ray Knight	.03
233	Gary Matthews	.03
234	Juan Bonilla	.03
235	Rod Scurry	.03
236	Atlee Hammaker	.03
237	Mike Caldwell	.03
238	Keith Hernandez	.10
239	Larry Bowa	.03
240	Tony Bernazard	.03
241	Damaso Garcia	.03
242	Tom Brunansky	.03
243	Dan Driessen	.03
244	Ron Kittle	.25
245	Tim Stoddard	.03
246	Bob Gibson	.03
247	Marty Castillo	.03
248	Don Mattingly	.50
249	Jeff Newman	.03
250	Alejandro Pena	.03
251	Toby Harrah	.03
252	Cesar Geronimo	.03
253	Tom Underwood	.03
254	Doug Flynn	.03
255	Andy Hassler	.03
256	Odell Jones	.03
257	Rudy Law	.03
258	Harry Spilman	.03
259	Marty Bystrom	.03
260	Dave Rucker	.03
261	Ruppert Jones	.03
262	Jeff Jones	.03
263	Gerald Perry	.03
264	Gene Tenace	.03
265	Brad Wellman	.03
266	Dickie Noles	.03
267	Jamie Allen	.03
268	Jim Gott	.03
269	Ron Davis	.03
270	Benny Ayala	.03
271	Ned Yost	.03
272	Dave Rozema	.03
273	Dave Stapleton	.03
274	Lou Piniella	.03
275	Jose Morales	.03
276	Brad Perkins	.03
277	Butch Davis	.03
278	Tony Phillips	.03
279	Jeff Reardon	.03
280	Ken Forsch	.03
281	Pete O'Brien	.03
282	Tom Paciorek	.03
283	Frank LaCorte	.03
284	Tim Lollar	.03
285	Greg Gross	.03
286	Alex Trevino	.03
287	Gene Garber	.03
288	Dave Parker	.10
289	Lee Smith	.05
290	Dave LaPoint	.03
291	John Shelby	.03
292	Charlie Moore	.03
293	Alan Trammell	.03
294	Tony Armas	.03
295	Shane Rawley	.03
296	Greg Brock	.05
297	Hal McRae	.03
298	Mike Davis	.03
299	Tim Raines	.10
300	Bucky Dent	.03
301	Tommy John	.05

302	Carlton Fisk	.10
303	Darrell Porter	.03
304	Dickie Thon	.05
305	Garry Maddox	.03
306	Cesar Cedeno	.03
307	Gary Lucas	.03
308	Johnny Ray	.05
309	Andy McGaffigan	.03
310	Claudell Washington	.03
311	Ryne Sandberg	.03
312	George Foster	.10
313	Spike Owens	.03
314	Gary Gaetti	.03
315	Willie Upshaw	.03
316	Al Williams	.03
317	Jorge Orta	.03
318	Orlando Mercado	.03
319	Junior Ortiz	.03
320	Mike Proly	.03
321	Randy Johnson	.03
322	Jim Morrison	.03
323	Max Venable	.03
324	Tony Gwynn	.03
325	Duane Walker	.03
326	Ozzie Virgil	.03
327	Jeff Lahti	.03
328	Bill Dawley	.03
329	Rob Wilfong	.03
330	Marc Hill	.03
331	Ray Burris	.03
332	Allan Ramirez	.03
333	Chuck Porter	.03
334	Wayne Krenchicki	.03
335	Gary Allenson	.03
336	Bob Meacham	.03
337	Joe Beckwith	.03
338	Rick Sutcliffe	.03
339	Mark Huismann	.03
340	Tim Conroy	.03
341	Scott Sanderson	.03
342	Larry Biittner	.03
343	Dave Stewart	.03
344	Darryl Motley	.03
345	Chris Codiroli	.03

346	Rich Behenna	.03
347	Andre Robertson	.03
348	Mike Marshall	.05
349	Larry Herndon	.03
350	Rich Dauer	.03
351	Cecil Cooper	.10
352	Rod Carew	.25
353	Willie McGee	.15
354	Phil Garner	.03
355	Joe Morgan	.10
356	Luis Salazar	.03
357	John Candelaria	.03
358	Bill Laskey	.03
359	Bob McClure	.03
360	Dave Kingman	.05
361	Ron Cey	.05
362	Matt Young	.03
363	Lloyd Moseby	.03
364	Frank Viola	.03
365	Eddie Milner	.03
366	Floyd Bannister	.03
367	Dan Ford	.03
368	Moose Haas	.03
369	Doug Bair	.03
370	Ray Fontenot	.05
371	Luis Aponte	.03
372	Jack Fimple	.03
373	Neal Heaton	.03
374	Greg Pryor	.03
375	Wayne Gross	.03
376	Charlie Lea	.03
377	Steve Lubratich	.03
378	Jon Matlack	.03
379	Julio Cruz	.03
380	John Mizerock	.03
381	Kevin Gross	.03
382	Mike Ramsey	.03
383	Doug Gwosdz	.03
384	Kelly Paris	.03
385	Pete Falcone	.03
386	Milt May	.03
387	Fred Breining	.03
388	Craig Lefferts	.03
389	Steve Henderson	.03

390	Randy Moffitt	.03	434	Danny Heep	.03
391	Ron Washington	.03	435	Ed Nunez	.03
392	Gary Roenicke	.03	436	Bobby Castillo	.03
393	Tom Candiotto	.03	437	Ernie Whitt	.03
394	Larry Pashnick	.03	438	Scott Ullger	.03
395	Dwight Evans	.03	439	Doyle Alexander	.03
396	Goose Gossage	.10	440	Domingo Ramos	.03
397	Derrel Thomas	.03	441	Craig Swan	.03
398	Juan Eichelberger	.03	442	Warren Brusstar	.03
399	Leon Roberts	.03	443	Len Barker	.03
400	Davey Lopes	.03	444	Mike Easler	.05
401	Bill Gullickson	.03	445	Renie Martin	.03
402	Geoff Zahn	.03	446	Dennis Rasmussen	.03
403	Billy Sample	.03	447	Ted Power	.03
404	Mike Squires	.03	448	Charlie Hudson	.03
405	Craig Reynolds	.03	449	Danny Cox	.03
406	Eric Show	.03	450	Kevin Bass	.03
407	John Denny	.03	451	Daryl Sconiers	.03
408	Dann Bilardello	.03	452	Scott Fletcher	.03
409	Bruce Benedict	.03	453	Bryn Smith	.03
410	Kent Tekulve	.03	454	Jim Dwyer	.03
411	Mel Hall	.20	455	Rob Picciolo	.03
412	John Stupor	.03	456	Enos Cabell	.03
413	Rick Dempsey	.03	457	Dennis Boyd	.03
414	Don Sutton	.05	458	Butch Wynegar	.03
415	Jack Morris	.03	459	Burt Hooton	.03
416	John Tudor	.03	460	Ron Hassey	.03
417	Willie Randolph	.03	461	Danny Jackson	.03
418	Jerry Reuss	.03	462	Bob Kearney	.03
419	Don Slaught	.03	463	Terry Francona	.03
420	Steve McCatty	.03	464	Wayne Tolleson	.03
421	Tim Wallach	.03	465	Mickey Rivers	.03
422	Larry Parrish	.03	466	John Wathan	.03
423	Brian Downing	.03	467	Bill Almon	.03
424	Britt Burns	.10	468	George Vukovich	.03
425	David Green	.10	469	Steve Kemp	.03
426	Jerry Mumphrey	.03	470	Ken Landreaux	.03
427	Ivan DeJesus	.03	471	Milt Wilcox	.03
428	Mario Soto	.03	472	Tippy Martinez	.03
429	Gene Richards	.03	473	Ted Simmons	.05
430	Dale Berra	.03	474	Tim Foli	.03
431	Darrell Evans	.03	475	George Hendrick	.05
432	Glenn Hubbard	.03	476	Terry Puhl	.03
433	Jody Davis	.03	477	Von Hayes	.03

478 Bobby Brown	.03	
479 Lee Lacy	.03	
480 Joel Youngblood	.03	
481 Jim Slaton	.03	
482 Mike Fitzgerald	.03	
483 Keith Moreland	.03	
484 Ron Roenicke	.03	
485 Luis Leal	.03	
486 Bryan Oelkers	.03	
487 Bruce Berenyi	.03	
488 LaMarr Hoyt	.10	
489 Joe Nolan	.03	
490 Marshall Edwards	.03	
491 Mike Laga	.03	
492 Rick Cerone	.03	
493 Rick Miller	.03	
494 Rick Honeycutt	.03	
495 Mike Hargrove	.03	
496 Joe Simpson	.03	
497 Keith Atherton	.03	
498 Chris Welsh	.03	
499 Bruce Kison	.03	
500 Bobby Johnson	.03	
501 Jerry Koosman	.03	
502 Frank Di Pino	.03	
503 Tony Perez	.03	
504 Ken Oberkfell	.03	
505 Mark Thurmond	.03	
506 Joe Price	.03	
507 Pascual Perez	.03	
508 Marvell Wynne	.05	
509 Mike Krukow	.03	
510 Dick Ruthven	.03	
511 Al Cowens	.03	
512 Cliff Johnson	.03	
513 Randy Bush	.03	
514 Sammy Stewart	.03	
515 Bill Schroeder	.03	
516 Aurelio Lopez	.03	
517 Mike Brown	.03	
518 Graig Nettles	.03	
519 Dave Sax	.03	
520 Gerry Willard	.03	
521 Paul Splittorff	.03	

522 Tom Burgmeier	.03
523 Chris Speier	.03
524 Bobby Clark	.03
525 George Wright	.03
526 Dennis Lamp	.03
527 Tony Scott	.03
528 Ed Whitson	.03
529 Ron Reed	.03
530 Charlie Puleo	.03
531 Jerry Royster	.03
532 Don Robinson	.03
533 Steve Trout	.03
534 Bruce Sutter	.05
535 Bob Horner	.15
536 Pat Tabler	.03
537 Chris Chambliss	.03
538 Bob Ojeda	.03
539 Alan Ashby	.03
540 Jay Johnstone	.03
541 Bob Dernier	.03
542 Brook Jacoby	.05
543 U. L. Washington	.03
544 Danny Darwin	.03
545 Kiko Garcia	.03
546 Vance Law	.03
547 Tug McGraw	.03
548 Dave Smith	.03
549 Len Matuszek	.03
550 Tom Hume	.03
551 Dave Dravecky	.03
552 Rick Rhoden	.03
553 Duane Kuiper	.03
554 Rusty Staub	.03
555 Bill Campbell	.03
556 Mike Torrez	.03
557 Dave Henderson	.03
558 Len Whitehouse	.03
559 Barry Bonnell	.03
560 Rick Lysander	.03
561 Garth Iorg	.03
562 Bryan Clark	.03
563 Brian Giles	.03
564 Vern Ruhle	.03
565 Steve Bedrosian	.03

566	Larry McWilliams	.03	**609**	Greg Walker	.03
567	Jeff Leonard	.03	**610**	Ken Singleton	.03
568	Alan Wiggins	.03	**611**	Mark Clear	.03
569	Jeff Russell	.03	**612**	Buck Martinez	.03
570	Salome Barojas	.03	**613**	Ken Griffey	.03
571	Dane Iorg	.03	**614**	Reid Nichols	.03
572	Bob Knepper	.03	**615**	Doug Sisk	.03
573	Gary Lavelle	.03	**616**	Bob Brenly	.03
574	Gorman Thomas	.03	**617**	Joey McLaughlin	.03
575	Manny Trillo	.03	**618**	Glen Wilson	.03
576	Jim Palmer	.03	**619**	Bob Stoddard	.03
577	Dale Murray	.03	**620**	Lenn Sakata	.03
578	Tom Brookens	.03	**621**	Mike Young	.03
579	Rich Gedman	.03	**622**	John Stefero	.03
580	Bill Doran	.03	**623**	Carmelo Martinez	.03
581	Steve Yeager	.03	**624**	Dave Bergman	.03
582	Dan Spillner	.03	**625**	Runnin' Redbirds	.03
583	Dan Quisenberry	.10	**626**	Rudy May	.03
584	Rance Mulliniks	.03	**627**	Matt Keough	.03
585	Storm Davis	.03	**628**	Jose DeLeon	.15
586	Dave Schmidt	.03	**629**	Jim Essian	.03
587	Bill Russell	.03	**630**	Darnell Coles	.03
588	Pat Sheridan	.03	**631**	Mike Warren	.03
589	Rafael Ramirez	.03	**632**	Del Crandall	.03
590	Bud Anderson	.03	**633**	Dennis Martinez	.03
591	George Frazier	.03	**634**	Mike Moore	.03
592	Lee Tunnell	.03	**635**	Lary Sorensen	.03
593	Kirk Gibson	.03	**636**	Rick Nelson	.03
594	Scott McGregor	.03	**637**	Omar Moreno	.03
595	Bob Bailor	.03	**638**	Charlie Hough	.03
596	Tommy Herr	.03	**639**	Dennis Eckersley	.03
597	Luis Sanchez	.03	**640**	Walt Terrell	.03
598	Dave Engel	.03	**641**	Denny Walling	.03
599	Craig McMurtry	.03	**642**	Dave Anderson	.03
600	Carlos Diaz	.03	**643**	Jose Oquendo	.03
601	Tom O'Malley	.03	**644**	Bob Stanley	.03
602	Nick Esasky	.03	**645**	Dave Geisel	.03
603	Ron Hodges	.03	**646**	Scott Garrelts	.03
604	Ed Vandeberg	.03	**647**	Gary Pettis	.03
605	Alfredo Griffin	.03	**648**	DUKE SNIDER PUZZLE	.10
606	Glenn Hoffman	.03	**649**	Johnnie LeMaster	.03
607	Hubie Brooks	.03	**650**	Dave Collins	.03
608	Richard Barnes	.03	**651**	THE CHICKEN	.25

Index

About the Authors

MARGO MCLOONE-BASTA, born and raised in rural Minnesota, is the coauthor of *The Herb & Spice Book for Kids, Sports Cards: Collecting, Trading, and Playing,* and *It's a Girl's Game Too.* She is a junior high school teacher in New York City, where she lives with her husband.

ALICE SIEGEL, coauthor of *The Herb & Spice Book for Kids, Sports Cards: Collecting, Trading, and Playing,* and *It's a Girl's Game Too,* is a reading specialist for the Greenwich, Connecticut public school system. She lives with her husband and three sons in Scarsdale, New York.